# Fourth Widening Natural Language Processing Workshop 2020

Seattle, Washington, USA
5 July 2020

ISBN: 978-1-7138-1380-4

# TABLE OF CONTENTS

ACL 2020

# The Fourth Widening Natural Language Processing Workshop

# Program of the Workshop

July 5, 2020
Seattle, USA

## Silver Sponsors

## Bronze Sponsors

**Bloomberg**
Engineering

# Introduction

Welcome to 2020 Widening NLP Workshop!

In 2016, a select group of people met at ACL in Berlin to discuss the underrepresentation of women and other minorities in the Natural Language Processing community. The outcome of this was the first Workshop for Women and underrepresented minorities in NLP at ACL 2017: a workshop specifically dedicated to highlighting the work of groups whose work is often overlooked. We are proud to continue this work with the 2020 Widening NLP workshop.

Every year, we strive to make the workshop more inclusive. After the 2017 iteration of WiNLP, we set up two submission deadlines, one for early submissions to accommodate those who need more time for visa applications and a later deadline for those who do not have such concerns.

Following the success of the 2018 workshop, in 2019 we sought to also highlight diversity in scientific background, discipline, training, obtained degrees, and seniority. In addition, we introduced a workshopping feature, where authors themselves opted in to give feedback to their fellow authors before the papers were sent out for review.

The year 2020 brought new challenges with a global pandemic canceling all in-person conferences and workshops but has also given us the opportunity to widen our audience and authorship further. Our travel funds have been repurposed to assist with higher speed internet connections and registration fees – since those are lower cost items it means we can offer assistance to even more people to join our virtual workshop.

Despite the rapid changes in 2020, we received 66 submissions! Of these submissions 54% were by women as first authors, 73% were by people of color, 54% of all papers came from outside of North America and Europe. Turning our attention to the papers which were accepted, equally encouraging numbers come up: 57% of all accepted submissions had women as their first authors, 75% of all accepted papers were by people of color, and 52% of the accepted papers came from outside of Europe and North America.

We are proud to have great invited speakers - Drs. Helena Caseli, Jose Eduardo Ochoa Luna, Verena Riesner, Rachel Tatman, as well as four excellent panelists - Drs. Anima Anandkumar, Luciana Benotti, Xanda Schofield, and MSc Jade Abbott.

We thus proudly present the 2020 Widening NLP workshop, and hope that you will enjoy the wonderful work of the authors, speakers, and panelists of this edition of the workshop.

Rossana, Samira, Erika, Ryan, Alicia, Antonios, and Khyathi.

**Organizers:**

Rossana Cunha, Federal University of Minas Gerais
Samira Shaikh, University of North Carolina at Charlotte
Erika Varis, Walt Disney Studios
Ryan Georgi, University of Washington
Antonios Anastasopoulos, Carnegie Mellon University
Khyathi Raghavi Chandu, Carnegie Mellon University
Alicia Tsai, UC Berkeley

**Advisory Board:**

Isabelle Augenstein, University of Copenhagen
Amittai Axelrod, University of Maryland
Libby Barak, Rutgers University
Daniel Beck, University of Melbourne
Chloé Braud, CNRS – LORIA
Hal Daumé III, Associate Professor, University of Maryland
Mourad Gridach, Ibn Zohr University, Agadir
Valia Kordoni, Humboldt University Berlin
Cisca Odalipo, Kampala International University
Martha Palmer, University of Colorado
Natalie Schluter, University of Copenhagen
Tiago Torrent, Federal University of Juiz de Fora,
Aline Villavicencio, Federal University of Rio Grande do Sul, University of Essex
Hanna Wallach, Microsoft Research
Zeerak Waseem, University of Sheffield

**Program Committee:**

Gavin Abercrombie, University of Manchester
Fernando Alva-Manchego, University of Sheffield
Antonios Anastasopoulos, Carnegie Mellon University
Gabor Angeli, Square Inc
Miguel Ballesteros, Amazon
Libby Barak, Rutgers University
Marco Baroni, ICREA
Maria Barrett, University of Copenhagen
Chloé Braud, IRIT - CNRS
Jose Camacho-Collados, Cardiff University
Khyathi Raghavi Chandu, Carnegie Mellon University
Colin Cherry, Google
George Chrysostomou, The University of Sheffield
Kenneth Church, Baidu, USA
Marta R. Costa-jussà, Universitat Politècnica de Catalunya
Rossana Cunha, Federal University of Minas Gerais
Walter Daelemans, University of Antwerp, CLiPS
Dipanjan Das, Google AI Language
Erika Doggett, Walt Disney Studios
Luis Espinosa Anke, Cardiff University
Jennifer Foster, Dublin City University
Ryan Georgi, University of Washington

Kevin Gimpel, Toyota Technological Institute at Chicago
Julia Hirschberg, Columbia University in the City of New York
Dirk Hovy, Bocconi University
Kristen Howell, University of Washington
Naoya Inoue, Tohoku University / RIKEN AIP
Cassandra L. Jacobs, University of Wisconsin, Madison
Huda Khayrallah, Johns Hopkins University
Kevin Knight, DiDi Labs
Rebecca Knowles, National Research Council Canada
Philipp Koehn, Johns Hopkins University
Rik Koncel-Kedziorski, University of Washington
Valia Kordoni, Humboldt-Universität zu Berlin
Ophélie Lacroix, Siteimprove
Els Lefever, LT3, Ghent University
Lucy H. Lin, University of Washington
Nitin Madnani, Educational Testing Service
Alex Marin, Microsoft Corporation
Héctor Martínez Alonso, Apple Inc
Arya D. McCarthy, Johns Hopkins University
Kourosh Meshgi, Riken AIP/ Kyoto University
Lisa Michaud, Interactions LLC
Sabrina J. Mielke, Johns Hopkins University
Aakanksha Naik, Carnegie Mellon University
Vincent Ng, University of Texas at Dallas
Debora Nozza, Bocconi University
Eda Okur, Intel Labs
Miles Osborne, Bloomberg
Gustavo Henrique Paetzold, Federal University of Technology - Paraná
Alexis Palmer, University of North Texas
Patrick Pantel, Facebook
Yannick Parmentier, University of Lorraine
Panupong Pasupat, Google
Roma Patel, Brown University
Viviana Patti, University of Turin, Dipartimento di Informatica
Amandalynne Paullada, University of Washington
Siyao Peng, Georgetown University
Hoifung Poon, Microsoft Research
Matthew Purver, Queen Mary University of London
Dragomir Radev, Yale University
Gabriela Ramirez-de-la-Rosa, Universidad Autónoma Metropolitana
Michael Roth, University of Stuttgart
Niloofar Safi Samghabadi, University of Houston
Sashank Santhanam, University of North Carolina at Charlotte
Naomi Saphra, University of Edinburgh
David Schlangen, University of Potsdam
Alexandra Schofield, Harvey Mudd College
Brandon Sepulvado, NORC at the University of Chicago
Samira Shaikh, UNC - Charlotte
Karin Sim Smith, University of Sheffield
Noah A. Smith, University of Washington
Marco Antonio Sobrevilla Cabezudo, University of São Paulo

Vivek Srikumar, University of Utah
Mark Steedman, University of Edinburgh
Madhumita Sushil, University of Antwerp
Jeniya Tabassum, The Ohio State University
Christoph Teichmann, Bloomberg LP
Elena Tutubalina, Kazan Federal University
Aline Villavicencio, University of Sheffield, UK
Bonnie Webber, University of Edinburgh
Wei Xu, The Ohio State University
Olga Zamaraeva, University of Washington


**Invited Speakers:**

Verena Rieser, Heriot-Watt University
Helena Caseli, Universidade Federal de São Carlos
José Eduardo Ochoa, Universidad Católica San Pablo
Rachael Tatman, Rasa

**Panelists:**

Anima Anandkumar, California Institute of Technology, NVIDIA
Jade Abbott, Retro Rabbit
Luciana Benotti, Universidad Nacional de Córdoba
Xanda Schofield, Harvey Mudd College

# Workshop Program

**Sunday, July 5, 2020**

**8:00–9:00**      **Sponsored "breakfast"**

**9:00–10:30**      **Session 1: Opening, Keynote, and Posters**

9:00–9:10      *Opening Remarks*

9:10–9:50      *Keynote 1:Verena Rieser*

9:50–10:30      *Poster Session A*

*Corpus based Amharic sentiment lexicon generation*
Girma Neshir Alemneh, Andreas Rauber and Solomon Atnafu

*Negation handling for Amharic sentiment classification*
Girma Neshir Alemneh, Andreas Rauber and Solomon Atnafu

*Embedding Oriented Adaptable Semantic Annotation Framework for Amharic Web Documents*
Kidane Woldemariyam and Dr. Fekade Getahun

*Similarity and Farness Based Bidirectional Neural Co-Attention for Amharic Natural Language Inference*
Abebawu Eshetu, Getenesh Teshome and Ribka Alemayehu

*Large Vocabulary Read Speech Corpora for Four Ethiopian Languages: Amharic, Tigrigna, Oromo, and Wolaytta*
Solomon Teferra Abate, Martha Yifiru Tachbelie, Michael Melese, Hafte Abera, Tewodros Gebreselassie, Wondwossen Mulugeta, Yaregal Assabie, Million Meshesha Beyene, Solomon Atinafu and Binyam Ephrem Seyoum

*SIMPLEX-PB 2.0: A Reliable Dataset for Lexical Simplification in Brazilian Portuguese*
Nathan Hartmann, Gustavo Henrique Paetzold and Sandra Aluísio

*Token Level Identification of Multiword Expressions Using Contextual Information*
REYHANEH HASHEMPOUR and Aline Villavicencio

*Multitask Models for Controlling the Complexity of Neural Machine Translation*
Sweta Agrawal and Marine Carpuat

*Using Social Media For Bitcoin Day Trading Behavior Prediction*
Anna Paula Pawlicka Maule and Kristen Johnson

*HausaMT v1.0: Towards English–Hausa Neural Machine Translation*
Adewale Akinfaderin

*Outcomes of coming out: Analyzing stories of LGBTQ+*
Krithika Ramesh and Tanvi Anand

*An Evaluation of Subword Segmentation Strategies for Neural Machine Translation of Morphologically Rich Languages*
Aquia Richburg, Ramy Eskander, Smaranda Muresan and Marine Carpuat

*Enhanced Urdu Word Segmentation using Conditional Random Fields and Morphological Context Features*
Aamir Farhan, Mashrukh Islam and Dipti Misra Sharma

*Flexible Non-Autoregressive Neural Machine Translation via Repositioning Edit Operations*
Weijia Xu and Marine Carpuat

**15:10–15:25**   ***Break (sponsored)***

# Corpus based Amharic sentiment lexicon generation

Girma Neshir
Addis Ababa University
IT Doctoral Program
Ethiopia
girma1978@gmail.com

Andreas Rauber
Technical Uni. of Vienna
Institute of Inf. Systems Eng.,
Austria
rauber@ifs.tuwien.ac.at

Solomon Atnafu
Addis Ababa University,
Dept. of Computer Science
Ethiopia
solomon.atnafu@aau.edu.et

## 1 Introduction

For carrying out Amharic sentiment classification, the availability of sentiment lexicons is crucial. To date, there are three Amharic sentiment lexicons. These are manually generated lexicon (1000) [Gebremeskel, 2010], dictionary-based Amharic SWN and SOCAL lexicons [Alemneh et al., 2019]. However, dictionary-based generated lexicons has short-comings in that it has difficulty in capturing cultural connotation and language-specific features of the language. This research builds corpus-based algorithm to handle language and culture specific words in the lexicons [Alessia et al., 2015]. However, it could probably be impossible to handle all the words in the language as the corpus is a limited-resource in almost all less-resourced languages like Amharic. But still it is possible to build sentiment lexicons in particular domain where large amount of Amharic corpus is available. Due to this reason, the lexicon built using this approach is usually used for lexicon-based sentiment analysis in the same domain from which it is built. The research questions to be addressed utilizing this approach are: (1) how can we build an approach to generate Amharic sentiment lexicon from corpus? (2) how do we evaluate the validity and quality of the generated lexicon?

Our work is similar to the work of [Passaro et al., 2015] which generated emotion lexicon by bootstrapping Facebook News corpus using word distributional semantics (i.e. using Positive Point-wise Mutual Information (PPMI)). However, our approach is different from [Passaro et al., 2015] in that we generated sentiment lexicon(i.e. scores might be either of positive, negative or neutral) rather than emotion lexicon(i.e. scores might be assigned different emotion categories: happy, sad, surprise, ugly, etc. ). The other thing is that the approach of propagating sentiment to expand the seeds using PPMI matrix is also different. The number of part of speech for our seed words are different in Amharic language. That means, Amharic has few adverb classes unlike Italian [Yimam, 2009]. Thus, our seed words do not contain adverbs.

## 2 Proposed approach

There are variety of corpus-based strategies that include count-based (e.g. PPMI) and predictive-based (e.g. word embedding) approaches. In this section, we present the proposed count-based approach to generate Amharic sentiment lexicon from a corpus as word embedding is not cost-effective with existing local resources. The proposed framework of corpus-based approach is able to generate Amharic sentiment lexicon. The framework has four components: (Amharic news) corpus collection, preprocessing module, PPMI matrix of word-context, algorithm to generate (Amharic) sentiment lexicon resulting in the generated (Amharic) sentiment lexicon.

We developed algorithms for constructing Amharic sentiment lexicons automatically from Amharic news corpus. Corpus-based approach is proposed relying on the word co-occurrence distributional embedding including frequency-based embedding (i.e. PPMI). First we build word-context unigram frequency count matrix and transform it to Point-wise Mutual Information matrix. For an experimentally chosen threshold value, the top closest words to the mean vector of seed list are added to the lexicon. Then, the mean vector of the new sentiment seed list is updated and process is repeated until we get lexicon with comparative size of lexicons in the semitic languages of the literature.



*Proceedings of the 55th Annual Meeting of the Association for Computational Linguistics*, pages 1–3
Florence, Italy, July 28th, 2019. ©2019 Association for Computational Linguistics

## 3   Results and Discussion

For evaluating the proposed framework, we used the datasets which consist of 2705 sentence/phrase level sentiment annotated facebook news users' comments collected from the Government Office Affairs Communication (GOAC) between 2008 and 2010. We also used the Amharic sentiment lexicons including manual(1000), SWN(13679) and SOCAL(5683) [ Neshir et al. , 2019]. Amharic seed words of size 519 are used to expand PPMI-based lexicons. With experimentally obtained threshold value of 100 and 200, we got corpus-based Amharic sentiment lexicons of size 1811 and 3794 respectively.

As discussed on dictionary-based lexicons in [Alemneh et al 2019] for lexicon-based sentiment classification, using stemming and negation handling are far improving the performance lexicon-based classification. Besides, combination of lexicons outperforms better than the individual lexicon. We evaluated the generated Amharic sentiment lexicon in two ways: external to lexicon and internal to lexicon. External to lexicon is to test the usefulness and the correctness of each of the lexicon to assign sentiment score of sentiment labeled Amharic comments corpus. Internal evaluation is compute the degree to which each of the generated lexicons are sentimentally agreed (or overlapped) with manual, SOCAL and SWN (Amharic) sentiment lexicons. Our lexicon detects subjectivity of Amharic Facebook comments which has shown an increment of detection accuracy of 3.73 more than the subjectivity detection rate of the manual lexicon. For sentiment classification, the performance of our generated lexicon for classifying sentiment of Amharic facebook comments has an increment of 6.71 than the manual sentiment lexicon as shown in Table 1.

Table 1: The Accuracy (in percent) of PPMI based Lexicons for Sentiment Classification

| Amharic Lexicons | Accuracy(%) | | |
|---|---|---|---|
| | NoStem+NoNeg. | Stem+NoNeg. | Stem+Neg. |
| Manual(baseline) | 16.7 | 42.9 | 42.16 |
| PPMI | - | - | 48.87 |
| SOCAL | 14.6 | 46.3 | 47.2 |
| SWN | 30.9 | 50.1 | 48.87 |
| SOCAL +SWN | 443.7 | 66.6 | 70.26 |
| Manual+SOCAL +SWN | 53.7 | 75.8 | 78.19 |
| PPMI+SOCAL+SWN+Manual | - | - | 83.51 |

Table 1 Evaluation of Corpus-based Generated Amharic lexicon for Amharic Facebook Sentiment Classification

In addition, the coverage result in a general web corpus with 20 million tokens helps to depict the coverage of PPMI based Amharic sentiment lexicon is better than the manual lexicon and SOCAL. However, it has less coverage than SWN. Unlike SWN, PPMI based lexicon is generated from corpus. Due to this reason its coverage to work on a general domain is limited. It also demonstrated that the positive and negative count in almost all lexicons seems to have balanced and uniform distribution of sentiment polarity terms in the corpus.

## 4   Conclusions

This study revealed that it is possible to create sentiment lexicon for low-resourced languages from corpus. This captures the language-specific features and connotations related to the culture where the language is spoken. This cannot be handled using dictionary-based approach that propagates labels from resource-rich languages. To the best of our knowledge, the PPMI-based approach to generate Amharic sentiment lexicon form corpus is performed for first time for Amharic language with minimal costs and time. Thus, the generated lexicons can be used in combination with other sentiment lexicons to enhance the performance of sentiment classificationsin Amharic language. The approach is a generic approach which can be adapted to other resource-limited languages to reduce cost of human annotation and saving the time of annotating the sentiment lexicons. Though the PPMI-based Amharic sentiment lexicon outperforms the manual lexicon, prediction (word embedding)-based approach is recommended to generate sentiment lexicon for Amharic language to handle context sensitive terms. Moreover, there are challenges to be addressed in the future researches including (i)selection of seed words matters, (ii)result is not quite good if either too big or too small threshold, (iii) semantic drift might occur if number of iterations is too big and (iv) the generated lexicon might not work in a general domain.

References

D Alessia, Fernando Ferri, Patrizia Grifoni  2015.  Approaches, tools and applications for sentiment analysis implementation, International Journal of Computer Applications, 125(3).

S. Gebremeskel. 2010. Sentiment mining model for opinionated Amharic texts. Unpublished Masters Thesis and Department of Computer Science and Addis Ababa University and Addis Ababa.

Girma Neshir Alemneh, Andreas Rauber, and Solomon Atnafu. 2019. Dictionary Based Amharic Sentiment Lexicon Generation. Springer LNS book Chapter, pages 311–326..

Lucia Passaro, Laura Pollacci, and Alessandro Lenci. 2015. Item: A vector space model to bootstrap an Italian emotive lexicon. In Second Italian Conference on Computational Linguistics CLiC-it, pages 215–220. Academia University Press.

Baye Yimam. 2009  yäamarIña säwasäw (Amharic Grammar).  Educational Materials Production and Distribution Enterprise(EMPDE).

# Negation handling for Amharic sentiment classification


**Girma Neshir**
Addis Ababa University
IT Doctoral Program
Ethiopia
girma1978@gmail.com

**Andreas Rauber**
Technical Uni. of Vienna
Institute of Inf. Systems Eng.,
Austria
rauber@ifs.tuwien.ac.at

**Solomon Atnafu**
Addis Ababa University,
Dept. of Computer Science
Ethiopia
solomon.atnafu@aau.edu.et


## 1  Introduction

Users usually express their feelings, emotions and opinions as comments in response to the posted news, photo, audio and video. Currently, opinionated sources are increasing in languages other than English. However, Amharic sentiment analysis researches are very few as it has no sufficient linguistic resources for linguistic preprocessing and sentiment analysis. There are several challenges in lexicon-based sentiment analysis. One of these is that handling negation in the text. The most common approach for negation-handling is carried out relying on negation keywords. However, it is complex to identify the scope of negation where the process of correctly identifying the part of the text affected by the presence of negation word. Negation-handling is never studied in Amharic language to the best of our knowledge. Thus, this research develops an automatic method to handle negation and combined with character ngram features for Amharic sentiment classification relying on these linguistic features. The research questions to be addressed in this work are as follows: (a) how can we automatically detect negation words in Amharic texts? (b) how can we design a framework for handling negation in Amharic sentiment analysis? (c) how to capture character level ngram features for improving Amharic sentiment analysis in social media(e.g. Facebook) and (d) how can we evaluate the performance of the framework?

In literature, Amalia et al. (2011) proposed rule based negation handling and its scope based on syntactic parsing of Indonesian language for machine learning based sentiment analysis in twitter and the result of support vector machine performs well as compared with other experiments. The F-Score on two Twitter data sets is improved by 1.79% and 2.69% from the existing baseline without negation handling. Similarly, Asmi and Ishaya (2012) proposed an approach that can detect negation and considers scope of negation relying on syntactic dependency for sentiment analysis. Using the linguistic features of the language, Farooq et al. (2017) developed negation scope handling strategies. The accuracy of negation scope identification is 83.3% which outperforms very well above the baseline. In Diamantini et al. (2016), develops negation scope detection using dependency parsing tree and semantic disambiguation technique which is tested on integrated social networks in real time. The performance of negation handling outperforms with accuracy of 6% more than the baseline. The work in Heerschop et al. (2011) developed negation handling relying on wordbank creation and document sentiment scoring for sentiment analysis and outperforms the human rating by an increase precision with 1.17%. Enger et al. (2017) developed negation clue and scope handling open source tool using dependency parser, negation clue (negation lists, prefix, suffix) as input to machine learning(e.g. SVM) and its performance is slightly unchanged from the baseline.

## 2  Proposed approach

The proposed framework consists of components including preprocessing and sentiment score calculation using negation detection and machine learning using character level ngrams features as shown in Fig. 1.

To compute sentiment score using negation detection, for each Amharic news comment, $C_i$, if each stemmed word $w_{ij}$ is found in either of the Amharic sentiment lexicons such as Manual [Gebremeskel,2010], SOCAL & SWN [Neshir et al, 2019], then the sentiment score $s_{ij}$ is retrieved.




*Proceedings of the 55th Annual Meeting of the Association for Computational Linguistics*, pages 4–6
Florence, Italy, July 28th, 2019. ©2019 Association for Computational Linguistics

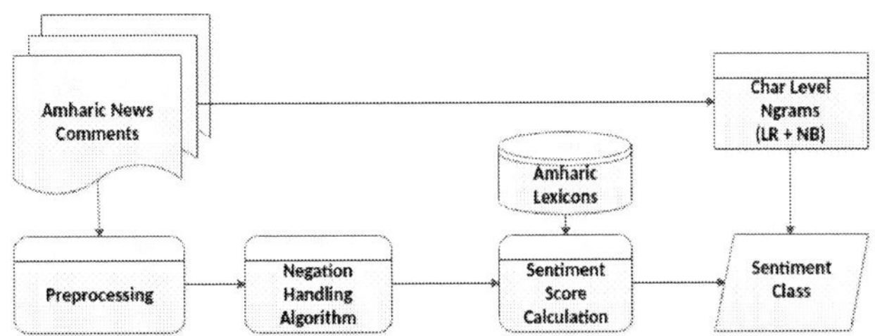

Figure 1: Amharic Negation Handling Framework

$s_{ij}$ and its position index in the comment is stored. To compute the sentiment of the comment, we apply positional weighting inversion(i.e. the sentiment weight of the comment that contains negation clue is inverted as many as the number of negation clue(s) ) if the comment contains any negation clue. If negation clue is not found, the score of the word is simply added.

Besides lexicon based negation handling approach, the usefulness of character aware language models is well suited to apply for language identification, reducing of text feature sparse dimensionality, helps to handle spelling errors, abbreviations, special characters, etc. [Heerschop et al., 2011]. That is why we proposed character level ngram approaches to reduce and address these issues for Amharic Facebook news comments' sentiment classification rather than word level ngram approaches. For example, the negation carrying Amharic word *"አልወደውም"/* "I donot like him"/ has 2-gram character level features includes አ-አል-ልወ-ወደ-ደው-ውም-ም, 3-gram character level features are አ-አል-አልወ-ልወደ-ወደው-ደውም-ውም-ም, etc. The negation marker/morpheme/ አል- is detected as feature of the negation word/*"አልወደውም"/*. That is probabilities negation clue n-grams are computed providing the sentiment of the term.

## 3   Results and discussions

For evaluating the proposed framework, we used the datasets which consist of 2705 sentence/phrase level sentiment annotated Facebook news users' comments collected from the Government Office Affairs Communication (GOAC) between 2008 and 2010 are randomly partitioned 70%(train set) and 30%(test set). We also used the Amharic sentiment lexicons including manual( size.1000), SWN(size.13679) and SOCAL(size.5683) [ Neshir et al. , 2019]. The proposed negation handling approach for Amharic sentiment classification outperforms very well when we compared to the character ngram-based machine learning classifiers. The char-ngram based machine learning is promising that it reduces the demand for linguistic resources for less dominant languages. The results are presented in Table 1 shown below. The hybrid approach (Negation Handling(NH) + Logistic regression(LR)+ Naive Bayesian(NB)) outperforms the best compared to the individual approach for sentiment classification on Amharic Facebook news comment texts with accuracy of 98.0.

Table 1: Classification Performance of Amharic Negation Handling

| Approach | Accuracy(%) | |
|---|---|---|
| | Wordlevel (Baseline) | Char Level |
| Negation Handling(NH) | 86.2 | - |
| NB + LR | 79.32 | 83.75 |
| Hybrid(NH+NB+LR) | 95.27 | 98.0 |

## 4   Conclusions

In general, extensive linguistic resources are expensive to build sentiment classification on the less dominant languages (e.g. Amharic). To reduce this problem, we proposed negation handling approach and character ngram approach for Sentiment analysis of Amharic face book news comments. We evaluated the usefulness of the combination of Negation Handling (NH) and character level ngram based machine learning models for sentiment classification of Amharic Facebook news comments. We call the combination (i.e. hybrid) of rule based NH and machine learning algorithms (logistic regression and Naïve Bayesian) using character ngram based tfidf features for Amharic sentiment classification. The proposed approaches are evaluated by measuring accuracy of individual and their combinations for Amharic text sentiment classification. Amharic negation scope identification and handling is recommended for further researches. We also suggest method to consider character ngram embedding features from corpus of the same domain(e.g. Facebook news comments).

## References


S. Gebremeskel. 2010. *Sentiment mining model for opinionated Amharic texts.* Unpublished Masters Thesis and Department of Computer Science and Addis Ababa University and Addis Ababa.

Rizkiana Amalia, Moch Arif Bijaksana, and Dhinta Darmantoro 2011. *Negation handling in sentiment classification using rule-based adapted from Indonesian language syntactic for Indonesian text in twitter,* In Journal of Physics: Conference Series, volume 971, page 012039. IOP Publishing.

Amna Asmi and Tanko Ishaya 2012. *Negation identification and calculation in sentiment analysis.* In The second international conference on advances in information mining and management, pages 1–7.

Girma Neshir Alemneh, Andreas Rauber, and Solomon Atnafu. 2019. *Dictionary Based Amharic Sentiment Lexicon Generation.* Springer LNS book Chapter, pages 311–326..

Claudia Diamantini, Alex Mircoli, and Domenico Potena. 2016. *A negation handling technique for sentiment analysis.* In 2016 International Conference on Collaboration Technologies and Systems (CTS), pages 188–195. IEEE.

Martine Enger, Erik Velldal, and Lilja Øvrelid.. 2017 *An open-source tool for negation detection: a maximum-margin approach.* In Proceedings of the Workshop Computational Semantics Beyond Events and Roles, pages 64–69.

Umar Farooq, Hasan Mansoor, Antoine Nongaillard, Yacine Ouzrout, and Muhammad Abdul Qadir. 2017 *Negation handling in sentiment analysis at sentence level.* JCP, 12(5):470–478.

Bas Heerschop, Paul van Iterson, Alexander Hogenboom, Flavius Frasincar, and Uzay Kaymak. 2011 *Accounting for negation in sentiment analysis.* In 11th DutchBelgian Information Retrieval Workshop (DIR 2011), pages 38–39.

# Instructions for WiNLP 2020


**First Author**
Affiliation / Address line 1
Affiliation / Address line 2
Affiliation / Address line 3
`email@domain`

**Second Author**
Affiliation / Address line 1
Affiliation / Address line 2
Affiliation / Address line 3
`email@domain`


## Abstract


This document contains the instructions for preparing a paper submitted to WiNLP 2019. The document itself conforms to its own specifications, and is therefore an example of what your manuscript should look like. These instructions should be used for both papers submitted for review and for final versions of accepted papers. Authors are asked to conform to all the directions reported in this document.


## 1   Credits

This document has been adapted from the instructions for COLING-2018 proceedings compiled by Xiaodan Zhu and Zhiyuan Liu, which are, in turn, based on the instructions for COLING-2016 proceedings, which are, in turn, based on the instructions for COLING-2014 proceedings compiled by Joachim Wagner, Liadh Kelly and Lorraine Goeuriot, which are, in turn, based on the instructions for earlier ACL proceedings, including those for ACL-2014 by Alexander Koller and Yusuke Miyao, those for ACL-2012 by Maggie Li and Michael White, those for ACL-2010 by Jing-Shing Chang and Philipp Koehn, those for ACL-2008 by Johanna D. Moore, Simone Teufel, James Allan, and Sadaoki Furui, those for ACL-2005 by Hwee Tou Ng and Kemal Oflazer, those for ACL-2002 by Eugene Charniak and Dekang Lin, and earlier ACL and EACL formats. Those versions were written by several people, including John Chen, Henry S. Thompson and Donald Walker. Additional elements were taken from the formatting instructions of the *International Joint Conference on Artificial Intelligence*.

## 2   Introduction

The following instructions are directed to authors of papers submitted to WiNLP 2019 or accepted for publication in its proceedings. All authors are required to adhere to these specifications. Authors are required to provide a Portable Document Format (PDF) version of their papers. **The proceedings are designed for printing on A4 paper.**

Authors from countries in which access to word-processing systems is limited should contact WiNLP Organizers `winlp-chairs@googlegroups.com` as soon as possible.

## 3   General Instructions

Manuscripts must be in single-column format. **Type single-spaced.** Start all pages directly under the top margin. See the guidelines later regarding formatting the first page. The lengths of manuscripts should not exceed the maximum page limit described in Section 5. Do not number the pages.

### 3.1   Electronically-available Resources

We strongly prefer that you prepare your PDF files using LaTeX with the official COLING 2018 style file (coling2018.sty) and bibliography style (acl.bst). These files are available in coling2018.zip at `http://coling2018.org/`. You will also find the document you are currently reading (coling2018.pdf) and its LaTeX source code (coling2018.tex) in coling2018.zip.

---

Place licence statement here for the camera-ready version. See Section 3.9 of the instructions for preparing a manuscript.




*Proceedings of the 55th Annual Meeting of the Association for Computational Linguistics*, pages 8–12
Florence, Italy, July 28th, 2019. ©2019 Association for Computational Linguistics

You can alternatively use Microsoft Word to produce your PDF file. In this case, we strongly recommend the use of the Word template file (coling2018.dot) in coling2018.zip. If you have an option, we recommend that you use the LaTeX2e version. If you will be using the Microsoft Word template, you must anonymise your source file so that the pdf produced does not retain your identity. This can be done by removing any personal information from your source document properties.

### 3.2 Format of Electronic Manuscript

For the production of the electronic manuscript you must use Adobe's Portable Document Format (PDF). PDF files are usually produced from LaTeX using the *pdflatex* command. If your version of LaTeX produces Postscript files, you can convert these into PDF using *ps2pdf* or *dvipdf*. On Windows, you can also use Adobe Distiller to generate PDF.

Please make sure that your PDF file includes all the necessary fonts (especially tree diagrams, symbols, and fonts for non-Latin characters). When you print or create the PDF file, there is usually an option in your printer setup to include none, all or just non-standard fonts. Please make sure that you select the option of including ALL the fonts. **Before sending it, test your PDF by printing it from a computer different from the one where it was created.** Moreover, some word processors may generate very large PDF files, where each page is rendered as an image. Such images may reproduce poorly. In this case, try alternative ways to obtain the PDF. One way on some systems is to install a driver for a postscript printer, send your document to the printer specifying "Output to a file", then convert the file to PDF.

It is of utmost importance to specify the **A4 format** (21 cm x 29.7 cm) when formatting the paper. When working with `dvips`, for instance, one should specify `-t a4`.

If you cannot meet the above requirements for the production of your electronic submission, please contact the publication co-chairs as soon as possible.

### 3.3 Layout

Format manuscripts with a single column to a page, in the manner these instructions are formatted. The exact dimensions for a page on A4 paper are:

- Left and right margins: 2.5 cm

- Top margin: 2.5 cm

- Bottom margin: 2.5 cm

- Width: 16.0 cm

- Height: 24.7 cm

Papers should not be submitted on any other paper size. If you cannot meet the above requirements for the production of your electronic submission, please contact the publication co-chairs above as soon as possible.

### 3.4 Fonts

For reasons of uniformity, Adobe's **Times Roman** font should be used. In LaTeX2e this is accomplished by putting

```
\usepackage{times}
\usepackage{latexsym}
```

in the preamble. If Times Roman is unavailable, use **Computer Modern Roman** (LaTeX2e's default). Note that the latter is about 10% less dense than Adobe's Times Roman font.

The **Times New Roman** font, which is configured for us in the Microsoft Word template (coling2018.dot) and which some Linux distributions offer for installation, can be used as well.

| Type of Text | Font Size | Style |
|---|---|---|
| paper title | 15 pt | bold |
| author names | 12 pt | bold |
| author affiliation | 12 pt | |
| the word "Abstract" | 12 pt | bold |
| section titles | 12 pt | bold |
| document text | 11 pt | |
| captions | 11 pt | |
| sub-captions | 9 pt | |
| abstract text | 11 pt | |
| bibliography | 10 pt | |
| footnotes | 9 pt | |

Table 1: Font guide.

### 3.5 The First Page

Centre the title, author's name(s) and affiliation(s) across the page. Do not use footnotes for affiliations. Do not include the paper ID number assigned during the submission process. Do not include the authors' names or affiliations in the version submitted for review.

**Title**: Place the title centred at the top of the first page, in a 15 pt bold font. (For a complete guide to font sizes and styles, see Table 1.) Long titles should be typed on two lines without a blank line intervening. Approximately, put the title at 2.5 cm from the top of the page, followed by a blank line, then the author's names(s), and the affiliation on the following line. Do not use only initials for given names (middle initials are allowed). Do not format surnames in all capitals (e.g., use "Schlangen" not "SCHLANGEN"). Do not format title and section headings in all capitals as well except for proper names (such as "BLEU") that are conventionally in all capitals. The affiliation should contain the author's complete address, and if possible, an electronic mail address. Start the body of the first page 7.5 cm from the top of the page.

The title, author names and addresses should be completely identical to those entered to the electronical paper submission website in order to maintain the consistency of author information among all publications of the conference. If they are different, the publication co-chairs may resolve the difference without consulting with you; so it is in your own interest to double-check that the information is consistent.

**Abstract**: Type the abstract between addresses and main body. The width of the abstract text should be smaller than main body by about 0.6 cm on each side. Centre the word **Abstract** in a 12 pt bold font above the body of the abstract. The abstract should be a concise summary of the general thesis and conclusions of the paper. It should be no longer than 200 words. The abstract text should be in 11 pt font.

**Text**: Begin typing the main body of the text immediately after the abstract, observing the single-column format as shown in the present document. Do not include page numbers.

**Indent** when starting a new paragraph. Use 11 pt for text and subsection headings, 12 pt for section headings and 15 pt for the title.

**Licence**: Include a licence statement as an unmarked (unnumbered) footnote on the first page of the final, camera-ready paper. See Section 3.9 below for details and motivation.

### 3.6 Sections

**Headings**: Type and label section and subsection headings in the style shown on the present document. Use numbered sections (Arabic numerals) in order to facilitate cross references. Number subsections with the section number and the subsection number separated by a dot, in Arabic numerals. Do not number subsubsections.

**Citations**: Citations within the text appear in parentheses as (Gusfield, 1997) or, if the author's name

appears in the text itself, as Gusfield (1997). Append lowercase letters to the year in cases of ambiguity. Treat double authors as in (Aho and Ullman, 1972), but write as in (Chandra et al., 1981) when more than two authors are involved. Collapse multiple citations as in (Gusfield, 1997; Aho and Ullman, 1972). Also refrain from using full citations as sentence constituents. We suggest that instead of

"(Gusfield, 1997) showed that ..."

you use

"Gusfield (1997) showed that ..."

If you are using the provided LaTeX and BibTeX style files, you can use the command \newcite to get "author (year)" citations.

As reviewing will be double-blind, the submitted version of the papers should not include the authors' names and affiliations. Furthermore, self-references that reveal the author's identity, e.g.,

"We previously showed (Gusfield, 1997) ..."

should be avoided. Instead, use citations such as

"Gusfield (1997) previously showed ... "

**Please do not use anonymous citations** and do not include any of the following when submitting your paper for review: acknowledgements, project names, grant numbers, and names or URLs of resources or tools that have only been made publicly available in the last 3 weeks or are about to be made public and would compromise the anonymity of the submission. Papers that do not conform to these requirements may be rejected without review. These details can, however, be included in the camera-ready, final paper.

**References**: Gather the full set of references together under the heading **References**; place the section before any Appendices, unless they contain references. Arrange the references alphabetically by first author, rather than by order of occurrence in the text. Provide as complete a citation as possible, using a consistent format, such as the one for *Computational Linguistics* or the one in the *Publication Manual of the American Psychological Association* (American Psychological Association, 1983). Use of full names for authors rather than initials is preferred. A list of abbreviations for common computer science journals can be found in the ACM *Computing Reviews* (Association for Computing Machinery, 1983).

The LaTeX and BibTeX style files provided roughly fit the American Psychological Association format, allowing regular citations, short citations and multiple citations as described above.

**Appendices**: Appendices, if any, directly follow the text and the references (but see above). Letter them in sequence and provide an informative title: **Appendix A. Title of Appendix**.

### 3.7 Footnotes

**Footnotes**: Put footnotes at the bottom of the page and use 9 pt text. They may be numbered or referred to by asterisks or other symbols.[1] Footnotes should be separated from the text by a line.[2]

### 3.8 Graphics

**Illustrations**: Place figures, tables, and photographs in the paper near where they are first discussed, rather than at the end, if possible. Colour illustrations are discouraged, unless you have verified that they will be understandable when printed in black ink.

**Captions**: Provide a caption for every illustration; number each one sequentially in the form: "Figure 1. Caption of the Figure." "Table 1. Caption of the Table." Type the captions of the figures and tables below the body, using 11 pt text.

Narrow graphics together with the single-column format may lead to large empty spaces, see for example the wide margins on both sides of Table 1. If you have multiple graphics with related content, it may be preferable to combine them in one graphic. You can identify the sub-graphics with sub-captions below the sub-graphics numbered (a), (b), (c) etc. and using 9 pt text. The LaTeX packages wrapfig, subfig, subtable and/or subcaption may be useful.

---

[1] This is how a footnote should appear.

[2] Note the line separating the footnotes from the text.

### 3.9 Licence Statement

As in COLING-2014 and COLING-2016, we require that authors license their camera-ready papers under a Creative Commons Attribution 4.0 International Licence (CC-BY). This means that authors (copyright holders) retain copyright but grant everybody the right to adapt and re-distribute their paper as long as the authors are credited and modifications listed. In other words, this license lets researchers use research papers for their research without legal issues. Please refer to `http://creativecommons.org/licenses/by/4.0/` for the licence terms.

Depending on whether you use British or American English in your paper, please include one of the following as an unmarked (unnumbered) footnote on page 1 of your paper. The LaTeX style file (coling2018.sty) adds a command `blfootnote` for this purpose, and usage of the command is prepared in the LaTeX source code (coling2018.tex) at the start of Section "Introduction".

- This work is licensed under a Creative Commons Attribution 4.0 International Licence. Licence details: `http://creativecommons.org/licenses/by/4.0/`.

- This work is licensed under a Creative Commons Attribution 4.0 International License. License details: `http://creativecommons.org/licenses/by/4.0/`.

We strongly prefer that you licence your paper as the CC license above. However, if it is impossible for you to use that license, please contact the publication co-chairs Xiaodan Zhu (`zhu2048@gmail.com`) and Zhiyuan Liu (`liuzy@tsinghua.edu.cn`), before you submit your final version of accepted papers. (Please note that this license statement is only related to the final versions of accepted papers. It is not required for papers submitted for review.)

## 4 Translation of non-English Terms

It is also advised to supplement non-English characters and terms with appropriate transliterations and/or translations since not all readers understand all such characters and terms. Inline transliteration or translation can be represented in the order of: original-form transliteration "translation".

## 5 Length of Submission

The maximum submission length is 2 pages (A4), plus an unlimited number of pages for references. Authors of accepted papers will be given additional space in the camera-ready version to reflect space needed for changes stemming from reviewers comments.

Papers that do not conform to the specified length and formatting requirements may be rejected without review.

## Acknowledgements

The acknowledgements should go immediately before the references. Do not number the acknowledgements section. Do not include this section when submitting your paper for review.

## References


Alfred V. Aho and Jeffrey D. Ullman. 1972. *The Theory of Parsing, Translation and Compiling*, volume 1. Prentice-Hall, Englewood Cliffs, NJ.

American Psychological Association. 1983. *Publications Manual*. American Psychological Association, Washington, DC.

Association for Computing Machinery. 1983. *Computing Reviews*, 24(11):503–512.

Ashok K. Chandra, Dexter C. Kozen, and Larry J. Stockmeyer. 1981. Alternation. *Journal of the Association for Computing Machinery*, 28(1):114–133.

Dan Gusfield. 1997. *Algorithms on Strings, Trees and Sequences*. Cambridge University Press, Cambridge, UK.

# Instructions for WiNLP 2020


**First Author**
Affiliation / Address line 1
Affiliation / Address line 2
Affiliation / Address line 3
email@domain

**Second Author**
Affiliation / Address line 1
Affiliation / Address line 2
Affiliation / Address line 3
email@domain


## Abstract


This document contains the instructions for preparing a paper submitted to WiNLP 2019. The document itself conforms to its own specifications, and is therefore an example of what your manuscript should look like. These instructions should be used for both papers submitted for review and for final versions of accepted papers. Authors are asked to conform to all the directions reported in this document.


## 1 Credits

This document has been adapted from the instructions for COLING-2018 proceedings compiled by Xiaodan Zhu and Zhiyuan Liu, which are, in turn, based on the instructions for COLING-2016 proceedings, which are, in turn, based on the instructions for COLING-2014 proceedings compiled by Joachim Wagner, Liadh Kelly and Lorraine Goeuriot, which are, in turn, based on the instructions for earlier ACL proceedings, including those for ACL-2014 by Alexander Koller and Yusuke Miyao, those for ACL-2012 by Maggie Li and Michael White, those for ACL-2010 by Jing-Shing Chang and Philipp Koehn, those for ACL-2008 by Johanna D. Moore, Simone Teufel, James Allan, and Sadaoki Furui, those for ACL-2005 by Hwee Tou Ng and Kemal Oflazer, those for ACL-2002 by Eugene Charniak and Dekang Lin, and earlier ACL and EACL formats. Those versions were written by several people, including John Chen, Henry S. Thompson and Donald Walker. Additional elements were taken from the formatting instructions of the *International Joint Conference on Artificial Intelligence*.

## 2 Introduction

The following instructions are directed to authors of papers submitted to WiNLP 2019 or accepted for publication in its proceedings. All authors are required to adhere to these specifications. Authors are required to provide a Portable Document Format (PDF) version of their papers. **The proceedings are designed for printing on A4 paper.**

Authors from countries in which access to word-processing systems is limited should contact WiNLP Organizers `winlp-chairs@googlegroups.com` as soon as possible.

## 3 General Instructions

Manuscripts must be in single-column format. **Type single-spaced.** Start all pages directly under the top margin. See the guidelines later regarding formatting the first page. The lengths of manuscripts should not exceed the maximum page limit described in Section 5. Do not number the pages.

### 3.1 Electronically-available Resources

We strongly prefer that you prepare your PDF files using LaTeX with the official COLING 2018 style file (coling2018.sty) and bibliography style (acl.bst). These files are available in coling2018.zip at `http://coling2018.org/`. You will also find the document you are currently reading (coling2018.pdf) and its LaTeX source code (coling2018.tex) in coling2018.zip.

---

Place licence statement here for the camera-ready version. See Section 3.9 of the instructions for preparing a manuscript.




*Proceedings of the 55th Annual Meeting of the Association for Computational Linguistics*, pages 13–17
Florence, Italy, July 28th, 2019. ©2019 Association for Computational Linguistics

You can alternatively use Microsoft Word to produce your PDF file. In this case, we strongly recommend the use of the Word template file (coling2018.dot) in coling2018.zip. If you have an option, we recommend that you use the LaTeX2e version. If you will be using the Microsoft Word template, you must anonymise your source file so that the pdf produced does not retain your identity. This can be done by removing any personal information from your source document properties.

## 3.2 Format of Electronic Manuscript

For the production of the electronic manuscript you must use Adobe's Portable Document Format (PDF). PDF files are usually produced from LaTeX using the *pdflatex* command. If your version of LaTeX produces Postscript files, you can convert these into PDF using *ps2pdf* or *dvipdf*. On Windows, you can also use Adobe Distiller to generate PDF.

Please make sure that your PDF file includes all the necessary fonts (especially tree diagrams, symbols, and fonts for non-Latin characters). When you print or create the PDF file, there is usually an option in your printer setup to include none, all or just non-standard fonts. Please make sure that you select the option of including ALL the fonts. **Before sending it, test your PDF by printing it from a computer different from the one where it was created.** Moreover, some word processors may generate very large PDF files, where each page is rendered as an image. Such images may reproduce poorly. In this case, try alternative ways to obtain the PDF. One way on some systems is to install a driver for a postscript printer, send your document to the printer specifying "Output to a file", then convert the file to PDF.

It is of utmost importance to specify the **A4 format** (21 cm x 29.7 cm) when formatting the paper. When working with `dvips`, for instance, one should specify `-t a4`.

If you cannot meet the above requirements for the production of your electronic submission, please contact the publication co-chairs as soon as possible.

## 3.3 Layout

Format manuscripts with a single column to a page, in the manner these instructions are formatted. The exact dimensions for a page on A4 paper are:

- Left and right margins: 2.5 cm

- Top margin: 2.5 cm

- Bottom margin: 2.5 cm

- Width: 16.0 cm

- Height: 24.7 cm

Papers should not be submitted on any other paper size. If you cannot meet the above requirements for the production of your electronic submission, please contact the publication co-chairs above as soon as possible.

## 3.4 Fonts

For reasons of uniformity, Adobe's **Times Roman** font should be used. In LaTeX2e this is accomplished by putting

```
\usepackage{times}
\usepackage{latexsym}
```

in the preamble. If Times Roman is unavailable, use **Computer Modern Roman** (LaTeX2e's default). Note that the latter is about 10% less dense than Adobe's Times Roman font.

The **Times New Roman** font, which is configured for us in the Microsoft Word template (coling2018.dot) and which some Linux distributions offer for installation, can be used as well.

| Type of Text | Font Size | Style |
|---|---|---|
| paper title | 15 pt | bold |
| author names | 12 pt | bold |
| author affiliation | 12 pt | |
| the word "Abstract" | 12 pt | bold |
| section titles | 12 pt | bold |
| document text | 11 pt | |
| captions | 11 pt | |
| sub-captions | 9 pt | |
| abstract text | 11 pt | |
| bibliography | 10 pt | |
| footnotes | 9 pt | |

Table 1: Font guide.

### 3.5 The First Page

Centre the title, author's name(s) and affiliation(s) across the page. Do not use footnotes for affiliations. Do not include the paper ID number assigned during the submission process. Do not include the authors' names or affiliations in the version submitted for review.

**Title**: Place the title centred at the top of the first page, in a 15 pt bold font. (For a complete guide to font sizes and styles, see Table 1.) Long titles should be typed on two lines without a blank line intervening. Approximately, put the title at 2.5 cm from the top of the page, followed by a blank line, then the author's names(s), and the affiliation on the following line. Do not use only initials for given names (middle initials are allowed). Do not format surnames in all capitals (e.g., use "Schlangen" not "SCHLANGEN"). Do not format title and section headings in all capitals as well except for proper names (such as "BLEU") that are conventionally in all capitals. The affiliation should contain the author's complete address, and if possible, an electronic mail address. Start the body of the first page 7.5 cm from the top of the page.

The title, author names and addresses should be completely identical to those entered to the electronical paper submission website in order to maintain the consistency of author information among all publications of the conference. If they are different, the publication co-chairs may resolve the difference without consulting with you; so it is in your own interest to double-check that the information is consistent.

**Abstract**: Type the abstract between addresses and main body. The width of the abstract text should be smaller than main body by about 0.6 cm on each side. Centre the word **Abstract** in a 12 pt bold font above the body of the abstract. The abstract should be a concise summary of the general thesis and conclusions of the paper. It should be no longer than 200 words. The abstract text should be in 11 pt font.

**Text**: Begin typing the main body of the text immediately after the abstract, observing the single-column format as shown in the present document. Do not include page numbers.

**Indent** when starting a new paragraph. Use 11 pt for text and subsection headings, 12 pt for section headings and 15 pt for the title.

**Licence**: Include a licence statement as an unmarked (unnumbered) footnote on the first page of the final, camera-ready paper. See Section 3.9 below for details and motivation.

### 3.6 Sections

**Headings**: Type and label section and subsection headings in the style shown on the present document. Use numbered sections (Arabic numerals) in order to facilitate cross references. Number subsections with the section number and the subsection number separated by a dot, in Arabic numerals. Do not number subsubsections.

**Citations**: Citations within the text appear in parentheses as (Gusfield, 1997) or, if the author's name

appears in the text itself, as Gusfield (1997). Append lowercase letters to the year in cases of ambiguity. Treat double authors as in (Aho and Ullman, 1972), but write as in (Chandra et al., 1981) when more than two authors are involved. Collapse multiple citations as in (Gusfield, 1997; Aho and Ullman, 1972). Also refrain from using full citations as sentence constituents. We suggest that instead of

> "(Gusfield, 1997) showed that ..."

you use

> "Gusfield (1997) showed that ..."

If you are using the provided LaTeX and BibTeX style files, you can use the command \newcite to get "author (year)" citations.

As reviewing will be double-blind, the submitted version of the papers should not include the authors' names and affiliations. Furthermore, self-references that reveal the author's identity, e.g.,

> "We previously showed (Gusfield, 1997) ..."

should be avoided. Instead, use citations such as

> "Gusfield (1997) previously showed ... "

**Please do not use anonymous citations** and do not include any of the following when submitting your paper for review: acknowledgements, project names, grant numbers, and names or URLs of resources or tools that have only been made publicly available in the last 3 weeks or are about to be made public and would compromise the anonymity of the submission. Papers that do not conform to these requirements may be rejected without review. These details can, however, be included in the camera-ready, final paper.

**References**: Gather the full set of references together under the heading **References**; place the section before any Appendices, unless they contain references. Arrange the references alphabetically by first author, rather than by order of occurrence in the text. Provide as complete a citation as possible, using a consistent format, such as the one for *Computational Linguistics* or the one in the *Publication Manual of the American Psychological Association* (American Psychological Association, 1983). Use of full names for authors rather than initials is preferred. A list of abbreviations for common computer science journals can be found in the ACM *Computing Reviews* (Association for Computing Machinery, 1983).

The LaTeX and BibTeX style files provided roughly fit the American Psychological Association format, allowing regular citations, short citations and multiple citations as described above.

**Appendices**: Appendices, if any, directly follow the text and the references (but see above). Letter them in sequence and provide an informative title: **Appendix A. Title of Appendix**.

### 3.7 Footnotes

**Footnotes**: Put footnotes at the bottom of the page and use 9 pt text. They may be numbered or referred to by asterisks or other symbols.[1] Footnotes should be separated from the text by a line.[2]

### 3.8 Graphics

**Illustrations**: Place figures, tables, and photographs in the paper near where they are first discussed, rather than at the end, if possible. Colour illustrations are discouraged, unless you have verified that they will be understandable when printed in black ink.

**Captions**: Provide a caption for every illustration; number each one sequentially in the form: "Figure 1. Caption of the Figure." "Table 1. Caption of the Table." Type the captions of the figures and tables below the body, using 11 pt text.

Narrow graphics together with the single-column format may lead to large empty spaces, see for example the wide margins on both sides of Table 1. If you have multiple graphics with related content, it may be preferable to combine them in one graphic. You can identify the sub-graphics with sub-captions below the sub-graphics numbered (a), (b), (c) etc. and using 9 pt text. The LaTeX packages wrapfig, subfig, subtable and/or subcaption may be useful.

---

[1] This is how a footnote should appear.

[2] Note the line separating the footnotes from the text.

### 3.9 Licence Statement

As in COLING-2014 and COLING-2016, we require that authors license their camera-ready papers under a Creative Commons Attribution 4.0 International Licence (CC-BY). This means that authors (copyright holders) retain copyright but grant everybody the right to adapt and re-distribute their paper as long as the authors are credited and modifications listed. In other words, this license lets researchers use research papers for their research without legal issues. Please refer to `http://creativecommons.org/licenses/by/4.0/` for the licence terms.

Depending on whether you use British or American English in your paper, please include one of the following as an unmarked (unnumbered) footnote on page 1 of your paper. The LaTeX style file (coling2018.sty) adds a command `blfootnote` for this purpose, and usage of the command is prepared in the LaTeX source code (coling2018.tex) at the start of Section "Introduction".

- This work is licensed under a Creative Commons Attribution 4.0 International Licence. Licence details: `http://creativecommons.org/licenses/by/4.0/`.

- This work is licensed under a Creative Commons Attribution 4.0 International License. License details: `http://creativecommons.org/licenses/by/4.0/`.

We strongly prefer that you licence your paper as the CC license above. However, if it is impossible for you to use that license, please contact the publication co-chairs Xiaodan Zhu (`zhu2048@gmail.com`) and Zhiyuan Liu (`liuzy@tsinghua.edu.cn`), before you submit your final version of accepted papers. (Please note that this license statement is only related to the final versions of accepted papers. It is not required for papers submitted for review.)

## 4 Translation of non-English Terms

It is also advised to supplement non-English characters and terms with appropriate transliterations and/or translations since not all readers understand all such characters and terms. Inline transliteration or translation can be represented in the order of: original-form transliteration "translation".

## 5 Length of Submission

The maximum submission length is 2 pages (A4), plus an unlimited number of pages for references. Authors of accepted papers will be given additional space in the camera-ready version to reflect space needed for changes stemming from reviewers comments.

Papers that do not conform to the specified length and formatting requirements may be rejected without review.

## Acknowledgements

The acknowledgements should go immediately before the references. Do not number the acknowledgements section. Do not include this section when submitting your paper for review.

## References


Alfred V. Aho and Jeffrey D. Ullman. 1972. *The Theory of Parsing, Translation and Compiling*, volume 1. Prentice-Hall, Englewood Cliffs, NJ.

American Psychological Association. 1983. *Publications Manual*. American Psychological Association, Washington, DC.

Association for Computing Machinery. 1983. *Computing Reviews*, 24(11):503–512.

Ashok K. Chandra, Dexter C. Kozen, and Larry J. Stockmeyer. 1981. Alternation. *Journal of the Association for Computing Machinery*, 28(1):114–133.

Dan Gusfield. 1997. *Algorithms on Strings, Trees and Sequences*. Cambridge University Press, Cambridge, UK.

# Instructions for WiNLP 2020


**First Author**
Affiliation / Address line 1
Affiliation / Address line 2
Affiliation / Address line 3
email@domain

**Second Author**
Affiliation / Address line 1
Affiliation / Address line 2
Affiliation / Address line 3
email@domain


## Abstract


This document contains the instructions for preparing a paper submitted to WiNLP 2019. The document itself conforms to its own specifications, and is therefore an example of what your manuscript should look like. These instructions should be used for both papers submitted for review and for final versions of accepted papers. Authors are asked to conform to all the directions reported in this document.


## 1 Credits

This document has been adapted from the instructions for COLING-2018 proceedings compiled by Xiaodan Zhu and Zhiyuan Liu, which are, in turn, based on the instructions for COLING-2016 proceedings, which are, in turn, based on the instructions for COLING-2014 proceedings compiled by Joachim Wagner, Liadh Kelly and Lorraine Goeuriot, which are, in turn, based on the instructions for earlier ACL proceedings, including those for ACL-2014 by Alexander Koller and Yusuke Miyao, those for ACL-2012 by Maggie Li and Michael White, those for ACL-2010 by Jing-Shing Chang and Philipp Koehn, those for ACL-2008 by Johanna D. Moore, Simone Teufel, James Allan, and Sadaoki Furui, those for ACL-2005 by Hwee Tou Ng and Kemal Oflazer, those for ACL-2002 by Eugene Charniak and Dekang Lin, and earlier ACL and EACL formats. Those versions were written by several people, including John Chen, Henry S. Thompson and Donald Walker. Additional elements were taken from the formatting instructions of the *International Joint Conference on Artificial Intelligence*.

## 2 Introduction

The following instructions are directed to authors of papers submitted to WiNLP 2019 or accepted for publication in its proceedings. All authors are required to adhere to these specifications. Authors are required to provide a Portable Document Format (PDF) version of their papers. **The proceedings are designed for printing on A4 paper.**

Authors from countries in which access to word-processing systems is limited should contact WiNLP Organizers `winlp-chairs@googlegroups.com` as soon as possible.

## 3 General Instructions

Manuscripts must be in single-column format. **Type single-spaced.** Start all pages directly under the top margin. See the guidelines later regarding formatting the first page. The lengths of manuscripts should not exceed the maximum page limit described in Section 5. Do not number the pages.

### 3.1 Electronically-available Resources

We strongly prefer that you prepare your PDF files using LaTeX with the official COLING 2018 style file (coling2018.sty) and bibliography style (acl.bst). These files are available in coling2018.zip at `http://coling2018.org/`. You will also find the document you are currently reading (coling2018.pdf) and its LaTeX source code (coling2018.tex) in coling2018.zip.

---

Place licence statement here for the camera-ready version. See Section 3.9 of the instructions for preparing a manuscript.




*Proceedings of the 55th Annual Meeting of the Association for Computational Linguistics*, pages 18–22
Florence, Italy, July 28th, 2019. ©2019 Association for Computational Linguistics

You can alternatively use Microsoft Word to produce your PDF file. In this case, we strongly recommend the use of the Word template file (coling2018.dot) in coling2018.zip. If you have an option, we recommend that you use the LaTeX2e version. If you will be using the Microsoft Word template, you must anonymise your source file so that the pdf produced does not retain your identity. This can be done by removing any personal information from your source document properties.

### 3.2  Format of Electronic Manuscript

For the production of the electronic manuscript you must use Adobe's Portable Document Format (PDF). PDF files are usually produced from LaTeX using the *pdflatex* command. If your version of LaTeX produces Postscript files, you can convert these into PDF using *ps2pdf* or *dvipdf*. On Windows, you can also use Adobe Distiller to generate PDF.

Please make sure that your PDF file includes all the necessary fonts (especially tree diagrams, symbols, and fonts for non-Latin characters). When you print or create the PDF file, there is usually an option in your printer setup to include none, all or just non-standard fonts. Please make sure that you select the option of including ALL the fonts. **Before sending it, test your PDF by printing it from a computer different from the one where it was created.** Moreover, some word processors may generate very large PDF files, where each page is rendered as an image. Such images may reproduce poorly. In this case, try alternative ways to obtain the PDF. One way on some systems is to install a driver for a postscript printer, send your document to the printer specifying "Output to a file", then convert the file to PDF.

It is of utmost importance to specify the **A4 format** (21 cm x 29.7 cm) when formatting the paper. When working with `dvips`, for instance, one should specify `-t a4`.

If you cannot meet the above requirements for the production of your electronic submission, please contact the publication co-chairs as soon as possible.

### 3.3  Layout

Format manuscripts with a single column to a page, in the manner these instructions are formatted. The exact dimensions for a page on A4 paper are:

- Left and right margins: 2.5 cm

- Top margin: 2.5 cm

- Bottom margin: 2.5 cm

- Width: 16.0 cm

- Height: 24.7 cm

Papers should not be submitted on any other paper size. If you cannot meet the above requirements for the production of your electronic submission, please contact the publication co-chairs above as soon as possible.

### 3.4  Fonts

For reasons of uniformity, Adobe's **Times Roman** font should be used. In LaTeX2e this is accomplished by putting

```
\usepackage{times}
\usepackage{latexsym}
```

in the preamble. If Times Roman is unavailable, use **Computer Modern Roman** (LaTeX2e's default). Note that the latter is about 10% less dense than Adobe's Times Roman font.

The **Times New Roman** font, which is configured for us in the Microsoft Word template (coling2018.dot) and which some Linux distributions offer for installation, can be used as well.

| Type of Text | Font Size | Style |
|---|---|---|
| paper title | 15 pt | bold |
| author names | 12 pt | bold |
| author affiliation | 12 pt | |
| the word "Abstract" | 12 pt | bold |
| section titles | 12 pt | bold |
| document text | 11 pt | |
| captions | 11 pt | |
| sub-captions | 9 pt | |
| abstract text | 11 pt | |
| bibliography | 10 pt | |
| footnotes | 9 pt | |

Table 1: Font guide.

## 3.5 The First Page

Centre the title, author's name(s) and affiliation(s) across the page. Do not use footnotes for affiliations. Do not include the paper ID number assigned during the submission process. Do not include the authors' names or affiliations in the version submitted for review.

**Title**: Place the title centred at the top of the first page, in a 15 pt bold font. (For a complete guide to font sizes and styles, see Table 1.) Long titles should be typed on two lines without a blank line intervening. Approximately, put the title at 2.5 cm from the top of the page, followed by a blank line, then the author's names(s), and the affiliation on the following line. Do not use only initials for given names (middle initials are allowed). Do not format surnames in all capitals (e.g., use "Schlangen" not "SCHLANGEN"). Do not format title and section headings in all capitals as well except for proper names (such as "BLEU") that are conventionally in all capitals. The affiliation should contain the author's complete address, and if possible, an electronic mail address. Start the body of the first page 7.5 cm from the top of the page.

The title, author names and addresses should be completely identical to those entered to the electronical paper submission website in order to maintain the consistency of author information among all publications of the conference. If they are different, the publication co-chairs may resolve the difference without consulting with you; so it is in your own interest to double-check that the information is consistent.

**Abstract**: Type the abstract between addresses and main body. The width of the abstract text should be smaller than main body by about 0.6 cm on each side. Centre the word **Abstract** in a 12 pt bold font above the body of the abstract. The abstract should be a concise summary of the general thesis and conclusions of the paper. It should be no longer than 200 words. The abstract text should be in 11 pt font.

**Text**: Begin typing the main body of the text immediately after the abstract, observing the single-column format as shown in the present document. Do not include page numbers.

**Indent** when starting a new paragraph. Use 11 pt for text and subsection headings, 12 pt for section headings and 15 pt for the title.

**Licence**: Include a licence statement as an unmarked (unnumbered) footnote on the first page of the final, camera-ready paper. See Section 3.9 below for details and motivation.

## 3.6 Sections

**Headings**: Type and label section and subsection headings in the style shown on the present document. Use numbered sections (Arabic numerals) in order to facilitate cross references. Number subsections with the section number and the subsection number separated by a dot, in Arabic numerals. Do not number subsubsections.

**Citations**: Citations within the text appear in parentheses as (Gusfield, 1997) or, if the author's name

appears in the text itself, as Gusfield (1997). Append lowercase letters to the year in cases of ambiguity. Treat double authors as in (Aho and Ullman, 1972), but write as in (Chandra et al., 1981) when more than two authors are involved. Collapse multiple citations as in (Gusfield, 1997; Aho and Ullman, 1972). Also refrain from using full citations as sentence constituents. We suggest that instead of

> "(Gusfield, 1997) showed that ..."

you use

> "Gusfield (1997) showed that ..."

If you are using the provided LaTeX and BibTeX style files, you can use the command \newcite to get "author (year)" citations.

As reviewing will be double-blind, the submitted version of the papers should not include the authors' names and affiliations. Furthermore, self-references that reveal the author's identity, e.g.,

> "We previously showed (Gusfield, 1997) ..."

should be avoided. Instead, use citations such as

> "Gusfield (1997) previously showed ... "

**Please do not use anonymous citations** and do not include any of the following when submitting your paper for review: acknowledgements, project names, grant numbers, and names or URLs of resources or tools that have only been made publicly available in the last 3 weeks or are about to be made public and would compromise the anonymity of the submission. Papers that do not conform to these requirements may be rejected without review. These details can, however, be included in the camera-ready, final paper.

**References**: Gather the full set of references together under the heading **References**; place the section before any Appendices, unless they contain references. Arrange the references alphabetically by first author, rather than by order of occurrence in the text. Provide as complete a citation as possible, using a consistent format, such as the one for *Computational Linguistics* or the one in the *Publication Manual of the American Psychological Association* (American Psychological Association, 1983). Use of full names for authors rather than initials is preferred. A list of abbreviations for common computer science journals can be found in the ACM *Computing Reviews* (Association for Computing Machinery, 1983).

The LaTeX and BibTeX style files provided roughly fit the American Psychological Association format, allowing regular citations, short citations and multiple citations as described above.

**Appendices**: Appendices, if any, directly follow the text and the references (but see above). Letter them in sequence and provide an informative title: **Appendix A. Title of Appendix**.

### 3.7 Footnotes

**Footnotes**: Put footnotes at the bottom of the page and use 9 pt text. They may be numbered or referred to by asterisks or other symbols.[1] Footnotes should be separated from the text by a line.[2]

### 3.8 Graphics

**Illustrations**: Place figures, tables, and photographs in the paper near where they are first discussed, rather than at the end, if possible. Colour illustrations are discouraged, unless you have verified that they will be understandable when printed in black ink.

**Captions**: Provide a caption for every illustration; number each one sequentially in the form: "Figure 1. Caption of the Figure." "Table 1. Caption of the Table." Type the captions of the figures and tables below the body, using 11 pt text.

Narrow graphics together with the single-column format may lead to large empty spaces, see for example the wide margins on both sides of Table 1. If you have multiple graphics with related content, it may be preferable to combine them in one graphic. You can identify the sub-graphics with sub-captions below the sub-graphics numbered (a), (b), (c) etc. and using 9 pt text. The LaTeX packages wrapfig, subfig, subtable and/or subcaption may be useful.

---

[1]This is how a footnote should appear.

[2]Note the line separating the footnotes from the text.

### 3.9 Licence Statement

As in COLING-2014 and COLING-2016, we require that authors license their camera-ready papers under a Creative Commons Attribution 4.0 International Licence (CC-BY). This means that authors (copyright holders) retain copyright but grant everybody the right to adapt and re-distribute their paper as long as the authors are credited and modifications listed. In other words, this license lets researchers use research papers for their research without legal issues. Please refer to `http://creativecommons.org/licenses/by/4.0/` for the licence terms.

Depending on whether you use British or American English in your paper, please include one of the following as an unmarked (unnumbered) footnote on page 1 of your paper. The LaTeX style file (coling2018.sty) adds a command `blfootnote` for this purpose, and usage of the command is prepared in the LaTeX source code (coling2018.tex) at the start of Section "Introduction".

- This work is licensed under a Creative Commons Attribution 4.0 International Licence. Licence details: `http://creativecommons.org/licenses/by/4.0/`.

- This work is licensed under a Creative Commons Attribution 4.0 International License. License details: `http://creativecommons.org/licenses/by/4.0/`.

We strongly prefer that you licence your paper as the CC license above. However, if it is impossible for you to use that license, please contact the publication co-chairs Xiaodan Zhu (`zhu2048@gmail.com`) and Zhiyuan Liu (`liuzy@tsinghua.edu.cn`), before you submit your final version of accepted papers. (Please note that this license statement is only related to the final versions of accepted papers. It is not required for papers submitted for review.)

## 4 Translation of non-English Terms

It is also advised to supplement non-English characters and terms with appropriate transliterations and/or translations since not all readers understand all such characters and terms. Inline transliteration or translation can be represented in the order of: original-form transliteration "translation".

## 5 Length of Submission

The maximum submission length is 2 pages (A4), plus an unlimited number of pages for references. Authors of accepted papers will be given additional space in the camera-ready version to reflect space needed for changes stemming from reviewers comments.

Papers that do not conform to the specified length and formatting requirements may be rejected without review.

## Acknowledgements

The acknowledgements should go immediately before the references. Do not number the acknowledgements section. Do not include this section when submitting your paper for review.

## References


Alfred V. Aho and Jeffrey D. Ullman. 1972. *The Theory of Parsing, Translation and Compiling*, volume 1. Prentice-Hall, Englewood Cliffs, NJ.

American Psychological Association. 1983. *Publications Manual*. American Psychological Association, Washington, DC.

Association for Computing Machinery. 1983. *Computing Reviews*, 24(11):503–512.

Ashok K. Chandra, Dexter C. Kozen, and Larry J. Stockmeyer. 1981. Alternation. *Journal of the Association for Computing Machinery*, 28(1):114–133.

Dan Gusfield. 1997. *Algorithms on Strings, Trees and Sequences*. Cambridge University Press, Cambridge, UK.

# Token Level Identification of Multiword Expressions Using Contextual Information


**Reyhaneh Hashempour**
University of Essex
rh18456@essex.ac.uk

**Aline Villavicencio**
University of Sheffield
a.villavicencio@sheffield.ac.uk



## Abstract

Studies on detecting idiomatic expressions mostly focus on discovering potentially idiomatic expressions disregarding the context. However, many idioms like *kick the bucket* could be idiomatic/literal depending on the context. In this work, we use Context2Vec model to include contextual information. The model learns a generic context embedding function from large corpora, using bidirectional LSTM. We build a simple nearest neighbor classification on Context2Vec which outperforms the popular context representation of average-of-word-embeddings. Through lexical substitution task, we further show that the Context2Vec model is able to place MWEs into distinct 'sense'(idiomatic/literal) regions of the embedding space, while traditional word embedding i.e. Skip Gram lacks this ability.


## 1 Introduction

Determining whether a sequence of words (MWE) is idiomatic i.e., type identification, has received lots of attention (Baldwin et al., 2003; Cordeiro et al., 2016). However, an idiom could have a literal interpretation depending on the context. This makes token classification of potential idioms crucial for NLP tasks, especially Machine Translation. For example, *held fire* must be translated differently in *The army **held** their fire* and *The worshippers **held** the fire up to the idol* (Fazly et al., 2009).

Local linguistic context can provide evidence to identify whether a multi-word expression (MWE) has a literal or idiomatic meaning. King and Cook (2018) proposed a model based on distributed representations (i.e., Skip-Gram (Mikolov et al., 2013)) to classify VNC usages as idiomatic/literal. They represented the embeddings of the context of a target MWE by simple averaging of the embeddings of its surrounding words in a sentence. They used accuracy score to evaluate their model. We argue that simple averaging is too simplistic to capture inter-dependencies between the words in a sentence whereas a bidirectional LSTM (i.e., Context2Vec (Melamud et al., 2016)) is more powerful as it also takes the order of words into account. Moreover, given that the dataset (Cook et al., 2008) is unbalanced, the accuracy is not a good measure to evaluate the proposed model. Having this in mind, we show that although simple averaging almost yields the same accuracy score as our proposed model's, it falls short by a noticeable margin when the model is evaluated using other metrics such as precision, recall, and F-Score.

## 2 Experimental Setup

| Sense | Sentence | Context2Vec | Skip-Gram |
|---|---|---|---|
| Literal | 1 | **smash**, stuck, flatten, drop, shoot | Be, have, do, think, say |
| Idiomatic | 2 | go, finish, **start,embark**,come | Say, do , will, go, get |

Table 1: Words suggested by Context2Vec and Skip-Gram models to replace *hit-the-road*

Following Melamud et al. (2016), who used the kNN classification algorithm (Cover and Hart, 1967) for the task of WSD, we also use the simple non-parametric version and for the distance measure, we rely on cosine distance of the vectors. We consider two senses (idiomatic/literal) for an MWE and make sure that both senses have been observed in training set for a target MWE. We use BNC corpus (Burnard,




*Proceedings of the 55th Annual Meeting of the Association for Computational Linguistics*, pages 23–25
Florence, Italy, July 28th, 2019. ©2019 Association for Computational Linguistics

2000) and first lemmatize it using spaCy (Honnibal and Johnson, 2015). Then we tokenize where each MWE is treated as a single token with an underline between the first and the second part (e.g., blow the whistle is mapped to blow-whistle).[1] We build two semantic spaces, one using Context2Vec and the other using Skip-Gram. Our goal is to determine the correct sense of an MWE in context, based on a manually tagged training set. To classify a test MWE instance in context, we consider all of the instances of the same MWE in the training set, and find the instance whose context embedding is the most similar to the context embedding of the test instance using the context-to-context similarity measure. Then, we use the label of that instance as the correct label for the MWE in the test set. We use the simplest form of a k-nearest-neighbor algorithm, with k = 1 as it was used by Melamud et al. (2016) for the task of WSD and we also experiment with two more values for k=3 and 5.

## 3   Data set and Evaluation

We use VNC-Tokens dataset (Cook et al., 2008) to evaluate our model. The dataset includes sentences containing VNC tokens labelled as either idiomatic (I) / literal (L) (or "unknown"). For our experiments, we only use VNCs that are annotated as I or L (as in Salton et al. (2016) and King and Cook (2018)). We evaluate Context2Vec and Skip-Gram both qualitatively and quantitatively. In the qualitative setting, we compare the models through lexical substitution task. In the lexical substitution task, the goal is to find a substitute word for a given target word in sentential context. To do so, we remove the MWE from a sentence and then get the embeddings of the remaining sentence which is in fact the context of the MWE. Then we investigate to see the embeddings of which words have the highest cosine similarity with the embeddings of the context. These words are suggested as a substitute for the removed MWE. Table 1 shows the suggested words by Context2Vec vs. Skip-Gram to replace hit-the-road in literal (1) and idiomatic (2) meanings. Similar examples for other MWEs are omitted to conserve space.

(1) The bullets were [hitting the road] and I could see them coming towards me a lot faster than I was able to reverse.

(2) The Ulster Society are about to [hit the road] on one of their magical history tours

In the quantitative setting (Table 2), we use five-fold cross-validation and calculate the accuracy, precision, recall, and F-score per each expression and then report the average scores. We consider the positive class to be the "I" (idiomatic) label (as in Salton et al. (2016)).

| Model | Contex2Vec | | | | Skip-Gram | | | |
|---|---|---|---|---|---|---|---|---|
| | Accuracy | Precision | Recall | F-Score | Accuracy | Precision | Recall | F-Score |
| KNN1 | **0.84** | **0.81** | **0.83** | **0.81** | 0.78 | 0.74 | 0.76 | 0.73 |
| KNN3 | 0.84 | 0.78 | 0.82 | 0.79 | 0.81 | 0.74 | 0.81 | 0.76 |
| KNN5 | 0.84 | 0.77 | 0.81 | 0.77 | 0.83 | 0.74 | 0.81 | 0.76 |

Table 2: Context2Vec versus Skip-Gram scores in Classifying Idiomatic Expressions Using 1,2, and 3 nearest neighbours.

Using Skip-Gram, we achieve the same accuracy score as that of King and Cook (2018) and Context2Vec seems to perform on-par with Skip-Gram in terms of accuracy score; however, the superiority of the model is more obvious when we consider other metrics e.g. F-score. Moreover, the results in Table 1 suggest that Context2Vec seem to distinguish between idiomatic and literal sense of an MWE by proposing appropriate lexical substitute for the removed MWE.

## 4   Conclusion and Future Work

Using qualitative and quantitative analyses, we demonstrated that Context2Vec outperforms traditional average-of-word-embeddings in representing the context for the task of Token-level identification of MWEs. In future, we would like to investigate the performance of recently-introduced word embeddings, e.g. BERT (Devlin et al., 2019) for the same task using the same experimental settings.

---

[1] We also experimented with non-tokenized version and got poor results which verify our hypothesis that each MWE needs to be treated as a single token before training our embedding models.

# References


Timothy Baldwin, Colin Bannard, Takaaki Tanaka, and Dominic Widdows. 2003. https://doi.org/10.3115/1119282.1119294 An empirical model of multiword expression decomposability. In *Proceedings of the ACL 2003 Workshop on Multiword Expressions: Analysis, Acquisition and Treatment - Volume 18*, MWE '03, pages 89–96, Stroudsburg, PA, USA. Association for Computational Linguistics.

Lou Burnard. 2000. The british national corpus users reference guide. Technical report, Oxford University Computing Services.

Paul Cook, Afsaneh Fazly, and Suzanne Stevenson. 2008. The vnctokens dataset. In *In Proceedings of the LREC Workshop on Towards a Shared Task for Multiword Expressions (MWE 2008)*, pages 19–22, Marrakech, Morocco. Association for Computational Linguistics.

Silvio Cordeiro, Carlos Ramisch, Marco Idiart, and Aline Villavicencio. 2016. https://doi.org/10.18653/v1/P16-1187 Predicting the compositionality of nominal compounds: Giving word embeddings a hard time. In *Proceedings of the 54th Annual Meeting of the Association for Computational Linguistics (Volume 1: Long Papers)*, pages 1986–1997, Berlin, Germany. Association for Computational Linguistics.

T. Cover and P. Hart. 1967. https://doi.org/10.1109/TIT.1967.1053964 Nearest neighbor pattern classification. *IEEE Trans. Inf. Theor.*, 13(1):21–27.

Jacob Devlin, Ming-Wei Chang, Kenton Lee, and Kristina Toutanova. 2019. https://doi.org/10.18653/v1/N19-1423 BERT: Pre-training of deep bidirectional transformers for language understanding. In *Proceedings of the 2019 Conference of the North American Chapter of the Association for Computational Linguistics: Human Language Technologies, Volume 1 (Long and Short Papers)*, pages 4171–4186, Minneapolis, Minnesota. Association for Computational Linguistics.

Afsaneh Fazly, Paul Cook, and Suzanne Stevenson. 2009. https://doi.org/10.1162/coli.08-010-R1-07-048 Unsupervised type and token identification of idiomatic expressions. *Computational Linguistics*, 35(1):61–103.

Matthew Honnibal and Mark Johnson. 2015. https://doi.org/10.18653/v1/D15-1162 An improved non-monotonic transition system for dependency parsing. In *Proceedings of the 2015 Conference on Empirical Methods in Natural Language Processing*, pages 1373–1378, Lisbon, Portugal. Association for Computational Linguistics.

Milton King and Paul Cook. 2018. https://www.aclweb.org/anthology/P18-2055 Leveraging distributed representations and lexico-syntactic fixedness for token-level prediction of the idiomaticity of english verb-noun combinations. In *Proceedings of the 56th Annual Meeting of the Association for Computational Linguistics (Volume 2: Short Papers)*, pages 345–350, Melbourne, Australia. Association for Computational Linguistics.

Oren Melamud, Jacob Goldberger, and Ido Dagan. 2016. https://doi.org/10.18653/v1/K16-1006 context2vec: Learning generic context embedding with bidirectional LSTM. In *Proceedings of The 20th SIGNLL Conference on Computational Natural Language Learning*, pages 51–61, Berlin, Germany. Association for Computational Linguistics.

Tomas Mikolov, Kai Chen, Greg Corrado, and Jeffrey Dean. 2013. http://arxiv.org/abs/1301.3781 Efficient estimation of word representations in vector space. In *1st International Conference on Learning Representations, ICLR 2013, Scottsdale, Arizona, USA, May 2-4, 2013, Workshop Track Proceedings*.

Giancarlo Salton, Robert Ross, and John Kelleher. 2016. https://doi.org/10.18653/v1/P16-1019 Idiom token classification using sentential distributed semantics. In *Proceedings of the 54th Annual Meeting of the Association for Computational Linguistics (Volume 1: Long Papers)*, pages 194–204, Berlin, Germany. Association for Computational Linguistics.

# Instructions for WiNLP 2020


**First Author**
Affiliation / Address line 1
Affiliation / Address line 2
Affiliation / Address line 3
email@domain

**Second Author**
Affiliation / Address line 1
Affiliation / Address line 2
Affiliation / Address line 3
email@domain


## Abstract


This document contains the instructions for preparing a paper submitted to WiNLP 2019. The document itself conforms to its own specifications, and is therefore an example of what your manuscript should look like. These instructions should be used for both papers submitted for review and for final versions of accepted papers. Authors are asked to conform to all the directions reported in this document.


## 1 Credits

This document has been adapted from the instructions for COLING-2018 proceedings compiled by Xiaodan Zhu and Zhiyuan Liu, which are, in turn, based on the instructions for COLING-2016 proceedings, which are, in turn, based on the instructions for COLING-2014 proceedings compiled by Joachim Wagner, Liadh Kelly and Lorraine Goeuriot, which are, in turn, based on the instructions for earlier ACL proceedings, including those for ACL-2014 by Alexander Koller and Yusuke Miyao, those for ACL-2012 by Maggie Li and Michael White, those for ACL-2010 by Jing-Shing Chang and Philipp Koehn, those for ACL-2008 by Johanna D. Moore, Simone Teufel, James Allan, and Sadaoki Furui, those for ACL-2005 by Hwee Tou Ng and Kemal Oflazer, those for ACL-2002 by Eugene Charniak and Dekang Lin, and earlier ACL and EACL formats. Those versions were written by several people, including John Chen, Henry S. Thompson and Donald Walker. Additional elements were taken from the formatting instructions of the *International Joint Conference on Artificial Intelligence*.

## 2 Introduction

The following instructions are directed to authors of papers submitted to WiNLP 2019 or accepted for publication in its proceedings. All authors are required to adhere to these specifications. Authors are required to provide a Portable Document Format (PDF) version of their papers. **The proceedings are designed for printing on A4 paper.**

Authors from countries in which access to word-processing systems is limited should contact WiNLP Organizers winlp-chairs@googlegroups.com as soon as possible.

## 3 General Instructions

Manuscripts must be in single-column format. **Type single-spaced.** Start all pages directly under the top margin. See the guidelines later regarding formatting the first page. The lengths of manuscripts should not exceed the maximum page limit described in Section 5. Do not number the pages.

### 3.1 Electronically-available Resources

We strongly prefer that you prepare your PDF files using LaTeX with the official COLING 2018 style file (coling2018.sty) and bibliography style (acl.bst). These files are available in coling2018.zip at `http://coling2018.org/`. You will also find the document you are currently reading (coling2018.pdf) and its LaTeX source code (coling2018.tex) in coling2018.zip.

---

Place licence statement here for the camera-ready version. See Section 3.9 of the instructions for preparing a manuscript.




*Proceedings of the 55th Annual Meeting of the Association for Computational Linguistics*, pages 26–30
Florence, Italy, July 28th, 2019. ©2019 Association for Computational Linguistics

You can alternatively use Microsoft Word to produce your PDF file. In this case, we strongly recommend the use of the Word template file (coling2018.dot) in coling2018.zip. If you have an option, we recommend that you use the LaTeX2e version. If you will be using the Microsoft Word template, you must anonymise your source file so that the pdf produced does not retain your identity. This can be done by removing any personal information from your source document properties.

### 3.2 Format of Electronic Manuscript

For the production of the electronic manuscript you must use Adobe's Portable Document Format (PDF). PDF files are usually produced from LaTeX using the *pdflatex* command. If your version of LaTeX produces Postscript files, you can convert these into PDF using *ps2pdf* or *dvipdf*. On Windows, you can also use Adobe Distiller to generate PDF.

Please make sure that your PDF file includes all the necessary fonts (especially tree diagrams, symbols, and fonts for non-Latin characters). When you print or create the PDF file, there is usually an option in your printer setup to include none, all or just non-standard fonts. Please make sure that you select the option of including ALL the fonts. **Before sending it, test your PDF by printing it from a computer different from the one where it was created.** Moreover, some word processors may generate very large PDF files, where each page is rendered as an image. Such images may reproduce poorly. In this case, try alternative ways to obtain the PDF. One way on some systems is to install a driver for a postscript printer, send your document to the printer specifying "Output to a file", then convert the file to PDF.

It is of utmost importance to specify the **A4 format** (21 cm x 29.7 cm) when formatting the paper. When working with `dvips`, for instance, one should specify `-t a4`.

If you cannot meet the above requirements for the production of your electronic submission, please contact the publication co-chairs as soon as possible.

### 3.3 Layout

Format manuscripts with a single column to a page, in the manner these instructions are formatted. The exact dimensions for a page on A4 paper are:

- Left and right margins: 2.5 cm

- Top margin: 2.5 cm

- Bottom margin: 2.5 cm

- Width: 16.0 cm

- Height: 24.7 cm

Papers should not be submitted on any other paper size. If you cannot meet the above requirements for the production of your electronic submission, please contact the publication co-chairs above as soon as possible.

### 3.4 Fonts

For reasons of uniformity, Adobe's **Times Roman** font should be used. In LaTeX2e this is accomplished by putting

```
\usepackage{times}
\usepackage{latexsym}
```

in the preamble. If Times Roman is unavailable, use **Computer Modern Roman** (LaTeX2e's default). Note that the latter is about 10% less dense than Adobe's Times Roman font.

The **Times New Roman** font, which is configured for us in the Microsoft Word template (coling2018.dot) and which some Linux distributions offer for installation, can be used as well.

| Type of Text | Font Size | Style |
|---|---|---|
| paper title | 15 pt | bold |
| author names | 12 pt | bold |
| author affiliation | 12 pt | |
| the word "Abstract" | 12 pt | bold |
| section titles | 12 pt | bold |
| document text | 11 pt | |
| captions | 11 pt | |
| sub-captions | 9 pt | |
| abstract text | 11 pt | |
| bibliography | 10 pt | |
| footnotes | 9 pt | |

Table 1: Font guide.

### 3.5 The First Page

Centre the title, author's name(s) and affiliation(s) across the page. Do not use footnotes for affiliations. Do not include the paper ID number assigned during the submission process. Do not include the authors' names or affiliations in the version submitted for review.

**Title**: Place the title centred at the top of the first page, in a 15 pt bold font. (For a complete guide to font sizes and styles, see Table 1.) Long titles should be typed on two lines without a blank line intervening. Approximately, put the title at 2.5 cm from the top of the page, followed by a blank line, then the author's names(s), and the affiliation on the following line. Do not use only initials for given names (middle initials are allowed). Do not format surnames in all capitals (e.g., use "Schlangen" not "SCHLANGEN"). Do not format title and section headings in all capitals as well except for proper names (such as "BLEU") that are conventionally in all capitals. The affiliation should contain the author's complete address, and if possible, an electronic mail address. Start the body of the first page 7.5 cm from the top of the page.

The title, author names and addresses should be completely identical to those entered to the electronical paper submission website in order to maintain the consistency of author information among all publications of the conference. If they are different, the publication co-chairs may resolve the difference without consulting with you; so it is in your own interest to double-check that the information is consistent.

**Abstract**: Type the abstract between addresses and main body. The width of the abstract text should be smaller than main body by about 0.6 cm on each side. Centre the word **Abstract** in a 12 pt bold font above the body of the abstract. The abstract should be a concise summary of the general thesis and conclusions of the paper. It should be no longer than 200 words. The abstract text should be in 11 pt font.

**Text**: Begin typing the main body of the text immediately after the abstract, observing the single-column format as shown in the present document. Do not include page numbers.

**Indent** when starting a new paragraph. Use 11 pt for text and subsection headings, 12 pt for section headings and 15 pt for the title.

**Licence**: Include a licence statement as an unmarked (unnumbered) footnote on the first page of the final, camera-ready paper. See Section 3.9 below for details and motivation.

### 3.6 Sections

**Headings**: Type and label section and subsection headings in the style shown on the present document. Use numbered sections (Arabic numerals) in order to facilitate cross references. Number subsections with the section number and the subsection number separated by a dot, in Arabic numerals. Do not number subsubsections.

**Citations**: Citations within the text appear in parentheses as (Gusfield, 1997) or, if the author's name

appears in the text itself, as Gusfield (1997). Append lowercase letters to the year in cases of ambiguity. Treat double authors as in (Aho and Ullman, 1972), but write as in (Chandra et al., 1981) when more than two authors are involved. Collapse multiple citations as in (Gusfield, 1997; Aho and Ullman, 1972). Also refrain from using full citations as sentence constituents. We suggest that instead of

> "(Gusfield, 1997) showed that ..."

you use

> "Gusfield (1997) showed that ..."

If you are using the provided LaTeX and BibTeX style files, you can use the command \newcite to get "author (year)" citations.

As reviewing will be double-blind, the submitted version of the papers should not include the authors' names and affiliations. Furthermore, self-references that reveal the author's identity, e.g.,

> "We previously showed (Gusfield, 1997) ..."

should be avoided. Instead, use citations such as

> "Gusfield (1997) previously showed ... "

**Please do not use anonymous citations** and do not include any of the following when submitting your paper for review: acknowledgements, project names, grant numbers, and names or URLs of resources or tools that have only been made publicly available in the last 3 weeks or are about to be made public and would compromise the anonymity of the submission. Papers that do not conform to these requirements may be rejected without review. These details can, however, be included in the camera-ready, final paper.

**References**: Gather the full set of references together under the heading **References**; place the section before any Appendices, unless they contain references. Arrange the references alphabetically by first author, rather than by order of occurrence in the text. Provide as complete a citation as possible, using a consistent format, such as the one for *Computational Linguistics* or the one in the *Publication Manual of the American Psychological Association* (American Psychological Association, 1983). Use of full names for authors rather than initials is preferred. A list of abbreviations for common computer science journals can be found in the ACM *Computing Reviews* (Association for Computing Machinery, 1983).

The LaTeX and BibTeX style files provided roughly fit the American Psychological Association format, allowing regular citations, short citations and multiple citations as described above.

**Appendices**: Appendices, if any, directly follow the text and the references (but see above). Letter them in sequence and provide an informative title: **Appendix A. Title of Appendix**.

## 3.7 Footnotes

**Footnotes**: Put footnotes at the bottom of the page and use 9 pt text. They may be numbered or referred to by asterisks or other symbols.[1] Footnotes should be separated from the text by a line.[2]

## 3.8 Graphics

**Illustrations**: Place figures, tables, and photographs in the paper near where they are first discussed, rather than at the end, if possible. Colour illustrations are discouraged, unless you have verified that they will be understandable when printed in black ink.

**Captions**: Provide a caption for every illustration; number each one sequentially in the form: "Figure 1. Caption of the Figure." "Table 1. Caption of the Table." Type the captions of the figures and tables below the body, using 11 pt text.

Narrow graphics together with the single-column format may lead to large empty spaces, see for example the wide margins on both sides of Table 1. If you have multiple graphics with related content, it may be preferable to combine them in one graphic. You can identify the sub-graphics with sub-captions below the sub-graphics numbered (a), (b), (c) etc. and using 9 pt text. The LaTeX packages wrapfig, subfig, subtable and/or subcaption may be useful.

---

[1]This is how a footnote should appear.

[2]Note the line separating the footnotes from the text.

### 3.9 Licence Statement

As in COLING-2014 and COLING-2016, we require that authors license their camera-ready papers under a Creative Commons Attribution 4.0 International Licence (CC-BY). This means that authors (copyright holders) retain copyright but grant everybody the right to adapt and re-distribute their paper as long as the authors are credited and modifications listed. In other words, this license lets researchers use research papers for their research without legal issues. Please refer to `http://creativecommons.org/licenses/by/4.0/` for the licence terms.

Depending on whether you use British or American English in your paper, please include one of the following as an unmarked (unnumbered) footnote on page 1 of your paper. The LaTeX style file (coling2018.sty) adds a command `blfootnote` for this purpose, and usage of the command is prepared in the LaTeX source code (coling2018.tex) at the start of Section "Introduction".

- This work is licensed under a Creative Commons Attribution 4.0 International Licence. Licence details: `http://creativecommons.org/licenses/by/4.0/`.

- This work is licensed under a Creative Commons Attribution 4.0 International License. License details: `http://creativecommons.org/licenses/by/4.0/`.

We strongly prefer that you licence your paper as the CC license above. However, if it is impossible for you to use that license, please contact the publication co-chairs Xiaodan Zhu (`zhu2048@gmail.com`) and Zhiyuan Liu (`liuzy@tsinghua.edu.cn`), before you submit your final version of accepted papers. (Please note that this license statement is only related to the final versions of accepted papers. It is not required for papers submitted for review.)

## 4 Translation of non-English Terms

It is also advised to supplement non-English characters and terms with appropriate transliterations and/or translations since not all readers understand all such characters and terms. Inline transliteration or translation can be represented in the order of: original-form transliteration "translation".

## 5 Length of Submission

The maximum submission length is 2 pages (A4), plus an unlimited number of pages for references. Authors of accepted papers will be given additional space in the camera-ready version to reflect space needed for changes stemming from reviewers comments.

Papers that do not conform to the specified length and formatting requirements may be rejected without review.

## Acknowledgements

The acknowledgements should go immediately before the references. Do not number the acknowledgements section. Do not include this section when submitting your paper for review.

## References


Alfred V. Aho and Jeffrey D. Ullman. 1972. *The Theory of Parsing, Translation and Compiling*, volume 1. Prentice-Hall, Englewood Cliffs, NJ.

American Psychological Association. 1983. *Publications Manual*. American Psychological Association, Washington, DC.

Association for Computing Machinery. 1983. *Computing Reviews*, 24(11):503–512.

Ashok K. Chandra, Dexter C. Kozen, and Larry J. Stockmeyer. 1981. Alternation. *Journal of the Association for Computing Machinery*, 28(1):114–133.

Dan Gusfield. 1997. *Algorithms on Strings, Trees and Sequences*. Cambridge University Press, Cambridge, UK.

# Effective questions in referential visual dialogue

**Mauricio Mazuecos (1), Alberto Testoni (2), Raffaella Bernardi (3) and Luciana Benotti (1)**
(1) FAMAF, Universidad Nacional de Córdoba, CONICET, Argentina
(2) DISI, University of Trento, Italy
(3) DISI, CIMEC, University of Trento, Italy
`mmazuecos@famaf.unc.edu.ar` `alberto.testoni@unitn.it`
`raffaella.bernardi@unitn.it` `luciana.benotti@unc.edu.ar`

## Abstract

An interesting challenge for situated dialogue systems is referential visual dialogue: by asking questions, the system has to identify the referent to which the user refers to. Task success is the standard metric used to evaluate these systems. However, it does not consider how *effective* each question is, that is how much each question contributes to the goal. We propose a new metric, that measures question effectiveness. As a preliminary study, we report the new metric for state of the art publicly available models on GuessWhat?!. Surprisingly, successful dialogues do not have a higher percentage of effective questions than failed dialogues. This suggests that a system with high task success is not necessarily one that generates good questions.

## 1 Introduction

GuessWhat?! (de Vries et al., 2017) is a cooperative two-player referential visual dialogue game. One player (the *Oracle*) is assigned a referent object in an image, the other player (the *Questioner*) has to guess the referent by asking yes/no questions. The GuessWhat?! dataset contains games of different complexity, ranging from easy images with a referent and 1 distractor to images with 19 distractors.

Referential visual dialogue has a clear task success metric: whether the Questioner is able or not to correctly identify the referent at the end of the dialogue. The need of going beyond this metric to evaluate the quality of the dialogues has already been observed. So far attention has been put on the linguistic skills of the models (Shukla et al., 2019; Shekhar et al., 2019) and their dialogue strategies (Abbasnejad et al., 2018; Shekhar et al., 2018). Recently, Sankar et al. (2019) showed that current SOTA dialogue systems do not take dialogue history into account, and new models were proposed to make questions more informative and consistent with the dialogue history (Shukla et al., 2019; Ray et al., 2019; Abbasnejad et al., 2019; Pang and Wang, 2020). But still the models are mostly evaluated without considering how much each question contributes to the goal. We propose a new metric to evaluate dialogue *effectiveness* as the percentage of effective questions it contains. Intuitively, a question is effective if it eliminates at least one possible distractor from the set of objects (Krahmer and van Deemter, 2012). Figure 1 gives a game played by humans as an example. In the image there are 8 candidate objects: the referent object is the cow marked in green and the distractors are the other 6 cows and the wooden stick. The dialogue is highly effective: 80% of the questions eliminate at least one distractor.

| Human question | Answer | # D | Effective |
|---|---|---|---|
| 1. is it a cow? | yes | 6 | True |
| 2. is it the big cow in the middle? | no | 5 | True |
| 3. a cow on the left? | no | 3 | True |
| 4. *on the right?* | yes | 3 | False |
| 5. first cow near us? | yes | 0 | True |

Figure 1: Human-human dialogue on the Guesswhat?! referential task extracted from (de Vries et al., 2017). The target is highlighted in green. # D is the number of candidates remaining after the question is answered. Four out of five questions eliminate distractors and, hence, are effective.



*Proceedings of the 55th Annual Meeting of the Association for Computational Linguistics*, pages 31–35
Florence, Italy, July 28th, 2019. ©2019 Association for Computational Linguistics

## 2 Previous work

Despite recent progress in the area of vision and language, recent work (Jain et al., 2019) in the navigation task (VLN) argues that current research leaves unclear how much of a role language plays in this task. They point out that dominant evaluation metrics have focused on goal completion rather than how each action contributes to the goal (Anderson et al., 2018). The nature of the path an agent takes, however, is of clear practical importance: it is undesirable for any robotic agent in the physical world to reach the destination by taking a lot of deviation or getting into dangerous zones. Jain et al. (2019) propose alternative metrics that evaluate the intermediate steps in the VLN task.

As argued by Lowe et al. (2019), the vast majority of recent papers on emergent communication show that adding a communication channel leads to an increase in task success. This is a useful indicator, but provides only a coarse measure of the agent's learned communication abilities. As we move towards more complex environments, it becomes imperative to have a set of finer tools that allow qualitative and quantitative insights into the emergence of communication.

Following this idea of not only focusing on goal completion but on evaluating how much each step contributes to the goal, in this paper we propose a new metric for referential dialogue. We agree with Thomason et al. (2019) that incremental evaluation metrics such as ours should look further back into the dialogue history. We believe that language and vision systems should also be evaluated on aspects such as grammatically, truthfulness, diversity and other aspects as done in previous work (Lee et al., 2018; Ray et al., 2019; Xie et al., 2020; Murahari et al., 2019). In this paper we focus on whether a question is effective considering the dialogue history and the visual context.

One of the motivations for referential visual dialogue is to provide robots with the ability to identify objects through dialogue with a humans. The task we address in this paper is a simplification. In our setup, the view of the robot is static (i.e. a picture). For our work we use the GuessWhat?! dataset (de Vries et al., 2017). We are particularly interested in models that generate questions explicitly modelling the dialogue history (Zhang et al., 2018; Shukla et al., 2019; Pang and Wang, 2020).[1]

## 3 Effective questions

Our definition of *effective* question is based on the set of candidate objects: the *reference set RS*. We compute $RS$ for each question $q_t$. The reference set before the dialogue starts, $RS(q_0)$, contains all the objects in the image. At each dialogue turn $t$, $RS(q_t)$ is defined as the set of objects in $RS(q_{t-1})$ such that the answer[2] to $q_t$ on those objects is the same than the answer to $q_t$ on the referent $r$. Formally:

$$RS(q_t) := \{o_i \in RS(q_{t-1}) \mid Answer(q_t, o_i) = Answer(q_t, r)\}$$

We say that a question $q_t$ is *not effective* iff $RS(q_t) = RS(q_{t-1})$. That is, the question does exclude any distractor. The *effectiveness* of the dialogue is given by the percentage of effective questions it has.

Table 1 reports the average *effectiveness* (Global column) for humans and SOTA models for which either the code or the dialogues with suitable annotations have been released. We also distinguish the effectiveness of dialogues finished in either Failure or Success. The baseline model (de Vries et al., 2017) represents the Questioner as two independent models, the question generator and the guesser, and train them by supervised learning. RL (Strub et al., 2017) further trains this baseline with a reinforcement learning phase. GDSE-SL differs from the baseline by having a joint encoder for the Questioner components and GDSE-CL exploits this joint architecture by letting the two components cooperate with each other (Shekhar et al., 2019). Last, VDST (Pang and Wang, 2020) extends the questioner with a probability distribution of each object being the referent and trains with reinforcement learning.

The results suggest that models make more non-effective questions than one may expect. Surprisingly, successful dialogues generated by models do not have a higher percentage of effective questions. Even for humans, effectiveness is not considerably higher for successful dialogues. Human effectiveness is

---

[1]Unfortunately, the code or test dialogues of some previous work are not available (Zhang et al., 2018; Shukla et al., 2019).

[2]Answers are provided by the Oracle model proposed in (de Vries et al., 2017) whose accuracy on the test set is 79%. As initial reference set, we take the list of objects annotated in the dataset (de Vries et al., 2017).

| | **VDST** | | **GDSE-CL** | |
|---|---|---|---|---|
| | 1. is it food? | yes | 1. is it food? | yes |
| | 2. is it in the left? | yes | 2. *is it a cake?* | yes |
| | 3. is it in the front? | yes | 3. *is it the dark brown?* | yes |
| | 4. *is it in the top?* | no | 4. *is it the entire cake?* | yes |
| | 5. *in the middle?* | no | 5. so the most left of the brown ones? | yes |

Figure 2: Dialogues generated by VDST and GDSE-CL in a successful game. Non effective in italics.

higher in almost every column of the table, the VDST model is close. Humans do not see the list of annotated objects as the Guesser models do. They rely on their sight on the image and they may ask questions that discard objects present in the image but not annotated in the dataset and hence not part of the reference set we calculate. All of these questions are marked as non-effective because they discard objects invisible to our metric and to the models. Hence, human effectiveness could be higher than we have calculated using the GuessWhat?! dataset object annotations.

| Model | Max Qs | Task success | Effectiveness | | |
|---|---|---|---|---|---|
| | | | Global | Failure | Success |
| Baseline (de Vries et al., 2017) | 8 | 40.7 | 26.4 | 27.5 | 24.7 |
| GDSE-SL (Shekhar et al., 2019) | 8 | 49.7 | 29.1 | 31.4 | 26.9 |
| RL (Strub et al., 2017) | 8 | 56.3 | 32.6 | 36.5 | 29.6 |
| GDSE-CL (Shekhar et al., 2019) | 8 | 58.4 | 30.2 | 32.3 | 28.6 |
| Baseline (de Vries et al., 2017) | 5 | 40.8 | 38.8 | 39.8 | 37.4 |
| GDSE-SL (Shekhar et al., 2019) | 5 | 47.8 | 42.2 | 44.6 | 39.9 |
| RL (Strub et al., 2017) | 5 | 58.4 | 48.6 | 52.9 | 45.1 |
| GDSE-CL (Shekhar et al., 2019) | 5 | 53.7 | 44.7 | 47.8 | 42.6 |
| VDST (Pang and Wang, 2020) | 5 | 64.4 | 52.9 | 57.4 | 51.0 |
| Humans (de Vries et al., 2017) | $\infty$ | 84.1 | 56.9 | 54.7 | 57.3 |

Table 1: Results comparing task success and effectiveness of generative systems for unseen images. Our manual inspections of human dialogues has shown that humans ask non-effective questions mostly at the end of the dialogue to reinforce their belief before guessing. We only show results of the 5 questions setup for VDST as we only had access to those dialogues.

Figure 2 shows an example of both metrics on a game on which VDST and GDSE-CL are successful. Effectiveness is 60 for VDST and 40 for GDSE-CL. Our definition of effectiveness not only accounts for question repetitions, but it also captures paraphrases and context-dependent redundancies. Examples of context dependent redundancy can be seen for both systems. In the VDST dialogue, 4 is redundant because, in this image, there is no cake that is both in the front and in the top. In GDSE-CL dialogue, question 2 is redundant because all cakes in the image are dark brown.

## 4   Conclusion and future work

We proposed a new metric for evaluating Guesswhat?! dialogues. Effectiveness, as we defined it, evaluates whether the question can rule out at least one possible distractor. We consider a question to be effective if it is able to make the reference set smaller. We observe that effectiveness decreases as dialogues advance and reaches its lowest level in the last turn. We also find that successful dialogues do not have a higher percentage of effective questions. This is surprising, and hints at the fact that there are other strategies to accomplish reference identification other than asking effective questions. We believe that our metric could be a heuristic that guides the training of end-to-end models.

# References


Ehsan Abbasnejad, Qi Wu, Iman Abbasnejad, Javen Shi, and Anton van den Hengel. 2018. An active information seeking model for goal-oriented vision-and-language tasks. *CoRR*, abs/1812.06398.

Ehsan Abbasnejad, Qi Wu, Javen Shi, and Anton van den Hengel. 2019. Whats to know? uncertainty as a guide to asking goal-oriented questions. In *IEEE Conference on Computer Vision and Pattern Recognition (CVPR)*.

Peter Anderson, Angel X. Chang, Devendra Singh Chaplot, Alexey Dosovitskiy, Saurabh Gupta, Vladlen Koltun, Jana Kosecka, Jitendra Malik, Roozbeh Mottaghi, Manolis Savva, and Amir Roshan Zamir. 2018. On evaluation of embodied navigation agents. *CoRR*, abs/1807.06757.

Harm de Vries, Florian Strub, Sarath Chandar, Olivier Pietquin, Hugo Larochelle, and Aaron C. Courville. 2017. Guesswhat?! visual object discovery through multi-modal dialogue. In *Conference on Computer Vision and Pattern Recognition (CVPR)*.

Vihan Jain, Gabriel Magalhaes, Alexander Ku, Ashish Vaswani, Eugene Ie, and Jason Baldridge. 2019. Stay on the path: Instruction fidelity in vision-and-language navigation. In *Proceedings of the 57th Annual Meeting of the Association for Computational Linguistics*, pages 1862–1872, Florence, Italy, July. Association for Computational Linguistics.

Emiel Krahmer and Kees van Deemter. 2012. Computational generation of referring expressions: A survey. *Computational Linguistics*, 38(1):173–218.

Sang-Woo Lee, Yu-Jung Heo, and Byoung-Tak Zhang. 2018. Answerer in questioner's mind: Information theoretic approach to goal-oriented visual dialog. In S. Bengio, H. Wallach, H. Larochelle, K. Grauman, N. Cesa-Bianchi, and R. Garnett, editors, *Advances in Neural Information Processing Systems 31*, pages 2579–2589. Curran Associates, Inc.

Ryan Lowe, Jakob Foerster, Y-Lan Boureau, Joelle Pineau, and Yann Dauphin. 2019. On the pitfalls of measuring emergent communication. In *Proceedings of the 18th International Conference on Autonomous Agents and MultiAgent Systems*, AAMAS '19, page 693–701, Richland, SC. International Foundation for Autonomous Agents and Multiagent Systems.

Vishvak Murahari, Prithvijit Chattopadhyay, Dhruv Batra, Devi Parikh, and Abhishek Das. 2019. Improving generative visual dialog by answering diverse questions. In *Proceedings of the 2019 Conference on Empirical Methods in Natural Language Processing and the 9th International Joint Conference on Natural Language Processing (EMNLP-IJCNLP)*, pages 1449–1454, Hong Kong, China, November. Association for Computational Linguistics.

Wei Pang and Xiaojie Wang. 2020. Visual dialogue state tracking for question generation. In *Proceedings of the Thirty-Fourth AAAI Conference on Artificial Intelligence (AAAI)*.

Arijit Ray, Karan Sikka, Ajay Divakaran, Stefan Lee, and Giedrius Burachas. 2019. Sunny and dark outside?! improving answer consistency in VQA through entailed question generation. In *Proceedings of the 2019 Conference on Empirical Methods in Natural Language Processing and the 9th International Joint Conference on Natural Language Processing (EMNLP-IJCNLP)*, pages 5860–5865, Hong Kong, China, November. Association for Computational Linguistics.

Chinnadhurai Sankar, Sandeep Subramanian, Chris Pal, Sarath Chandar, and Yoshua Bengio. 2019. Do neural dialog systems use the conversation history effectively? an empirical study. In *Proceedings of the 57th Annual Meeting of the Association for Computational Linguistics*, pages 32–37, Florence, Italy, July. Association for Computational Linguistics.

Ravi Shekhar, Tim Baumgärtner, Aashish Venkatesh, Elia Bruni, Raffaella Bernardi, and Raquel Fernandez. 2018. Ask no more: Deciding when to guess in referential visual dialogue. In *Proceedings of the 27th International Conference on Computational Linguistics*, pages 1218–1233, Santa Fe, New Mexico, USA, August. Association for Computational Linguistics.

Ravi Shekhar, Aashish Venkatesh, Tim Baumgärtner, Elia Bruni, Barbara Plank, Raffaella Bernardi, and Raquel Fernández. 2019. Beyond task success: A closer look at jointly learning to see, ask, and GuessWhat. In *Proceedings of the 2019 Conference of the North American Chapter of the Association for Computational Linguistics: Human Language Technologies, Volume 1 (Long and Short Papers)*, pages 2578–2587, Minneapolis, Minnesota, June. Association for Computational Linguistics.

Pushkar Shukla, Carlos Elmadjian, Richika Sharan, Vivek Kulkarni, Matthew Turk, and William Yang Wang. 2019. What should I ask? using conversationally informative rewards for goal-oriented visual dialog. In *Proceedings of the 57th Annual Meeting of the Association for Computational Linguistics*, pages 6442–6451, Florence, Italy, July. Association for Computational Linguistics.

Florian Strub, Harm de Vries, Jeremie Mary, Bilal Piot, Aaron C. Courville, and Olivier Pietquin. 2017. End-to-end optimization of goal-driven and visually grounded dialogue systems. In *International Joint Conference on Artificial Intelligence (IJCAI)*.

Jesse Thomason, Michael Murray, Maya Cakmak, and Luke Zettlemoyer. 2019. Vision-and-dialog navigation. In *Conference on Robot Learning*, Osaka, Japan.

Huiyuan Xie, Tom Sherborne, Alexander Kuhnle, and Ann Copestake. 2020. Going beneath the surface: Evaluating image captioning for grammaticality, truthfulness and diversity. In *Workshop on Evaluating AI Systems (AAAI 2020)*.

Junjie Zhang, Qi Wu, Chunhua Shen, Jian Zhang, Jianfeng Lu, and Anton van den Hengel. 2018. Goal-oriented visual question generation via intermediate rewards. In Vittorio Ferrari, Martial Hebert, Cristian Sminchisescu, and Yair Weiss, editors, *Computer Vision - ECCV 2018 - 15th European Conference, Munich, Germany, September 8-14, Proceedings, Part V*, volume 11209 of *Lecture Notes in Computer Science*, pages 189–204. Springer.

# Instructions for WiNLP 2020


**First Author**
Affiliation / Address line 1
Affiliation / Address line 2
Affiliation / Address line 3
`email@domain`

**Second Author**
Affiliation / Address line 1
Affiliation / Address line 2
Affiliation / Address line 3
`email@domain`


## Abstract


This document contains the instructions for preparing a paper submitted to WiNLP 2019. The document itself conforms to its own specifications, and is therefore an example of what your manuscript should look like. These instructions should be used for both papers submitted for review and for final versions of accepted papers. Authors are asked to conform to all the directions reported in this document.


## 1 Credits

This document has been adapted from the instructions for COLING-2018 proceedings compiled by Xiaodan Zhu and Zhiyuan Liu, which are, in turn, based on the instructions for COLING-2016 proceedings, which are, in turn, based on the instructions for COLING-2014 proceedings compiled by Joachim Wagner, Liadh Kelly and Lorraine Goeuriot, which are, in turn, based on the instructions for earlier ACL proceedings, including those for ACL-2014 by Alexander Koller and Yusuke Miyao, those for ACL-2012 by Maggie Li and Michael White, those for ACL-2010 by Jing-Shing Chang and Philipp Koehn, those for ACL-2008 by Johanna D. Moore, Simone Teufel, James Allan, and Sadaoki Furui, those for ACL-2005 by Hwee Tou Ng and Kemal Oflazer, those for ACL-2002 by Eugene Charniak and Dekang Lin, and earlier ACL and EACL formats. Those versions were written by several people, including John Chen, Henry S. Thompson and Donald Walker. Additional elements were taken from the formatting instructions of the *International Joint Conference on Artificial Intelligence*.

## 2 Introduction

The following instructions are directed to authors of papers submitted to WiNLP 2019 or accepted for publication in its proceedings. All authors are required to adhere to these specifications. Authors are required to provide a Portable Document Format (PDF) version of their papers. **The proceedings are designed for printing on A4 paper.**

Authors from countries in which access to word-processing systems is limited should contact WiNLP Organizers `winlp-chairs@googlegroups.com` as soon as possible.

## 3 General Instructions

Manuscripts must be in single-column format. **Type single-spaced.** Start all pages directly under the top margin. See the guidelines later regarding formatting the first page. The lengths of manuscripts should not exceed the maximum page limit described in Section 5. Do not number the pages.

### 3.1 Electronically-available Resources

We strongly prefer that you prepare your PDF files using LaTeX with the official COLING 2018 style file (coling2018.sty) and bibliography style (acl.bst). These files are available in coling2018.zip at `http://coling2018.org/`. You will also find the document you are currently reading (coling2018.pdf) and its LaTeX source code (coling2018.tex) in coling2018.zip.

---


Place licence statement here for the camera-ready version. See Section 3.9 of the instructions for preparing a manuscript.





*Proceedings of the 55th Annual Meeting of the Association for Computational Linguistics*, pages 36–40
Florence, Italy, July 28th, 2019. ©2019 Association for Computational Linguistics

You can alternatively use Microsoft Word to produce your PDF file. In this case, we strongly recommend the use of the Word template file (coling2018.dot) in coling2018.zip. If you have an option, we recommend that you use the LaTeX2e version. If you will be using the Microsoft Word template, you must anonymise your source file so that the pdf produced does not retain your identity. This can be done by removing any personal information from your source document properties.

### 3.2 Format of Electronic Manuscript

For the production of the electronic manuscript you must use Adobe's Portable Document Format (PDF). PDF files are usually produced from LaTeX using the *pdflatex* command. If your version of LaTeX produces Postscript files, you can convert these into PDF using *ps2pdf* or *dvipdf*. On Windows, you can also use Adobe Distiller to generate PDF.

Please make sure that your PDF file includes all the necessary fonts (especially tree diagrams, symbols, and fonts for non-Latin characters). When you print or create the PDF file, there is usually an option in your printer setup to include none, all or just non-standard fonts. Please make sure that you select the option of including ALL the fonts. **Before sending it, test your PDF by printing it from a computer different from the one where it was created.** Moreover, some word processors may generate very large PDF files, where each page is rendered as an image. Such images may reproduce poorly. In this case, try alternative ways to obtain the PDF. One way on some systems is to install a driver for a postscript printer, send your document to the printer specifying "Output to a file", then convert the file to PDF.

It is of utmost importance to specify the **A4 format** (21 cm x 29.7 cm) when formatting the paper. When working with `dvips`, for instance, one should specify `-t a4`.

If you cannot meet the above requirements for the production of your electronic submission, please contact the publication co-chairs as soon as possible.

### 3.3 Layout

Format manuscripts with a single column to a page, in the manner these instructions are formatted. The exact dimensions for a page on A4 paper are:

- Left and right margins: 2.5 cm

- Top margin: 2.5 cm

- Bottom margin: 2.5 cm

- Width: 16.0 cm

- Height: 24.7 cm

Papers should not be submitted on any other paper size. If you cannot meet the above requirements for the production of your electronic submission, please contact the publication co-chairs above as soon as possible.

### 3.4 Fonts

For reasons of uniformity, Adobe's **Times Roman** font should be used. In LaTeX2e this is accomplished by putting

```
\usepackage{times}
\usepackage{latexsym}
```

in the preamble. If Times Roman is unavailable, use **Computer Modern Roman** (LaTeX2e's default). Note that the latter is about 10% less dense than Adobe's Times Roman font.

The **Times New Roman** font, which is configured for us in the Microsoft Word template (coling2018.dot) and which some Linux distributions offer for installation, can be used as well.

| Type of Text | Font Size | Style |
|---|---|---|
| paper title | 15 pt | bold |
| author names | 12 pt | bold |
| author affiliation | 12 pt | |
| the word "Abstract" | 12 pt | bold |
| section titles | 12 pt | bold |
| document text | 11 pt | |
| captions | 11 pt | |
| sub-captions | 9 pt | |
| abstract text | 11 pt | |
| bibliography | 10 pt | |
| footnotes | 9 pt | |

Table 1: Font guide.

### 3.5 The First Page

Centre the title, author's name(s) and affiliation(s) across the page. Do not use footnotes for affiliations. Do not include the paper ID number assigned during the submission process. Do not include the authors' names or affiliations in the version submitted for review.

**Title**: Place the title centred at the top of the first page, in a 15 pt bold font. (For a complete guide to font sizes and styles, see Table 1.) Long titles should be typed on two lines without a blank line intervening. Approximately, put the title at 2.5 cm from the top of the page, followed by a blank line, then the author's names(s), and the affiliation on the following line. Do not use only initials for given names (middle initials are allowed). Do not format surnames in all capitals (e.g., use "Schlangen" not "SCHLANGEN"). Do not format title and section headings in all capitals as well except for proper names (such as "BLEU") that are conventionally in all capitals. The affiliation should contain the author's complete address, and if possible, an electronic mail address. Start the body of the first page 7.5 cm from the top of the page.

The title, author names and addresses should be completely identical to those entered to the electronical paper submission website in order to maintain the consistency of author information among all publications of the conference. If they are different, the publication co-chairs may resolve the difference without consulting with you; so it is in your own interest to double-check that the information is consistent.

**Abstract**: Type the abstract between addresses and main body. The width of the abstract text should be smaller than main body by about 0.6 cm on each side. Centre the word **Abstract** in a 12 pt bold font above the body of the abstract. The abstract should be a concise summary of the general thesis and conclusions of the paper. It should be no longer than 200 words. The abstract text should be in 11 pt font.

**Text**: Begin typing the main body of the text immediately after the abstract, observing the single-column format as shown in the present document. Do not include page numbers.

**Indent** when starting a new paragraph. Use 11 pt for text and subsection headings, 12 pt for section headings and 15 pt for the title.

**Licence**: Include a licence statement as an unmarked (unnumbered) footnote on the first page of the final, camera-ready paper. See Section 3.9 below for details and motivation.

### 3.6 Sections

**Headings**: Type and label section and subsection headings in the style shown on the present document. Use numbered sections (Arabic numerals) in order to facilitate cross references. Number subsections with the section number and the subsection number separated by a dot, in Arabic numerals. Do not number subsubsections.

**Citations**: Citations within the text appear in parentheses as (Gusfield, 1997) or, if the author's name

appears in the text itself, as Gusfield (1997). Append lowercase letters to the year in cases of ambiguity. Treat double authors as in (Aho and Ullman, 1972), but write as in (Chandra et al., 1981) when more than two authors are involved. Collapse multiple citations as in (Gusfield, 1997; Aho and Ullman, 1972). Also refrain from using full citations as sentence constituents. We suggest that instead of

> "(Gusfield, 1997) showed that ..."

you use

> "Gusfield (1997) showed that ..."

If you are using the provided LaTeX and BibTeX style files, you can use the command `\newcite` to get "author (year)" citations.

As reviewing will be double-blind, the submitted version of the papers should not include the authors' names and affiliations. Furthermore, self-references that reveal the author's identity, e.g.,

> "We previously showed (Gusfield, 1997) ..."

should be avoided. Instead, use citations such as

> "Gusfield (1997) previously showed ... "

**Please do not use anonymous citations** and do not include any of the following when submitting your paper for review: acknowledgements, project names, grant numbers, and names or URLs of resources or tools that have only been made publicly available in the last 3 weeks or are about to be made public and would compromise the anonymity of the submission. Papers that do not conform to these requirements may be rejected without review. These details can, however, be included in the camera-ready, final paper.

**References**: Gather the full set of references together under the heading **References**; place the section before any Appendices, unless they contain references. Arrange the references alphabetically by first author, rather than by order of occurrence in the text. Provide as complete a citation as possible, using a consistent format, such as the one for *Computational Linguistics* or the one in the *Publication Manual of the American Psychological Association* (American Psychological Association, 1983). Use of full names for authors rather than initials is preferred. A list of abbreviations for common computer science journals can be found in the ACM *Computing Reviews* (Association for Computing Machinery, 1983).

The LaTeX and BibTeX style files provided roughly fit the American Psychological Association format, allowing regular citations, short citations and multiple citations as described above.

**Appendices**: Appendices, if any, directly follow the text and the references (but see above). Letter them in sequence and provide an informative title: **Appendix A. Title of Appendix**.

### 3.7 Footnotes

**Footnotes**: Put footnotes at the bottom of the page and use 9 pt text. They may be numbered or referred to by asterisks or other symbols.[1] Footnotes should be separated from the text by a line.[2]

### 3.8 Graphics

**Illustrations**: Place figures, tables, and photographs in the paper near where they are first discussed, rather than at the end, if possible. Colour illustrations are discouraged, unless you have verified that they will be understandable when printed in black ink.

**Captions**: Provide a caption for every illustration; number each one sequentially in the form: "Figure 1. Caption of the Figure." "Table 1. Caption of the Table." Type the captions of the figures and tables below the body, using 11 pt text.

Narrow graphics together with the single-column format may lead to large empty spaces, see for example the wide margins on both sides of Table 1. If you have multiple graphics with related content, it may be preferable to combine them in one graphic. You can identify the sub-graphics with sub-captions below the sub-graphics numbered (a), (b), (c) etc. and using 9 pt text. The LaTeX packages wrapfig, subfig, subtable and/or subcaption may be useful.

---

[1]This is how a footnote should appear.

[2]Note the line separating the footnotes from the text.

### 3.9 Licence Statement

As in COLING-2014 and COLING-2016, we require that authors license their camera-ready papers under a Creative Commons Attribution 4.0 International Licence (CC-BY). This means that authors (copyright holders) retain copyright but grant everybody the right to adapt and re-distribute their paper as long as the authors are credited and modifications listed. In other words, this license lets researchers use research papers for their research without legal issues. Please refer to `http://creativecommons.org/licenses/by/4.0/` for the licence terms.

Depending on whether you use British or American English in your paper, please include one of the following as an unmarked (unnumbered) footnote on page 1 of your paper. The LaTeX style file (coling2018.sty) adds a command `blfootnote` for this purpose, and usage of the command is prepared in the LaTeX source code (coling2018.tex) at the start of Section "Introduction".

- This work is licensed under a Creative Commons Attribution 4.0 International Licence. Licence details: `http://creativecommons.org/licenses/by/4.0/`.

- This work is licensed under a Creative Commons Attribution 4.0 International License. License details: `http://creativecommons.org/licenses/by/4.0/`.

We strongly prefer that you licence your paper as the CC license above. However, if it is impossible for you to use that license, please contact the publication co-chairs Xiaodan Zhu (`zhu2048@gmail.com`) and Zhiyuan Liu (`liuzy@tsinghua.edu.cn`), before you submit your final version of accepted papers. (Please note that this license statement is only related to the final versions of accepted papers. It is not required for papers submitted for review.)

## 4 Translation of non-English Terms

It is also advised to supplement non-English characters and terms with appropriate transliterations and/or translations since not all readers understand all such characters and terms. Inline transliteration or translation can be represented in the order of: original-form transliteration "translation".

## 5 Length of Submission

The maximum submission length is 2 pages (A4), plus an unlimited number of pages for references. Authors of accepted papers will be given additional space in the camera-ready version to reflect space needed for changes stemming from reviewers comments.

Papers that do not conform to the specified length and formatting requirements may be rejected without review.

## Acknowledgements

The acknowledgements should go immediately before the references. Do not number the acknowledgements section. Do not include this section when submitting your paper for review.

## References


Alfred V. Aho and Jeffrey D. Ullman. 1972. *The Theory of Parsing, Translation and Compiling*, volume 1. Prentice-Hall, Englewood Cliffs, NJ.

American Psychological Association. 1983. *Publications Manual*. American Psychological Association, Washington, DC.

Association for Computing Machinery. 1983. *Computing Reviews*, 24(11):503–512.

Ashok K. Chandra, Dexter C. Kozen, and Larry J. Stockmeyer. 1981. Alternation. *Journal of the Association for Computing Machinery*, 28(1):114–133.

Dan Gusfield. 1997. *Algorithms on Strings, Trees and Sequences*. Cambridge University Press, Cambridge, UK.

# Instructions for WiNLP 2020

**First Author**
Affiliation / Address line 1
Affiliation / Address line 2
Affiliation / Address line 3
`email@domain`

**Second Author**
Affiliation / Address line 1
Affiliation / Address line 2
Affiliation / Address line 3
`email@domain`


## Abstract


This document contains the instructions for preparing a paper submitted to WiNLP 2019. The document itself conforms to its own specifications, and is therefore an example of what your manuscript should look like. These instructions should be used for both papers submitted for review and for final versions of accepted papers. Authors are asked to conform to all the directions reported in this document.


## 1 Credits

This document has been adapted from the instructions for COLING-2018 proceedings compiled by Xiaodan Zhu and Zhiyuan Liu, which are, in turn, based on the instructions for COLING-2016 proceedings, which are, in turn, based on the instructions for COLING-2014 proceedings compiled by Joachim Wagner, Liadh Kelly and Lorraine Goeuriot, which are, in turn, based on the instructions for earlier ACL proceedings, including those for ACL-2014 by Alexander Koller and Yusuke Miyao, those for ACL-2012 by Maggie Li and Michael White, those for ACL-2010 by Jing-Shing Chang and Philipp Koehn, those for ACL-2008 by Johanna D. Moore, Simone Teufel, James Allan, and Sadaoki Furui, those for ACL-2005 by Hwee Tou Ng and Kemal Oflazer, those for ACL-2002 by Eugene Charniak and Dekang Lin, and earlier ACL and EACL formats. Those versions were written by several people, including John Chen, Henry S. Thompson and Donald Walker. Additional elements were taken from the formatting instructions of the *International Joint Conference on Artificial Intelligence*.

## 2 Introduction

The following instructions are directed to authors of papers submitted to WiNLP 2019 or accepted for publication in its proceedings. All authors are required to adhere to these specifications. Authors are required to provide a Portable Document Format (PDF) version of their papers. **The proceedings are designed for printing on A4 paper.**

Authors from countries in which access to word-processing systems is limited should contact WiNLP Organizers `winlp-chairs@googlegroups.com` as soon as possible.

## 3 General Instructions

Manuscripts must be in single-column format. **Type single-spaced.** Start all pages directly under the top margin. See the guidelines later regarding formatting the first page. The lengths of manuscripts should not exceed the maximum page limit described in Section 5. Do not number the pages.

### 3.1 Electronically-available Resources

We strongly prefer that you prepare your PDF files using LaTeX with the official COLING 2018 style file (coling2018.sty) and bibliography style (acl.bst). These files are available in coling2018.zip at `http://coling2018.org/`. You will also find the document you are currently reading (coling2018.pdf) and its LaTeX source code (coling2018.tex) in coling2018.zip.

---

Place licence statement here for the camera-ready version. See Section 3.9 of the instructions for preparing a manuscript.




*Proceedings of the 55th Annual Meeting of the Association for Computational Linguistics*, pages 41–45
Florence, Italy, July 28th, 2019. ©2019 Association for Computational Linguistics

You can alternatively use Microsoft Word to produce your PDF file. In this case, we strongly recommend the use of the Word template file (coling2018.dot) in coling2018.zip. If you have an option, we recommend that you use the LaTeX2e version. If you will be using the Microsoft Word template, you must anonymise your source file so that the pdf produced does not retain your identity. This can be done by removing any personal information from your source document properties.

## 3.2 Format of Electronic Manuscript

For the production of the electronic manuscript you must use Adobe's Portable Document Format (PDF). PDF files are usually produced from LaTeX using the *pdflatex* command. If your version of LaTeX produces Postscript files, you can convert these into PDF using *ps2pdf* or *dvipdf*. On Windows, you can also use Adobe Distiller to generate PDF.

Please make sure that your PDF file includes all the necessary fonts (especially tree diagrams, symbols, and fonts for non-Latin characters). When you print or create the PDF file, there is usually an option in your printer setup to include none, all or just non-standard fonts. Please make sure that you select the option of including ALL the fonts. **Before sending it, test your PDF by printing it from a computer different from the one where it was created.** Moreover, some word processors may generate very large PDF files, where each page is rendered as an image. Such images may reproduce poorly. In this case, try alternative ways to obtain the PDF. One way on some systems is to install a driver for a postscript printer, send your document to the printer specifying "Output to a file", then convert the file to PDF.

It is of utmost importance to specify the **A4 format** (21 cm x 29.7 cm) when formatting the paper. When working with `dvips`, for instance, one should specify `-t a4`.

If you cannot meet the above requirements for the production of your electronic submission, please contact the publication co-chairs as soon as possible.

## 3.3 Layout

Format manuscripts with a single column to a page, in the manner these instructions are formatted. The exact dimensions for a page on A4 paper are:

- Left and right margins: 2.5 cm

- Top margin: 2.5 cm

- Bottom margin: 2.5 cm

- Width: 16.0 cm

- Height: 24.7 cm

Papers should not be submitted on any other paper size. If you cannot meet the above requirements for the production of your electronic submission, please contact the publication co-chairs above as soon as possible.

## 3.4 Fonts

For reasons of uniformity, Adobe's **Times Roman** font should be used. In LaTeX2e this is accomplished by putting

```
\usepackage{times}
\usepackage{latexsym}
```

in the preamble. If Times Roman is unavailable, use **Computer Modern Roman** (LaTeX2e's default). Note that the latter is about 10% less dense than Adobe's Times Roman font.

The **Times New Roman** font, which is configured for us in the Microsoft Word template (coling2018.dot) and which some Linux distributions offer for installation, can be used as well.

| Type of Text | Font Size | Style |
|---|---|---|
| paper title | 15 pt | bold |
| author names | 12 pt | bold |
| author affiliation | 12 pt | |
| the word "Abstract" | 12 pt | bold |
| section titles | 12 pt | bold |
| document text | 11 pt | |
| captions | 11 pt | |
| sub-captions | 9 pt | |
| abstract text | 11 pt | |
| bibliography | 10 pt | |
| footnotes | 9 pt | |

Table 1: Font guide.

## 3.5 The First Page

Centre the title, author's name(s) and affiliation(s) across the page. Do not use footnotes for affiliations. Do not include the paper ID number assigned during the submission process. Do not include the authors' names or affiliations in the version submitted for review.

**Title**: Place the title centred at the top of the first page, in a 15 pt bold font. (For a complete guide to font sizes and styles, see Table 1.) Long titles should be typed on two lines without a blank line intervening. Approximately, put the title at 2.5 cm from the top of the page, followed by a blank line, then the author's names(s), and the affiliation on the following line. Do not use only initials for given names (middle initials are allowed). Do not format surnames in all capitals (e.g., use "Schlangen" not "SCHLANGEN"). Do not format title and section headings in all capitals as well except for proper names (such as "BLEU") that are conventionally in all capitals. The affiliation should contain the author's complete address, and if possible, an electronic mail address. Start the body of the first page 7.5 cm from the top of the page.

The title, author names and addresses should be completely identical to those entered to the electronical paper submission website in order to maintain the consistency of author information among all publications of the conference. If they are different, the publication co-chairs may resolve the difference without consulting with you; so it is in your own interest to double-check that the information is consistent.

**Abstract**: Type the abstract between addresses and main body. The width of the abstract text should be smaller than main body by about 0.6 cm on each side. Centre the word **Abstract** in a 12 pt bold font above the body of the abstract. The abstract should be a concise summary of the general thesis and conclusions of the paper. It should be no longer than 200 words. The abstract text should be in 11 pt font.

**Text**: Begin typing the main body of the text immediately after the abstract, observing the single-column format as shown in the present document. Do not include page numbers.

**Indent** when starting a new paragraph. Use 11 pt for text and subsection headings, 12 pt for section headings and 15 pt for the title.

**Licence**: Include a licence statement as an unmarked (unnumbered) footnote on the first page of the final, camera-ready paper. See Section 3.9 below for details and motivation.

## 3.6 Sections

**Headings**: Type and label section and subsection headings in the style shown on the present document. Use numbered sections (Arabic numerals) in order to facilitate cross references. Number subsections with the section number and the subsection number separated by a dot, in Arabic numerals. Do not number subsubsections.

**Citations**: Citations within the text appear in parentheses as (Gusfield, 1997) or, if the author's name

appears in the text itself, as Gusfield (1997). Append lowercase letters to the year in cases of ambiguity. Treat double authors as in (Aho and Ullman, 1972), but write as in (Chandra et al., 1981) when more than two authors are involved. Collapse multiple citations as in (Gusfield, 1997; Aho and Ullman, 1972). Also refrain from using full citations as sentence constituents. We suggest that instead of

> "(Gusfield, 1997) showed that ..."

you use

> "Gusfield (1997) showed that ..."

If you are using the provided LaTeX and BibTeX style files, you can use the command \newcite to get "author (year)" citations.

As reviewing will be double-blind, the submitted version of the papers should not include the authors' names and affiliations. Furthermore, self-references that reveal the author's identity, e.g.,

> "We previously showed (Gusfield, 1997) ..."

should be avoided. Instead, use citations such as

> "Gusfield (1997) previously showed ... "

**Please do not use anonymous citations** and do not include any of the following when submitting your paper for review: acknowledgements, project names, grant numbers, and names or URLs of resources or tools that have only been made publicly available in the last 3 weeks or are about to be made public and would compromise the anonymity of the submission. Papers that do not conform to these requirements may be rejected without review. These details can, however, be included in the camera-ready, final paper.

**References**: Gather the full set of references together under the heading **References**; place the section before any Appendices, unless they contain references. Arrange the references alphabetically by first author, rather than by order of occurrence in the text. Provide as complete a citation as possible, using a consistent format, such as the one for *Computational Linguistics* or the one in the *Publication Manual of the American Psychological Association* (American Psychological Association, 1983). Use of full names for authors rather than initials is preferred. A list of abbreviations for common computer science journals can be found in the ACM *Computing Reviews* (Association for Computing Machinery, 1983).

The LaTeX and BibTeX style files provided roughly fit the American Psychological Association format, allowing regular citations, short citations and multiple citations as described above.

**Appendices**: Appendices, if any, directly follow the text and the references (but see above). Letter them in sequence and provide an informative title: **Appendix A. Title of Appendix**.

### 3.7   Footnotes

**Footnotes**: Put footnotes at the bottom of the page and use 9 pt text. They may be numbered or referred to by asterisks or other symbols.[1] Footnotes should be separated from the text by a line.[2]

### 3.8   Graphics

**Illustrations**: Place figures, tables, and photographs in the paper near where they are first discussed, rather than at the end, if possible. Colour illustrations are discouraged, unless you have verified that they will be understandable when printed in black ink.

**Captions**: Provide a caption for every illustration; number each one sequentially in the form: "Figure 1. Caption of the Figure." "Table 1. Caption of the Table." Type the captions of the figures and tables below the body, using 11 pt text.

Narrow graphics together with the single-column format may lead to large empty spaces, see for example the wide margins on both sides of Table 1. If you have multiple graphics with related content, it may be preferable to combine them in one graphic. You can identify the sub-graphics with sub-captions below the sub-graphics numbered (a), (b), (c) etc. and using 9 pt text. The LaTeX packages wrapfig, subfig, subtable and/or subcaption may be useful.

---

[1]This is how a footnote should appear.

[2]Note the line separating the footnotes from the text.

### 3.9 Licence Statement

As in COLING-2014 and COLING-2016, we require that authors license their camera-ready papers under a Creative Commons Attribution 4.0 International Licence (CC-BY). This means that authors (copyright holders) retain copyright but grant everybody the right to adapt and re-distribute their paper as long as the authors are credited and modifications listed. In other words, this license lets researchers use research papers for their research without legal issues. Please refer to `http://creativecommons.org/licenses/by/4.0/` for the licence terms.

Depending on whether you use British or American English in your paper, please include one of the following as an unmarked (unnumbered) footnote on page 1 of your paper. The LaTeX style file (coling2018.sty) adds a command `blfootnote` for this purpose, and usage of the command is prepared in the LaTeX source code (coling2018.tex) at the start of Section "Introduction".

- This work is licensed under a Creative Commons Attribution 4.0 International Licence. Licence details: `http://creativecommons.org/licenses/by/4.0/`.

- This work is licensed under a Creative Commons Attribution 4.0 International License. License details: `http://creativecommons.org/licenses/by/4.0/`.

We strongly prefer that you licence your paper as the CC license above. However, if it is impossible for you to use that license, please contact the publication co-chairs Xiaodan Zhu (`zhu2048@gmail.com`) and Zhiyuan Liu (`liuzy@tsinghua.edu.cn`), before you submit your final version of accepted papers. (Please note that this license statement is only related to the final versions of accepted papers. It is not required for papers submitted for review.)

## 4 Translation of non-English Terms

It is also advised to supplement non-English characters and terms with appropriate transliterations and/or translations since not all readers understand all such characters and terms. Inline transliteration or translation can be represented in the order of: original-form transliteration "translation".

## 5 Length of Submission

The maximum submission length is 2 pages (A4), plus an unlimited number of pages for references. Authors of accepted papers will be given additional space in the camera-ready version to reflect space needed for changes stemming from reviewers comments.

Papers that do not conform to the specified length and formatting requirements may be rejected without review.

## Acknowledgements

The acknowledgements should go immediately before the references. Do not number the acknowledgements section. Do not include this section when submitting your paper for review.

## References


Alfred V. Aho and Jeffrey D. Ullman. 1972. *The Theory of Parsing, Translation and Compiling*, volume 1. Prentice-Hall, Englewood Cliffs, NJ.

American Psychological Association. 1983. *Publications Manual*. American Psychological Association, Washington, DC.

Association for Computing Machinery. 1983. *Computing Reviews*, 24(11):503–512.

Ashok K. Chandra, Dexter C. Kozen, and Larry J. Stockmeyer. 1981. Alternation. *Journal of the Association for Computing Machinery*, 28(1):114–133.

Dan Gusfield. 1997. *Algorithms on Strings, Trees and Sequences*. Cambridge University Press, Cambridge, UK.

# Instructions for WiNLP 2020


**First Author**
Affiliation / Address line 1
Affiliation / Address line 2
Affiliation / Address line 3
`email@domain`

**Second Author**
Affiliation / Address line 1
Affiliation / Address line 2
Affiliation / Address line 3
`email@domain`



## Abstract

This document contains the instructions for preparing a paper submitted to WiNLP 2019. The document itself conforms to its own specifications, and is therefore an example of what your manuscript should look like. These instructions should be used for both papers submitted for review and for final versions of accepted papers. Authors are asked to conform to all the directions reported in this document.


## 1 Credits

This document has been adapted from the instructions for COLING-2018 proceedings compiled by Xiaodan Zhu and Zhiyuan Liu, which are, in turn, based on the instructions for COLING-2016 proceedings, which are, in turn, based on the instructions for COLING-2014 proceedings compiled by Joachim Wagner, Liadh Kelly and Lorraine Goeuriot, which are, in turn, based on the instructions for earlier ACL proceedings, including those for ACL-2014 by Alexander Koller and Yusuke Miyao, those for ACL-2012 by Maggie Li and Michael White, those for ACL-2010 by Jing-Shing Chang and Philipp Koehn, those for ACL-2008 by Johanna D. Moore, Simone Teufel, James Allan, and Sadaoki Furui, those for ACL-2005 by Hwee Tou Ng and Kemal Oflazer, those for ACL-2002 by Eugene Charniak and Dekang Lin, and earlier ACL and EACL formats. Those versions were written by several people, including John Chen, Henry S. Thompson and Donald Walker. Additional elements were taken from the formatting instructions of the *International Joint Conference on Artificial Intelligence*.

## 2 Introduction

The following instructions are directed to authors of papers submitted to WiNLP 2019 or accepted for publication in its proceedings. All authors are required to adhere to these specifications. Authors are required to provide a Portable Document Format (PDF) version of their papers. **The proceedings are designed for printing on A4 paper.**

Authors from countries in which access to word-processing systems is limited should contact WiNLP Organizers `winlp-chairs@googlegroups.com` as soon as possible.

## 3 General Instructions

Manuscripts must be in single-column format. **Type single-spaced.** Start all pages directly under the top margin. See the guidelines later regarding formatting the first page. The lengths of manuscripts should not exceed the maximum page limit described in Section 5. Do not number the pages.

### 3.1 Electronically-available Resources

We strongly prefer that you prepare your PDF files using LaTeX with the official COLING 2018 style file (coling2018.sty) and bibliography style (acl.bst). These files are available in coling2018.zip at `http://coling2018.org/`. You will also find the document you are currently reading (coling2018.pdf) and its LaTeX source code (coling2018.tex) in coling2018.zip.

---

Place licence statement here for the camera-ready version. See Section 3.9 of the instructions for preparing a manuscript.




*Proceedings of the 55th Annual Meeting of the Association for Computational Linguistics*, pages 46–50
Florence, Italy, July 28th, 2019. ©2019 Association for Computational Linguistics

You can alternatively use Microsoft Word to produce your PDF file. In this case, we strongly recommend the use of the Word template file (coling2018.dot) in coling2018.zip. If you have an option, we recommend that you use the LaTeX2e version. If you will be using the Microsoft Word template, you must anonymise your source file so that the pdf produced does not retain your identity. This can be done by removing any personal information from your source document properties.

### 3.2 Format of Electronic Manuscript

For the production of the electronic manuscript you must use Adobe's Portable Document Format (PDF). PDF files are usually produced from LaTeX using the *pdflatex* command. If your version of LaTeX produces Postscript files, you can convert these into PDF using *ps2pdf* or *dvipdf*. On Windows, you can also use Adobe Distiller to generate PDF.

Please make sure that your PDF file includes all the necessary fonts (especially tree diagrams, symbols, and fonts for non-Latin characters). When you print or create the PDF file, there is usually an option in your printer setup to include none, all or just non-standard fonts. Please make sure that you select the option of including ALL the fonts. **Before sending it, test your PDF by printing it from a computer different from the one where it was created.** Moreover, some word processors may generate very large PDF files, where each page is rendered as an image. Such images may reproduce poorly. In this case, try alternative ways to obtain the PDF. One way on some systems is to install a driver for a postscript printer, send your document to the printer specifying "Output to a file", then convert the file to PDF.

It is of utmost importance to specify the **A4 format** (21 cm x 29.7 cm) when formatting the paper. When working with `dvips`, for instance, one should specify `-t a4`.

If you cannot meet the above requirements for the production of your electronic submission, please contact the publication co-chairs as soon as possible.

### 3.3 Layout

Format manuscripts with a single column to a page, in the manner these instructions are formatted. The exact dimensions for a page on A4 paper are:

- Left and right margins: 2.5 cm

- Top margin: 2.5 cm

- Bottom margin: 2.5 cm

- Width: 16.0 cm

- Height: 24.7 cm

Papers should not be submitted on any other paper size. If you cannot meet the above requirements for the production of your electronic submission, please contact the publication co-chairs above as soon as possible.

### 3.4 Fonts

For reasons of uniformity, Adobe's **Times Roman** font should be used. In LaTeX2e this is accomplished by putting

```
\usepackage{times}
\usepackage{latexsym}
```

in the preamble. If Times Roman is unavailable, use **Computer Modern Roman** (LaTeX2e's default). Note that the latter is about 10% less dense than Adobe's Times Roman font.

The **Times New Roman** font, which is configured for us in the Microsoft Word template (coling2018.dot) and which some Linux distributions offer for installation, can be used as well.

| Type of Text | Font Size | Style |
|---|---|---|
| paper title | 15 pt | bold |
| author names | 12 pt | bold |
| author affiliation | 12 pt | |
| the word "Abstract" | 12 pt | bold |
| section titles | 12 pt | bold |
| document text | 11 pt | |
| captions | 11 pt | |
| sub-captions | 9 pt | |
| abstract text | 11 pt | |
| bibliography | 10 pt | |
| footnotes | 9 pt | |

Table 1: Font guide.

### 3.5 The First Page

Centre the title, author's name(s) and affiliation(s) across the page. Do not use footnotes for affiliations. Do not include the paper ID number assigned during the submission process. Do not include the authors' names or affiliations in the version submitted for review.

**Title**: Place the title centred at the top of the first page, in a 15 pt bold font. (For a complete guide to font sizes and styles, see Table 1.) Long titles should be typed on two lines without a blank line intervening. Approximately, put the title at 2.5 cm from the top of the page, followed by a blank line, then the author's names(s), and the affiliation on the following line. Do not use only initials for given names (middle initials are allowed). Do not format surnames in all capitals (e.g., use "Schlangen" not "SCHLANGEN"). Do not format title and section headings in all capitals as well except for proper names (such as "BLEU") that are conventionally in all capitals. The affiliation should contain the author's complete address, and if possible, an electronic mail address. Start the body of the first page 7.5 cm from the top of the page.

The title, author names and addresses should be completely identical to those entered to the electronical paper submission website in order to maintain the consistency of author information among all publications of the conference. If they are different, the publication co-chairs may resolve the difference without consulting with you; so it is in your own interest to double-check that the information is consistent.

**Abstract**: Type the abstract between addresses and main body. The width of the abstract text should be smaller than main body by about 0.6 cm on each side. Centre the word **Abstract** in a 12 pt bold font above the body of the abstract. The abstract should be a concise summary of the general thesis and conclusions of the paper. It should be no longer than 200 words. The abstract text should be in 11 pt font.

**Text**: Begin typing the main body of the text immediately after the abstract, observing the single-column format as shown in the present document. Do not include page numbers.

**Indent** when starting a new paragraph. Use 11 pt for text and subsection headings, 12 pt for section headings and 15 pt for the title.

**Licence**: Include a licence statement as an unmarked (unnumbered) footnote on the first page of the final, camera-ready paper. See Section 3.9 below for details and motivation.

### 3.6 Sections

**Headings**: Type and label section and subsection headings in the style shown on the present document. Use numbered sections (Arabic numerals) in order to facilitate cross references. Number subsections with the section number and the subsection number separated by a dot, in Arabic numerals. Do not number subsubsections.

**Citations**: Citations within the text appear in parentheses as (Gusfield, 1997) or, if the author's name

appears in the text itself, as Gusfield (1997). Append lowercase letters to the year in cases of ambiguity. Treat double authors as in (Aho and Ullman, 1972), but write as in (Chandra et al., 1981) when more than two authors are involved. Collapse multiple citations as in (Gusfield, 1997; Aho and Ullman, 1972). Also refrain from using full citations as sentence constituents. We suggest that instead of

"(Gusfield, 1997) showed that ..."

you use

"Gusfield (1997) showed that ..."

If you are using the provided LaTeX and BibTeX style files, you can use the command \newcite to get "author (year)" citations.

As reviewing will be double-blind, the submitted version of the papers should not include the authors' names and affiliations. Furthermore, self-references that reveal the author's identity, e.g.,

"We previously showed (Gusfield, 1997) ..."

should be avoided. Instead, use citations such as

"Gusfield (1997) previously showed ... "

**Please do not use anonymous citations** and do not include any of the following when submitting your paper for review: acknowledgements, project names, grant numbers, and names or URLs of resources or tools that have only been made publicly available in the last 3 weeks or are about to be made public and would compromise the anonymity of the submission. Papers that do not conform to these requirements may be rejected without review. These details can, however, be included in the camera-ready, final paper.

**References**: Gather the full set of references together under the heading **References**; place the section before any Appendices, unless they contain references. Arrange the references alphabetically by first author, rather than by order of occurrence in the text. Provide as complete a citation as possible, using a consistent format, such as the one for *Computational Linguistics* or the one in the *Publication Manual of the American Psychological Association* (American Psychological Association, 1983). Use of full names for authors rather than initials is preferred. A list of abbreviations for common computer science journals can be found in the ACM *Computing Reviews* (Association for Computing Machinery, 1983).

The LaTeX and BibTeX style files provided roughly fit the American Psychological Association format, allowing regular citations, short citations and multiple citations as described above.

**Appendices**: Appendices, if any, directly follow the text and the references (but see above). Letter them in sequence and provide an informative title: **Appendix A. Title of Appendix**.

### 3.7 Footnotes

**Footnotes**: Put footnotes at the bottom of the page and use 9 pt text. They may be numbered or referred to by asterisks or other symbols.[1] Footnotes should be separated from the text by a line.[2]

### 3.8 Graphics

**Illustrations**: Place figures, tables, and photographs in the paper near where they are first discussed, rather than at the end, if possible. Colour illustrations are discouraged, unless you have verified that they will be understandable when printed in black ink.

**Captions**: Provide a caption for every illustration; number each one sequentially in the form: "Figure 1. Caption of the Figure." "Table 1. Caption of the Table." Type the captions of the figures and tables below the body, using 11 pt text.

Narrow graphics together with the single-column format may lead to large empty spaces, see for example the wide margins on both sides of Table 1. If you have multiple graphics with related content, it may be preferable to combine them in one graphic. You can identify the sub-graphics with sub-captions below the sub-graphics numbered (a), (b), (c) etc. and using 9 pt text. The LaTeX packages wrapfig, subfig, subtable and/or subcaption may be useful.

---

[1] This is how a footnote should appear.

[2] Note the line separating the footnotes from the text.

### 3.9 Licence Statement

As in COLING-2014 and COLING-2016, we require that authors license their camera-ready papers under a Creative Commons Attribution 4.0 International Licence (CC-BY). This means that authors (copyright holders) retain copyright but grant everybody the right to adapt and re-distribute their paper as long as the authors are credited and modifications listed. In other words, this license lets researchers use research papers for their research without legal issues. Please refer to `http://creativecommons.org/licenses/by/4.0/` for the licence terms.

Depending on whether you use British or American English in your paper, please include one of the following as an unmarked (unnumbered) footnote on page 1 of your paper. The LaTeX style file (coling2018.sty) adds a command `blfootnote` for this purpose, and usage of the command is prepared in the LaTeX source code (coling2018.tex) at the start of Section "Introduction".

- This work is licensed under a Creative Commons Attribution 4.0 International Licence. Licence details: `http://creativecommons.org/licenses/by/4.0/`.

- This work is licensed under a Creative Commons Attribution 4.0 International License. License details: `http://creativecommons.org/licenses/by/4.0/`.

We strongly prefer that you licence your paper as the CC license above. However, if it is impossible for you to use that license, please contact the publication co-chairs Xiaodan Zhu (`zhu2048@gmail.com`) and Zhiyuan Liu (`liuzy@tsinghua.edu.cn`), before you submit your final version of accepted papers. (Please note that this license statement is only related to the final versions of accepted papers. It is not required for papers submitted for review.)

## 4 Translation of non-English Terms

It is also advised to supplement non-English characters and terms with appropriate transliterations and/or translations since not all readers understand all such characters and terms. Inline transliteration or translation can be represented in the order of: original-form transliteration "translation".

## 5 Length of Submission

The maximum submission length is 2 pages (A4), plus an unlimited number of pages for references. Authors of accepted papers will be given additional space in the camera-ready version to reflect space needed for changes stemming from reviewers comments.

Papers that do not conform to the specified length and formatting requirements may be rejected without review.

## Acknowledgements

The acknowledgements should go immediately before the references. Do not number the acknowledgements section. Do not include this section when submitting your paper for review.

## References


Alfred V. Aho and Jeffrey D. Ullman. 1972. *The Theory of Parsing, Translation and Compiling*, volume 1. Prentice-Hall, Englewood Cliffs, NJ.

American Psychological Association. 1983. *Publications Manual.* American Psychological Association, Washington, DC.

Association for Computing Machinery. 1983. *Computing Reviews*, 24(11):503–512.

Ashok K. Chandra, Dexter C. Kozen, and Larry J. Stockmeyer. 1981. Alternation. *Journal of the Association for Computing Machinery*, 28(1):114–133.

Dan Gusfield. 1997. *Algorithms on Strings, Trees and Sequences.* Cambridge University Press, Cambridge, UK.

# Variants of Vector Space Reductions for Predicting the Compositionality of English Noun Compounds


**Pegah Alipoormolabashi**
Sharif University of Technology
Islamic Republic of Iran
`palipoor@ce.sharif.edu`

**Sabine Schulte im Walde**
Institute for Natural Language Processing
University of Stuttgart, Germany
`schulte@ims.uni-stuttgart.de`


## Abstract


Predicting the degree of compositionality of noun compounds is a crucial ingredient for lexicography and NLP applications, to know whether the compound should be treated as a whole, or through its constituents. Computational approaches for an automatic prediction typically represent compounds and their constituents within a vector space to have a numeric relatedness measure for the words. This paper provides a systematic evaluation of using different vector-space reduction variants for the prediction. We demonstrate that Word2vec and nouns-only dimensionality reductions are the most successful and stable vector space reduction variants for our task.[1]


## 1 Introduction

The semantic relations between compounds and their constituents do not follow a strict rule. Compare, for example, the English noun compounds *snowball* –a ball consisting of snow, where clearly both constituents *snow* and *ball* contribute to the meaning of the compound– and *butterfly* –where the semantic contribution of the modifier noun *butter* is not obvious without knowing about the etymology of the compound. Computational approaches to predict the degree of compositionality typically represent compounds and their constituents within a vector space, and then compare the compound vectors with the constituent vectors as a proxy to the compounds' degree of compositionality (Reddy et al., 2011b; Reddy et al., 2011a; Salehi and Cook, 2013; Schulte im Walde et al., 2013; Salehi et al., 2014; Schulte im Walde et al., 2016; Cordeiro et al., 2019). Previous works have explored variants of vector space models in different ways. Our contribution in this paper was to provide a systematic evaluation of vector-space reductions across kinds, i.e., exploring part-of-speech-based reduction, Principal Components Analysis using Singular Value Decomposition, and Word2vec embeddings. As the gold standard, we used the dataset of English noun compounds created by Reddy et al. (2011b). This dataset contains a random list of English noun compounds annotated by compositionality ratings on the semantic contribution of the modifier to the compound meaning, the semantic contribution of the head noun to the compound meaning, and the compositionality of the compound as a whole phrase. Table 1 shows an example set of the gold data.

| Compound | Word1 | Word2 | Phrase |
|---|---|---|---|
| climate change | 4.90±0.30 | 4.83±0.38 | 4.97±0.18 |
| polo shirt | 1.73±1.41 | 5.00±0.00 | 3.37±1.38 |
| search engine | 4.62±0.96 | 2.25±1.70 | 3.32±1.16 |

Table 1: Examples of compounds and judgements on their compositionality (mean value and standard deviation, based on 30 annotators) from Reddy et al. (2011b).

---

[1]In accordance with the multiple-submission policy of WiNLP 2020 this work has already been published in (Alipoor and Schulte im Walde, 2020)




*Proceedings of the 55th Annual Meeting of the Association for Computational Linguistics*, pages 51–54
Florence, Italy, July 28th, 2019. ©2019 Association for Computational Linguistics

| Vector Space Variant | Prediction Function | Correlation Coefficient |
|---|---|---|
| All | ADD/COMB | 0.630 |
| VV | ADD | 0.581 |
| NN | ADD/MULT | 0.658 |
| **Word2vec** | **COMB** | **0.689** |

| Vector Space Variant | Prediction Function | Correlation Coefficient |
|---|---|---|
| NN | ADD/MULT | 0.658 |
| NN-1000 | COMB | 0.483 |
| NN-10000 | ADD | 0.638 |
| NN-20000 | ADD | 0.661 |
| **NN-30000** | **MULT** | **0.663** |
| NN-40000 | MULT | 0.659 |

| Vector Space Variant | Prediction Function | Correlation Coefficient |
|---|---|---|
| **All** | **ADD/COMB** | **0.630** |
| All-PCA-100 | ADD | 0.527 |
| All-PCA-200 | ADD | 0.577 |
| All-PCA-500 | ADD | 0.584 |
| All-PCA-1000 | MULT | 0.574 |
| All-PCA-2000 | COMB | 0.609 |
| All-PCA-5000 | ADD/COMB | 0.616 |

| Vector Space Variant | Prediction Function | Correlation Coefficient |
|---|---|---|
| **NN** | **ADD/MULT** | **0.658** |
| NN-PCA-100 | ADD | 0.620 |
| NN-PCA-200 | COMB | 0.595 |
| NN-PCA-500 | MULT | 0.631 |
| NN-PCA-1000 | COMB | 0.640 |
| NN-PCA-2000 | MULT | 0.657 |
| NN-PCA-5000 | MULT | 0.654 |

Table 2: Best results for each vector space variant

## 2 Experiment

We experimented with several vector space variants for representing the compounds and the constituents. All of these vector space variants were created based on the ENCOW16[2] corpus with a window size of 10. We also applied the *TreeTagger* for part-of-speech (pos) tagging and lemmatisation (Schmid, 1994). The vector space variants are listed below.

- **ALL** The whole co-occurrence matrix of the words as the baseline.

- **POS** Subsets of the co-occurrence matrix with only context dimensions of specific parts-of-speech (specifying on nouns/NN vs. verbs/VV).

- **PCA** All and nouns-only matrices after Principle Component Analysis reduction.

- **WORD2VEC** Standard Word2vec embedding (Mikolov et al., 2013) with 300-dimensional vectors.

- **NN-K** Noun-only matrix reduced to contain only neighbour nouns within the k most frequent nouns.

We used **cosine** as a similarity measure between compounds and constituents, assuming that the stronger the distributional similarity (i.e., the higher the cosine values), the stronger the semantic relatedness and therefore the degree of compositionality. Next to assessing the individual contributions of compound–modifier and compound–head relatedness, we applied the same functions as in (Reddy et al., 2011b) to combine the compound–constituent cosine scores for predicting the degree of compositionality of the compounds. Given that each component within the functions might provide a different weight to the overall prediction, we applied a linear regression model to find the corresponding coefficients, and here we report the best results from three-fold cross-validation with human judgments. The vector space predictions were evaluated against the mean human ratings on the degree of compositionality, using the Spearman Rank-Order Correlation Coefficient $\rho$ (Siegel and Castellan, 1988). Table 2 shows the best results among prediction functions using each vector-space variant.

- **WORD1** Use only the compound–modifier cosine score

- **WORD2** Use only the compound–head cosine score

- **ADD** Add the compound–modifier and compound–head cosine scores

- **MULT** Multiply the compound–modifier and compound–head cosine scores

- **COMB** Add the compound–modifier, compound–head and the multiplication of both cosine scores

| | All | | | NN | | | All-PCA-5000 | | | NN-PCA-2000 | | | Word2vec | | |
|---|---|---|---|---|---|---|---|---|---|---|---|---|---|---|---|
| | high | mid | low | high | mid | low | high | mid | low | high | mid | low | high | mid | low |
| Compound Frequency Range | 0.409 | **0.470** | 0.268 | 0.372 | **0.606** | 0.330 | 0.396 | **0.484** | 0.196 | 0.447 | **0.616** | 0.262 | **0.678** | 0.585 | 0.352 |
| Modifier Productivity Range | 0.594 | **0.619** | 0.394 | 0.543 | 0.543 | **0.653** | **0.600** | 0.554 | 0.414 | 0.543 | 0.625 | **0.636** | **0.631** | 0.571 | 0.584 |
| Head Productivity Range | 0.555 | **0.784** | 0.245 | 0.648 | **0.840** | 0.337 | 0.559 | **0.746** | 0.227 | 0.677 | **0.827** | 0.316 | 0.701 | **0.801** | 0.474 |
| Compound Compositionality Range | 0.240 | 0.256 | **0.525** | 0.293 | 0.290 | **0.469** | **0.409** | 0.196 | 0.196 | 0.375 | **0.614** | 0.259 | **0.631** | 0.571 | 0.584 |
| Modifier Compositionality Range | 0.498 | **0.560** | 0.434 | 0.620 | **0.662** | 0.343 | 0.535 | **0.601** | 0.434 | 0.649 | **0.681** | 0.363 | **0.650** | 0.585 | 0.417 |
| Head Compositionality Range | **0.777** | 0.476 | 0.361 | **0.752** | 0.589 | 0.496 | **0.779** | 0.519 | 0.253 | **0.753** | 0.585 | 0.468 | **0.761** | 0.592 | 0.288 |

Table 3: Best results for vector space variants across compound and constituent properties.

In order to zoom into specific strengths of individual vector space variants, we applied the variants to subsets of our compound targets according to the targets' compositionality, compound frequency, modifier productivity, and head productivity. For each of these conditions, we created three disjunctive subsets of the 90 compound targets with 30 targets each. We observed that training the regression on the whole set and testing it on the subsets has the same results as training it on the subsets. The subsets contain the strongest, weakest and in-between targets as based on the respective condition, e.g., regarding the compound frequency condition we distinguish between high-frequency, mid-frequency and low-frequency compounds. The empirical information relies on a refinement of the Reddy et al. dataset by Schulte im Walde et al. (2016) using ENCOW14 (the predecessor of ENCOW16 used in this study). The best results are shown in table 3.

## 3   Summary of Results

This study provided a systematic evaluation of vector-space reductions across kinds, for the task of predicting the compositionality degree of noun compounds. Our vector-space variant experiments identified Word2vec with 300 dimensions as the clear winner. Similarly good and stable predictions have been achieved when using a large subset of context nouns, even without any further PCA reduction. As a result, we suggest using these vectors in NLP applications. The baseline with using all context dimensions is worse in comparison to all optimised reduced conditions other than running PCA on the whole matrix. Therefore, next to identifying a clear winner (Word2vec) we can induce from our results that using only the most frequent noun dimensions is a reasonable alternative.

Regarding the prediction functions, ADD, MULT and COMB (with only marginal differences between them in most cases) generally outperformed WORD1 and WORD2. So combining the relatedness information for compound–modifier and compound–head pairs is better for the prediction of the compounds' degree of compositionality than relying on just one or the other.

These results vary strongly across subsets representing different ranges of compositionality, frequency and productivity. We observed that predictions for mid-frequency compounds are better than on average and predictions for low-frequency compounds are particularly bad. For head productivity ranges we observed very high prediction results for mid-productivity and very low prediction results for low-productivity subsets. Finally, regarding compositionality the predictions were better for overall mid- and high-compositional in comparison to low-compositional compounds; and generally good for compounds with mid-compositional compound-modifier relatedness and compounds with strongly compositional compound-head relatedness.

---

[2]`http://corporafromtheweb.org/encow16/`

## Acknowledgements

We thank Anna Hätty for her help on training the Word2vec and Gabriella Lapesa for guiding through the SVD reductions.


## References

Pegah Alipoor and Sabine Schulte im Walde. 2020. Variants of vector space reductions for predicting the compositionality of english noun compounds. In *Proceedings of The 12th Language Resources and Evaluation Conference*, pages 4379–4387, Marseille, France, May. European Language Resources Association.

Silvio Cordeiro, Aline Villavicencio, Marco Idiart, and Carlos Ramisch. 2019. Unsupervised Compositionality Prediction of Nominal Compounds. *Computational Linguistics*, 45(1):1–57.

Tomas Mikolov, Wen tau Yih, and Geoffrey Zweig. 2013. Linguistic Regularities in Continuous Space Word Representations. In *Proceedings of the Conference of the North American Chapter of the Association for Computational Linguistics: Human Language Technologies*, pages 746–751, Atlanta, GA, USA.

Siva Reddy, Ioannis P. Klapaftis, Diana McCarthy, and Suresh Manandhar. 2011a. Dynamic and Static Prototype Vectors for Semantic Composition. In *Proceedings of the 5th International Joint Conference on Natural Language Processing*, pages 705–713, Chiang Mai, Thailand.

Siva Reddy, Diana McCarthy, and Suresh Manandhar. 2011b. An Empirical Study on Compositionality in Compound Nouns. In *Proceedings of the 5th International Joint Conference on Natural Language Processing*, pages 210–218, Chiang Mai, Thailand.

Bahar Salehi and Paul Cook. 2013. Predicting the Compositionality of Multiword Expressions Using Translations in Multiple Languages. In *Proceedings of the 2nd Joint Conference on Lexical and Computational Semantics*, pages 266–275, Atlanta, GA, USA.

Bahar Salehi, Paul Cook, and Timothy Baldwin. 2014. Using Distributional Similarity of Multi-way Translations to Predict Multiword Expression Compositionality. In *Proceedings of the 14th Conference of the European Chapter of the Association for Computational Linguistics*, pages 472–481, Gothenburg, Sweden.

Helmut Schmid. 1994. Probabilistic Part-of-Speech Tagging using Decision Trees. In *Proceedings of the 1st International Conference on New Methods in Language Processing*.

Sabine Schulte im Walde, Stefan Müller, and Stephen Roller. 2013. Exploring Vector Space Models to Predict the Compositionality of German Noun-Noun Compounds. In *Proceedings of the 2nd Joint Conference on Lexical and Computational Semantics*, pages 255–265, Atlanta, GA, USA.

Sabine Schulte im Walde, Anna Hätty, and Stefan Bott. 2016. The Role of Modifier and Head Properties in Predicting the Compositionality of English and German Noun-Noun Compounds: A Vector-Space Perspective. In *Proceedings of the 5th Joint Conference on Lexical and Computational Semantics*, pages 148–158, Berlin, Germany.

Sidney Siegel and N. John Castellan. 1988. *Nonparametric Statistics for the Behavioral Sciences*. McGraw-Hill, Boston, MA, USA.

# SentiTel: TABSA for Twitter reviews on Uganda Telecoms


**David Kabiito**
Makerere University
dkabiito@cis.mak.ac.ug

**Joyce Nakatumba-Nabende**
Makerere University
jnakatumba@cis.mak.ac.ug



## Abstract

In this paper, we present a fine-grained opinion mining dataset called SentiTel. SentiTel is human annotated for targeted aspect-based sentiment analysis (TABSA). SentiTel contains Twitter reviews about three major Ugandan telecoms posted in the period between February 2019 and September 2019. The dataset contains reviews that are in English or have a codemix of English and Luganda. SentiTel contains 6 320 reviews that are annotated with the target telecom, aspect and sentiment towards the aspect of the target telecom. The reviews contain at least one target telecom. We present two models on the TABSA task; random forest (RF) which is the baseline model and the BERT based model. The best result is presented by the BERT model with an AUC of 0.950 and 0.965 on the aspect category detection task and sentiment classification task respectively. The results show that a great performance can be obtained on a downstream task by fine-tuning the pre-trained BERT model. Finally, the results also confirm that fine-grained information can be extracted from the short and unstructured text from Twitter with limited cues.


## 1 Introduction

Sentiment analysis (SA) is the computational analysis of people's opinions, sentiments, attitudes and emotions toward target entities such as products, services, organizations, individuals, topics, and their different aspects (Abdulaziz et al., 2015). With the rise of the social media era, people are always connected and they share opinions through tweets, comments, reviews and chats. However due to the high velocity and voluminous nature of data from social media, it is difficult to process and analyse the data. Automated opinion mining is thus needed to overcome these limitations. SA has previously been studied at three levels: document, sentence and fine-grained level (Yinglin and Ming, 2018). Fine-grained sentiment analysis considers the aspects and target entities in the review while document and sentence level resolve the overall sentiment in the review.

Previously, fine-grained opinion mining has been discussed at two levels that is aspect-based sentiment analysis (ABSA) (Titov and McDonald, 2008) and targeted sentiment classification. Recently, Saeidi et al., (2016) introduced the task of targeted aspect-based sentiment analysis (TABSA) which aims at identifying the fine-grained opinion polarity towards a specific aspect associated with a given target entity. TABSA attempts to tackle the challenges of both ABSA and targeted sentiment classification. TABSA is an important task since it provides a more detailed summary of the opinion.

The goal of this paper is three-fold: 1) to provide a human-annotated dataset for TABSA, 2) to show that despite the informal text structure, short text and limited cues, Twitter data is rich in information and can be used for fine-grained opinion mining, 3) to provide baseline models for TABSA on Twitter data.

## 2 Dataset

We present the SentiTel[1] dataset that was annotated by three undergraduate software engineering students using the BRAT annotation tool. The Dataset is annotated with target telecom, aspect and sentiment to wards the aspects of the target telecom. The reviews in this dataset were extracted using the Twitter

---

[1]The dataset is available on: https://github.com/davidkabiito/Sentitel/tree/master/Dataset




*Proceedings of the 55th Annual Meeting of the Association for Computational Linguistics*, pages 55–57
Florence, Italy, July 28th, 2019. ©2019 Association for Computational Linguistics

api with language value set to "en". The Twitter handles *"mtnug"*, *"Airtel_Ug"* and *"africellUG"* were used to query the reviews from Twitter. The reviews were collected for the period between February 2019 and September 2019. Telecoms being one of the largest service providers in Uganda, there are many discussions on Twitter regarding aspects of these telecoms.

SentiTel contains 6 320 English and Luganda[2] code-mixed reviews. 5 973 reviews in SentiTel contain a single telecom entity while 347 reviews mention two or three telecom entities. The total number of opinions in SentiTel is 6 683 since some reviews have multiple opinions. The telecom entity names in the reviews are all normalised to *"MTN"*, *"Airtel"* and *"Africell"*. The predefined aspect categories are *data, customer service, general, network, calls, mobile money* and *application*. These are the most discussed aspects about telecoms on Twitter in Uganda. The aspect *general* refers to a generic opinion about the target telecom in the review. Table 1 shows the distributions of opinions across the aspect categories.

| | Aspects | | | | | | |
|---|---|---|---|---|---|---|---|
| Sentiment | **data** | **customer service** | **general** | **network** | **calls** | **mobile money** | **application** |
| Positive | 377 | 74 | 450 | 81 | 35 | 23 | 8 |
| Negative | 2 064 | 928 | 418 | 740 | 442 | 244 | 139 |

Table 1: SentiTel sentiment distribution over the aspect categories.

## 3  Word Representation and Models

For training and evaluating our models, we used five most frequent aspects; *data, customer service, general, network* and *calls* from SentiTel. These are also the five most frequent aspects in the telecom domain. We split the dataset into three subsets train, validation and test set with each having 70%, 10% and 20% of the data respectively. The validation set is used to select the best model parameters before applying the models to the test set.

**Training the RF model:** The RF model is our baseline model. Before training the RF model, all the words in the reviews are first converted to lowercase then all punctuations and stopwords are removed except the word "not" which reverses the opinion polarity. The nltk inbuilt stopword list is used for this purpose. Since we had an imbalanced dataset, we used oversampling while training the models. The RF experiments were conducted using two word representations; tf-idf and word2vec (Mikolov et al., 2013). The TABSA task was modelled as a sentence-pair classification (NLI-M) problem as suggested by Sun et al., (2019) where the opinion polarity "None" is introduced on top of the "Positive" and "Negative" opinion polarities. The opinion polarity "None" is used to jointly detect the aspect category and the opinion polarity. The opinion polarity "None" indicates absence of the aspect in the review. The best model in both word representations was obtained using 100 trees.

**Training the BERT Model:** We constructed the BERT model using the sentence pair input representation. The BERT-pair-NLI-M auxiliary sentence construction was used as described by Sun et al., (2019). We used the pre-trained uncased $BERT_{BASE}$[3] model for fine tuning on TABSA downstream task. The following hyperparameters were used to obtain the best model; number of Transformer blocks:12, hidden layers size:768, number of self-attention heads:12, and total number of parameters for the pre-trained model:110M. When fine-tuning, we kept the dropout probability at 0.1, set the number of epochs to 6. The initial learning rate was 2e-5, and the batch size is 24. The training was done using one GPU on google colab.

Following Sun et al., (2019), the aspect category detection task is evaluated using strict accuracy and Macro-F1, the AUC score is also reported. For sentiment classification, accuracy and AUC score are reported. The Macro-F1 and AUC scores are used since they provide a better evaluation of imbalanced dataset like we have in the case of SentiTel.

---

[2]Luganda is a popular language spoken in Uganda.
[3]`https://storage.googleapis.com/bert_models/2018_10_18/uncased_L-12_H-768_A-12.zip`

## 4 Results and Conclusion

Table 2 and Table 3 show the results obtained by the models. The results were obtained after running the models on the test set. Table 2 shows the results in terms of $F_1$, accuracy and AUC. Table 3 shows the break down of AUC scores for each aspect.

|  | Aspect | | | Sentiment | |
| --- | --- | --- | --- | --- | --- |
| Model | *Acc.* | $F_1$ | *AUC* | *Acc.* | *AUC* |
| RF-tf-idf | 0.509 | 0.442 | 0.883 | **0.967** | 0.915 |
| RF-word2vec | 0.337 | 0.190 | 0.694 | 0.965 | 0.820 |
| BERT | **0.773** | **0.781** | **0.950** | 0.940 | **0.965** |

Table 2: Model performance on the SentiTel dataset. (Boldfaced values are the overall best scores by the models on the dataset.)

| | Aspect | | | | |
| --- | --- | --- | --- | --- | --- |
| **Model** | Calls | CustomerService | Data | General | Network |
| RF-tf-idf | 0.893 | 0.864 | 0.869 | 0.916 | 0.874 |
| RF-word2vec | 0.701 | 0.669 | 0.675 | 0.754 | 0.669 |
| BERT | **0.967** | **0.960** | **0.941** | **0.956** | **0.926** |

Table 3: Aspect level model performance using the AUC evaluation metric.

In this study, we shows that although the TABSA task is more complicated than SA due to additional target and aspect information thus requiring more cues, the results from the models demonstrate that TABSA level information can be extracted from Twitter reviews despite the limited cues and informal text structure. Furthermore the better performance presented by the BERT model shows that by fine-tuning a pre-trained BERT model promising results can be obtained on downstream tasks.

However based on previous research (Abdulaziz et al., 2015; Yinglin and Ming, 2018), we expected the RF-word2vec model to perform better than the RF-tf-idf model. The RF-word2vec model can be improved by training a word2vec model on generic Twitter data and finally training it on SentiTel. This will enable the word2vec model to obtain more semantic information on words from Twitter.

## References


Abdulaziz Alghunaim, Mitra Mohtarami, Scott Cyphers and James Glass 2015. A Vector Space Approach for Aspect Based Sentiment Analysis. *Proceedings of NAACL-HLT 2015*, Denver, Colorado:116–122. Association for Computational Linguistics.

Chi Sun, Luyao Huang, and Xipeng Qiu 2019. Utilizing BERT for Aspect-Based Sentiment Analysis via Constructing Auxiliary Sentence. *In the Proceedings of the 2019 Conference of the North American Chapter of the Association for Computational Linguistics: Human Language Technologies*, Minneapolis, Minnesota:380–385.

Jacob Devlin, Ming-Wei Chang, Kenton Lee and Kristina Toutanova. 2019. BERT: Pre-training of Deep Bidirectional Transformers for Language Understanding. http://arxiv.org/abs/1810.04805.

Ivan Titov and Ryan McDonald. 2008. Modeling online reviews with multi-grain topic models. *In Proceedings of the 17th international conference on World Wide Web*, (ACM):111–120.

Marzieh Saeidi, Guillaume Bouchard, Maria Liakata and Sebastian Riedel. 2016. SentiHood: Targeted Aspect Based Sentiment Analysis Dataset for Urban Neighbourhoods. *International Conference on Computational Linguistics*, (COLING 2016) Osaka Japan:1546–1556.

Tomas Mikolov, Kai Chen, Greg Corrado, and Jeffrey Dean. 2013. Efficient estimation of word representations in vector space. http://arxiv.org/pdf/l1301.3781.pdf.

Wang Yinglin and Wang Ming 2018. Fine-Grained Opinion Extraction from Chinese Car Reviews with an Integrated Strategy. *Journal of Shanghai Jiaotong University (Science)*, 23(5):620–626.

# An Assessment of Language Identification Methods on Tweets and Wikipedia Articles


**Pedro V. Gonçalves**
CDTec
UFPel – Brazil
pvgoncalves@inf.ufpel.edu.br

**Larissa A. de Freitas**
CDTec
UFPel – Brazil
larissa@inf.ufpel.edu.br



## Abstract

Language identification is the task of determining the language which a given text is written. This task is important for Natural Language Processing and Information Retrieval activities. Two popular approaches for language identification are the N-grams and stopwords models. In this paper, these two models were tested on different types of documents such as short, irregular texts (tweets) and long, regular texts (Wikipedia articles).


## 1 Introduction

The language identification task is a very important step in many Natural Language Processing (NLP) pipelines and Information Retrieval (IR) systems. Text processing techniques developed in NLP and IR generally pre-suppose that the language of the input text is known, and many techniques assume that all documents are in the same language (Jauhiainen et al., 2019). To identify the language of a text two approaches are commonly used: the N-grams (typically trigrams) (Zubiaga et al., 2014; Grag et al., 2014) and the stopwords models (Truica et al., 2015).

The first approach consists of tokenizing the text into its N-grams, then checking the language(s), one or more, for which each N-gram is particularly common, adding to the chances of each of those languages of being the one to be identified.

The second approach consists of tokenizing the text into what seems to be words, then, for each known stopword found among the tokens, add to the chances of the related language(s) of being the one to be identified.

This paper aims to compare the results obtained with each of those methods for two distinct types of linguistic content, which are encyclopedia articles collected from Wikipedia and short messages (tweets) collected from Twitter.

For such comparison, both models have been implemented in C++ as a single command-line tool.

## 2 The Models

Both language identification models covered by this work are based on language statistics. That essentially means they work by comparing information about the frequencies of some linguistic elements in a given text with previously known information, in turn, extracted from multiple corpora whose language is known.

### 2.1 N-grams Model

The N-grams model uses the fact that for each written language, there are some contiguous sequences of words which, particularly for that language, occur much more frequently than others. Based on that, one can extract a list of the most frequent sequences of N-grams from a text and compare it to previously known lists. Those sequences are called N-grams where, usually, $2 \leq N \leq 4$ and words mean, actually, graphemes, which are the smallest units of a writing system.

N-grams are hardly exclusive to one single language. As a consequence of that, the N-grams model tends lower confidence scores and smaller differences among confidence scores for each identified language. On the other hand, since any piece of writing contains at least a few N-grams and even a mis-




*Proceedings of the 55th Annual Meeting of the Association for Computational Linguistics*, pages 58–60
Florence, Italy, July 28th, 2019. ©2019 Association for Computational Linguistics

spelled word may also contain some recognizable ones, this model can work even for short and irregular inputs, such as tweets.

## 2.2 Stopwords Model

The stopwords model, on the other hand, uses the fact that for each language, there are some words use to occur very frequently only for that language, while being virtually absent in others. Those words are usually called stopwords in the context of NLP and consist, in most cases, of things such as articles, personal pronouns, prepositions, conjunctions and, auxiliary verbs. Even among languages with high degrees of similarity and shared vocabulary, like those spoken in Scandinavia or the Iberian Peninsula, for example, the spelling of such words still differs.

As opposed to the N-grams model, the one based on stopwords gets unsuitable and inaccurate as inputs get small since smaller pieces of text mean fewer words and, consequently, less stopwords. Also, given that language identification usually occurs early in NLP pipelines, before complex things such as spell checking, and that misspelled words tend not to match the ones extracted from the corpora, this model gets unsuitable as inputs get less regular.

Stopwords models show higher confidence scores and tends to overcome or at least catch up with the accuracy of other approaches for bigger and well-written inputs.

## 2.3 Comparing the models

The N-grams approach is a more universal one, keeping good results with all types of input, while the stopwords one loses its ability to deliver correct results as inputs get smaller. The stopwords model, however, is simpler and, therefore, faster, given that it involves fewer comparisons than the N-grams model.

## 3 Datasets

Datasets[1] used for the tests were automatically collected and built using publicly available Python modules. For the Wikipedia articles, the Python API[2] works in such a way that one has to set the desired language before downloading the articles. Tweets, on the other hand, can not be fetched by language, so they were collected from users known to speak the desired language and then classified using a popular Python module for language identification[3]. Tweets were stored and made available as lines of normalized Unicode text in one file for each language, while Wikipedia articles were stored as separate files named after their respective languages.

In total, 130505 tweets and 26570 Wikipedia articles have been collected to the two datasets, with counts by language as listed in **Tables 1** and **2**.

Table 1: Results for the N-grams and stopwords Models on Tweets, by language.

| | | | N-grams Model | | Stopwords Model | |
|---|---|---|---|---|---|---|
| **Language** | **ISO 639-2B code** | **Count** | **Acc.** | **Avg. Confidence** | **Acc.** | **Avg. Confidence** |
| TOTAL | - | - | 90% | 67% | 87% | 79% |
| English | eng | 52532 | 91% | 64% | 92% | 81% |
| Portuguese | por | 71849 | 88% | 68% | 84% | 79% |
| Spanish | spa | 6124 | 92% | 69% | 86% | 76% |

## 4 Results

Accuracy (Acc.) and Average Confidence (Avg. Confidence) metrics have been calculated by language, for each dataset and model (**Tables 1** and **2**). Those values have been generated by running the imple-

---

[1]Datasets are available at https://github.com/pedrovernetti/nlp-datasets
[2]Wikipedia Python module: https://pypi.org/project/wikipedia/
[3]Polyglot Python module: https://pypi.org/project/polyglot/

Table 2: Results for the N-grams and stopwords Models on Wikipedia Articles, by language.

| Language | ISO 639-2B code | Count | N-grams Model | | Stopwords Model | |
| --- | --- | --- | --- | --- | --- | --- |
| | | | Acc. | Avg. Confidence | Acc. | Avg. Confidence |
| TOTAL | - | - | 97% | 69% | 95% | 90% |
| Arabic | ara | 1574 | 100% | 86% | 97% | 92% |
| Danish | dan | 1555 | 98% | 69% | 94% | 89% |
| Dutch | dut | 1566 | 98% | 70% | 99% | 96% |
| English | eng | 1604 | 97% | 61% | 100% | 94% |
| Finnish | fin | 1551 | 98% | 64% | 92% | 83% |
| French | fre | 1528 | 98% | 67% | 100% | 91% |
| German | ger | 1574 | 99% | 70% | 99% | 93% |
| Irish | gle | 1607 | 95% | 74% | 91% | 93% |
| Greek | gre | 1578 | 99% | 91% | 99% | 94% |
| Hungarian | hun | 1533 | 96% | 60% | 87% | 83% |
| Italian | ita | 1548 | 98% | 66% | 96% | 88% |
| Portuguese | por | 1598 | 91% | 65% | 93% | 87% |
| Romanian | rum | 1571 | 94% | 66% | 98% | 94% |
| Spanish | spa | 1547 | 99% | 68% | 99% | 94% |
| Swedish | swe | 1533 | 98% | 71% | 99% | 89% |
| Turkish | tur | 1529 | 95% | 65% | 80% | 64% |
| Vietnamese | vie | 1574 | 97% | 63% | 100% | 97% |

mented tool[4].

Given each language identification process results in a list of language-confidence pairs, what was taken as the final result was the language for which the confidence value was the highest. The measured Acc. stands here for how many times, out of the total run tests, the final results matched the actual language.

The best results obtained in this task are from the 92% Acc. reported for irregular texts (tweets), or the 100% Acc. reported for regular text (Wikipedia articles) from the N-gram and stopwords models.

There are still many aspects of this topic for one to focus on, such as the effects of the number of supported languages on the confidence and accuracy of the results. Experimenting with some common problems involving similarities between closely related languages and their possible workarounds could deliver new results to be analyzed. Assessments on the performance and time efficiency of each model could also be of interest.

# References


Zubiaga, Arkaitz and San Vicente, Iñaki and Gamallo, Pablo and Pichel, José R. and Alegria, Iñaki and Aranberri, Nora and Ezeiza, Aitzol and Fresno, Víctor. 2014. Overview of TweetLID: Tweet Language Identification at SEPLN 2014. *Twitter Language Identification Workshop at SEPLN 2014*, 1–11.

Garg, Archana and Gupta, Vishal and Jindal, Manish. 2014. A Survey of Language Identification Techniques and Applications. *Journal of the Emerging Technologies in Web Intelligence*, 6(4):388–400.

Jauhiainen, Tommi and Lui, Marco and Zampieri, Marcos and Baldwin, Timothy and Lindén, Krister. 2019. Automatic Language Identification in Texts: A Survey. *Journal of the Artificial Intelligence Research*, 65:675–782.

Truica, Ciprian-Octavian and Velcin, Julien and Boicea, Alexandru. 2015. Automatic Language Identification for Romance Languages Using Stop Words and Diacritics. *17th International Symposium on Symbolic and Numeric Algorithms for Scientific Computing*, 243–246.


---

[4]Codes are available at https://github.com/pedrovernetti/omnglot

# A Comparison of Identification Methods of Brazilian Music Styles by Lyrics


**Patrick Guimarães**  
CDTec  
UFPel – Brazil

**Jader Froes**  
CDTec  
UFPel – Brazil

**Douglas Costa**  
CDTec  
UFPel – Brazil

**Larissa A. de Freitas**  
CDTec  
UFPel – Brazil

`pgdvargas,jfdsrosa,dwdcosta,larissa@inf.ufpel.edu.br`



## Abstract

In this paper we apply different techniques to text classification using song lyrics. We explore the following styles of Brazilian music: *Sertanejo, Forró, MPB, Samba, Gospel/Religioso, Bossa Nova*, and *Axé*. Finally, we compare the use of some machine learning approaches for text classification task, exploring the most used methods in the field.


## 1 Introduction

Problems that involve text classification are Natural Language Processing (NLP) problems. Nowadays, text classification is becoming a crucial task to analysts in different areas. Still, this task provide facilities that will save time and money for users and companies (Silva and Ribeiro, 2010). In this study, the goal is to classify the music styles using song lyrics, a problem that was also explored by other related works, such as (Tsaptsinos, 2017) and (Mayer et al., 2008). Some approaches like Random Forest (RF), Decision Tree (DT) and others can be applied to the text classification task (Liaw and Wiener, 2002). With the increased computational power, Deep Learning (DL) techniques can be applied in this task too (Young et al., 2018).

## 2 Methods

In this section we introduce the dataset created for our experiments and our pre-processing.

The song lyrics used in this study were acquired from the website Letras[1], where we collected around 6000 lyrics in CSV format, divided into seven Brazilian music styles. The dataset is available at https://github.com/patrickguima/PLN/trabalho final/lyrics_style_classifier.

The pre-processing is simple. First, we turn all the letters to lower case. Then we remove all the dots and commas from sentences. Finally, we remove Portuguese stopwords and, tokenize the dataset using NLTK[2].

## 3 Experiments

In this section we show the model configuration that we used. We further present the results of our experiments.

The best results were achieved using an Long Short-Term Memory (LSTM) word-level (Hochreiter and Schmidhuber, 1997). The model uses a maximum of 200 words per segment and a maximum of 100 segments. The LSTM applies a sigmoid activation function. We also used dropout (Srivastava et al., 2014) and gradient clipping (Pascanu et al., 2013). We dropout at each layer with probability $p = 0.5$ and gradients are clipped at a maximum norm of 1 in the propogation. For the loss and optimizer, we used categorical cross-entropy and RMSprop (Tieleman et al., 2012) with a learning rate of 0.01, respectively. In the output, a softmax function is used. We run the model for 10 epochs for better visualization, but after the 40 epochs, the validation accuracy tends to decrease. We applied different batch sizes in the experiments. We utilise for a mini-batch of 16 as it shows the best results. The dataset was divided by 70% for training, 10% for validation, and 20% for testing.

---

[1] https://letras.mus.br  
[2] http://www.nltk.org/




*Proceedings of the 55th Annual Meeting of the Association for Computational Linguistics*, pages 61–63  
Florence, Italy, July 28th, 2019. ©2019 Association for Computational Linguistics

We applied six different models in our experiments, LSTM, FastText, XGBoost, RF, DT, and Multi-layer Perceptron (MLP). The LSTM model achieves the best result with a 50% accuracy on the dataset, FastText with 49%, XGBoost with 48%, RF with 45%, DT with 38%, and MLP with 15%.

**Figure 1** shows the accuracy and loss of the LSTM model. The LSTM model, which takes into account word order and tries to implement a memory of these words, tends to overfit in the training dataset after the 5th epoch.

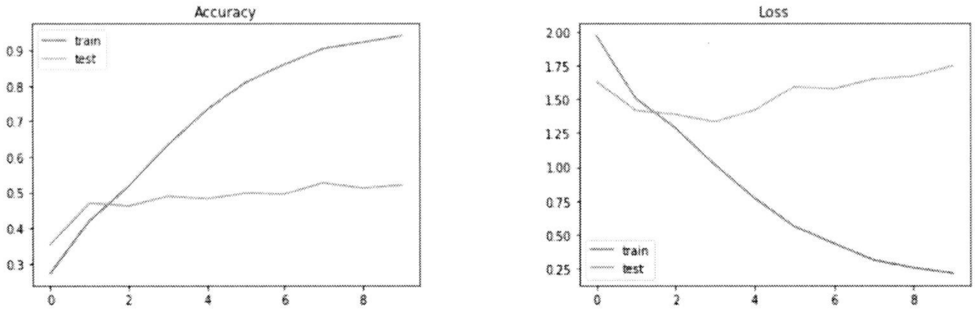

Figure 1: Accuracy and Loss for the LSTM model.

The confusion matrix for the testing dataset can be seen in **Figure 2**. We also present the most frequent words on two of the lyrics styles from our dataset in **Table 1**. We can see that even though the *Forró* and *Bossa Nova* are completely different musically, they share many words in their lyrics (e.g.: *amor* [love], *coração* [heart], *gente* [people], *Você* [you], *vida* [life], *dia* [day]). So it is no surprise that the model is confused as to their classification.

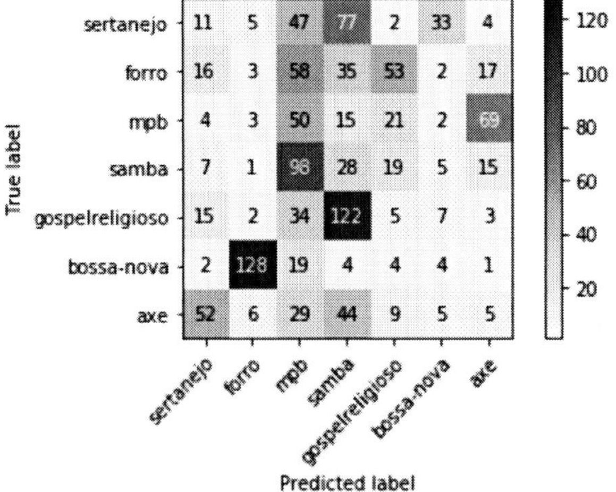

Figure 2: Confusion Matrix for the testing dataset.

## 4   Conclusion

Brazilian music styles by lyrics classification is presented as a hard task. As some of the styles share many similar words, it is unclear if whether a person would be able to distinguish between the lyrics of these genres. To produce a better classifier, we must take into account more than just the lyrics. A combination of audio and lyrics could be applied for bigger accuracy. As future work, we intend to

Table 1: Most frequent word from *Forró* and *Bossa Nova*.

<table>
<tr><td colspan="2" align="center">(a) Forró</td><td colspan="2" align="center">(b) Bossa Nova</td></tr>
<tr><td>word</td><td>frequency</td><td>word</td><td>frequency</td></tr>
<tr><td>amor</td><td>1220</td><td>amor</td><td>851</td></tr>
<tr><td>coração</td><td>560</td><td>vida</td><td>351</td></tr>
<tr><td>quero</td><td>443</td><td>ser</td><td>295</td></tr>
<tr><td>gente</td><td>434</td><td>tão</td><td>246</td></tr>
<tr><td>Você</td><td>407</td><td>sei</td><td>245</td></tr>
<tr><td>Me</td><td>405</td><td>bem</td><td>243</td></tr>
<tr><td>vida</td><td>388</td><td>coração</td><td>243</td></tr>
<tr><td>tudo</td><td>376</td><td>gente</td><td>239</td></tr>
<tr><td>dia</td><td>333</td><td>dia</td><td>236</td></tr>
<tr><td>tá</td><td>331</td><td>Você</td><td>234</td></tr>
</table>

increase our sample with more lyrics and to explore more of the similarity of the genres at the moment of classification.

## References


Silva, Catarina and Ribeiro, Bernadete. 2010. Inductive Inference for Large Scale Text Classification: Kernel Approaches and Techniques (Studies in Computational Intelligence) . Springer.

Tsaptsinos, Alexandros. 2017. Lyrics-Based Music Genre Classification Using A Hierarchical Attention Network. *In Proceedings of the 18th International Society for Music Information Retrieval Conference.*

Mayer, Rudolf and Neumayer, Robert and Rauber, Andreas. 2008. Combination of Audio and Lyrics Features for Genre Classification in Digital Audio Collections. *In Proceedings of the 16th ACM International Conference on Multimedia.*

Liaw, Andy and Wiener, Matthew. 2002. Classification and Regression by randomForest. *R News*, 2(3): 18–22.

Young, Tom and Hazarika, Devamanyu and Poria, Soujanya and Cambria, Erik. 2018. Recent trends in deep learning based natural language processing. *IEEE Computational Intelligence Magazine*, 13(3):55–75.

Hochreiter, Sepp and Schmidhuber, Jürgen. 1997. Long short-term memory. *Neural computation*, 9(8): 1735–1780.

Srivastava, Nitish and Hinton, Geoffrey and Krizhevsky, Alex and Sutskever, Ilya and Salakhutdinov, Ruslan. 2014. Dropout: A Simple Way to Prevent Neural Networks from Overfitting. *Journal of Machine Learning Research*, 15(1): 1929–1958.

Pascanu, Razvan and Mikolov, Tomas and Bengio, Yoshua. 2013. On the difficulty of training recurrent neural networks. *ICML*, 28:1310–1318.

Tieleman, Tijmen and Hinton, Geoffrey. 2012. Lecture 6.5-rmsprop: Divide the gradient by a running average of its recent magnitud. *COURSERA: Neural networks for machine learning*, 4(2).

# Enabling fast and correct typing in 'Leichte Sprache' (Easy Language)


**Ina Steinmetz**
Universität Koblenz-Landau
Computer Science Faculty
Universitätsstraße 1
56070 Koblenz
Germany
inaschroeder@uni-koblenz.de

**Karin Harbusch**
Universität Koblenz-Landau
Computer Science Faculty
Universitätsstraße 1
56070 Koblenz
Germany
harbusch@uni-koblenz-de



## Abstract

Simplified languages are instruments for inclusion aiming to overcome language barriers. *Leichte Sprache* (LS), for instance, is a variety of German with reduced complexity (cf. Basic English). So far, LS is mainly provided for, but rarely written by, its target groups, e.g. people with cognitive impairments. One reason may be the lack of technical support during the process from message conceptualization to sentence realization. In the following, we present a system for assisted typing in LS whose accuracy and speed is largely due to the deployment of real time natural-language processing enabling efficient prediction and context-sensitive grammar support.


## 1 Motivation

Written language is essential to integration and autonomous participation in social and economic life (Bingel, 2018; Siegel and Lieske, 2014). An established instrument to overcome language barriers for people with cognitive impairment is *Leichte Sprache* (LS) (Maaß and Bredel, 2016; Bock, 2015; Maaß et al., 2014). This is a simplified variety of written German which follows a set of rules to reduce language complexity in order to simplify understandability (cf. Basic English).

In many languages, systems for automatic text simplification are available: e.g., see Bingel (2018) (English), Suter et al. (2016) (German) or Seretan (2012) (French). See the survey by Shardlow (2014) for more examples. However, few systems aiming to assist people who primarily rely on LS in correctly committing their thoughts in writing, deploy advanced natural-language processing-techniques. Many people with communication impairments use solutions for *Alternative and Augmentative Communication* (*AAC*) that combine symbols and words. For people with basic written German language skills, these solutions range from tools which only allow manual inflection (*MYCore13*) to systems featuring automatic inflection for simple subjects, different verb tenses, basic adjective declination and adaptive word prediction (*MindExpress4, Tobii Gateway*) and the construction of subordinate clauses (*Tobii Gateway*)[1].

The more complex the system, the more grammatical knowledge is required. For instance, the user is forced to select noun cases (*MindExpress4*) or to manually correct errors caused by incorrect predictions (*Tobii Gateway*). This inspired our research question: To which extent can natural-language processing by computer support users in producing coherent text in LS at the user's personal level of proficiency in spelling and clause construction?

In the following, we describe our prototype *EasyTalk* – as it can also read-out the typed texts – that supports fast and correct typing of complex content messages, with main emphasis on extensive use of linguistic processing and on interactive user guidance aiming to compensate for lack of grammatical knowledge and to ensure understandability and syntactic correctness.

## 2 *EasyTalk*: an ACC system for fast and syntactically correct typing in LS

Our system, called *EasyTalk*, uses a paraphrase generator (cf. Harbusch et al. (2014; 2007)) based on a lexicalized, unification-based Performance Grammar  (Harbusch and Kempen, 2002; Kempen and

---



[1]MyCore13: http://www.my-core.de/, MindExpress4: http://www.mindexpress.be/ and Tobii Gateway: http://www.tobiidynavox.de/compass/gateway/




*Proceedings of the 55th Annual Meeting of the Association for Computational Linguistics*, pages 64–67
Florence, Italy, July 28th, 2019. ©2019 Association for Computational Linguistics

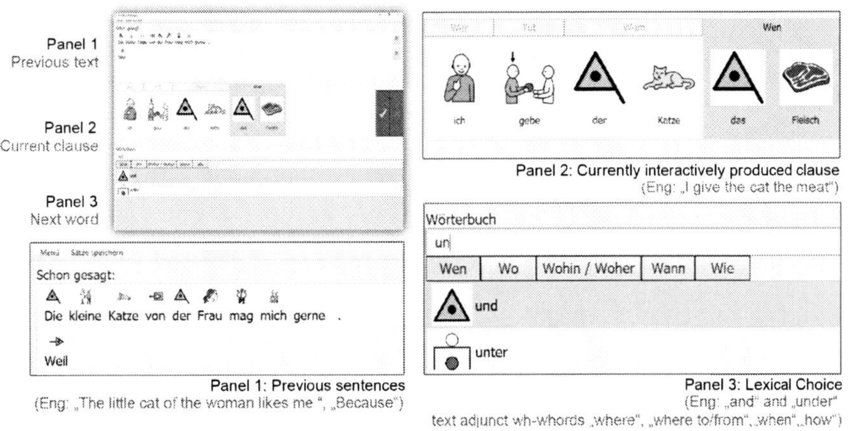



Figure 1: Top left: The overall organization of the three panels *EasyTalk* provides. Others: closeups.

Harbusch, 2002). It deploys a restricted set of grammar rules defined by the rule books of LS (Netzwerk Leichte Sprachel, 2013; Inclusion Europe, 2014; BITV 2.0, 2011) and their implicit linguistic effects (Maaß and Bredel, 2016). LS–rules such as *"Do not use commas"*, *"Avoid inversions"* and *"Use clear sentence structure"* are translated into main-clause patterns with a fixed subject-verb-argument-adjunct order. Genitive constructions (e.g. "the woman's cat") are avoided in favor of prepositional phrases ("the cat of the woman").

Figure 1 shows a snapshot of a text-production session with active elements highlighted in blue. Panel 1 contains the previously typed text: A statement followed by a cohesion marker. After each sentence the writer is reminded to select a cohesion marker from a set of conjunctions resembling RST connectors (Mann et al., 1992). These help users to write coherent texts. Panel 2 shows the currently produced sentence in the form of a skeleton of the clause structure in terms of headers for all obligatory grammatical functions couched in wh-words (cf. *wer* ('who'), *wem* ('whom'), *wen* ('what') according to the valency of the chosen verb *geben* ('give')). The finite verb is cued by *tut ('does')*. The blue area indicates the currently active position/inflection. To finish a sentence the user clicks the button with the green check mark. As a result, the sentence is displayed in panel 1. To discard the current sentence and start anew, the user clicks the blue button with the red X. Panel 3 displays a completion list of the currently typed prefix of the next word retrieved from the lexicon. The dictionary contains a list of all wordforms allowed in the currently constructed constituent. All suggestions are augmented by AAC symbols and the same RST-function cues used in panel 2. Further wh-cues of adjunct functions remind the user to specify the extensions explicitly. To write a sentence, the user selects words one-by-one from the suggestion list in panel 3. The linguistic context for the completion list is kept up to date at all times by our natural-language generator that yields the set of unified derivation trees. This way the user is always presented with a context-sensitive set of all wordforms that are syntactically correct choices. These choices can be further filtered by clicking on the cues mentioned above, thus recruiting additional syntactic support. If the word processing routine detects linguistic ambiguities, we temporarily replace panel 3 with a decision dialogue applying concepts of audience design (e.g. two cats mentioned in the text should be uniquely referred to or anaphorized, respectively) (Bell, 1984). The combination of interactive user guidance and inflected predictions provides reliable grammar support and speeds up typing.

A challenge with respect to the linear order of building a sentence is presented by complex verb constructions such as verb clusters including auxiliary or modal verbs. In order to satisfy the valency requirements of these verbs, our system asks the users if they want to add a second verb and updates the list of arguments accordingly. Striving for a correct and complete clause, we hereby knowingly urge the user to think in an unusual word order: In German, the arguments of the full verb often precede the verb, thus our system needs to know this verb in order to determine and support the formulation of its extensions.

Figure 2: Snapshot of the users being presented with a decision dialogue, in which they may directly continue with the argument of the verb (top) or first choose a second verb (bottom).

Figure 2 illustrates the dialogue for handling complex verb constructions: As soon as the user chooses a verb that allows complex verb constructions – in the example the modal verb *will* ('want') – they are asked to decide whether to continue with the arguments of the first verb or to choose another verb. The grammar rules permit recursion here, i.e. the dialogue can produce a verb chain. As soon as the verb chain ends, the user fills the arguments in the usual manner as depicted in Figure 1. In Figure 2 this happens after the verb *essen* ('to eat') is selected. Our system automatically adjusts the position of the verb after each successively entered wordform of all possible arguments. By highlighting the current constituent the user is not distracted by the verb(s) at the end of the sentence.

## 3  Discussion and Conclusion

We have presented *EasyTalk*, a new AAC app for fast and correct LS typing which is largely based on linguistic processing by computer. We strive for correct and understandable text by providing a context-sensitively filtered list of wordforms and interactive user guidance tailored to minimize the grammatical knowledge needed to produce correct and coherent complex contents.

We performed preliminary tests aiming to mature the finally tested version: A group of five German learners at CEFR-level A2 explored the efficacy of the user interface and the linguistic writing support. Interviews with a group of five AAC-/LS-experts (consisting of one LS consumer/validator, two LS translators and two experts of AAC methods familiar with LS) enabled us to eliminate pitfalls in our system caused by too complex actions before testing with impaired users. Both groups were satisfied with the interactive grammar support and the customizable AAC symbols. Accordingly, we primarily got feedback on the syntactic correctness and the grammatical guidance by the German learners. The LS experts' concerns focused mainly on evaluating the usability of our system in day-to-day use and facilities for personalization and adaptations to special needs. As for the issue of verb clusters mentioned above, the language learners could easily manage. Learners coming from SVO languages even appreciated the decision dialogue to remind them of the SOV word order in German verb clusters. The expert group gave positive feedback, too: They did not voice any reservations about the verb-cluster dialogue while exploring the system. Elaborate testing with AAC users to achieve quantifiable results is projected.

As for future work and open problems, we want to elaborate user-customization: Not all users need LS at its utmost simplification. We plan facilities to tailor our rule set to the personalized skill level of the user. Moreover, the knowledge representation of typed text in our system (cf. panel 1) allows to transform the text into unrestricted German, so that the users can choose the language level of the expected reader. Our system canonically implements the rules of LS. However, these rules are still under discussion (Maaß and Bredel, 2016; Zurstrassen, 2017; Bock, 2019) and the textual implementation often differs from the rule books. Therefore we plan an in-depth analysis of a broad set of LS texts in order to offer the user optional grammar expansions of structures commonly used in LS texts.

## References

Allan Bell. 1984. Language style as audience design. *Language in Society*, 13(2):145–204.

Joachim Bingel. 2018. *Personalized and Adaptive Text Simplification*. PhD Thesis. Department of Computer Science, Faculty of Science, University of Copenhagen, Denmark.

BITV 2.0. 2011. Verordnung zur Schaffung barrierefreier Informationstechnik nach dem Behindertengleich-stellungsgesetz (BarrierefreieInformationstechnik-Verordnung - BITV 2.0). *Barrierefreie-Informationstechnik-Verordnung vom 12. September 2011 (BGBl. I S. 1843), die zuletzt durch Artikel 1 der Verordnung vom 21Mai 2019 (BGBl. I S. 738) geändert worden ist.*

Bettina M. Bock. 2019. *"Leichte Sprache"–Kein Regelwerk: Sprachwissenschaftliche Ergebnisse und Praxisempfehlungen aus dem LeiSA-Projekt.(Vol. 5)* Frank & Timme, Berlin, Germany.

Bettina M. Bock. 2015. *Leichte Texte schreiben*. Frank & Timme, Berlin, Germany.

Karin Harbusch, Johannes Härtel, and Cristel-Joy Cameran. 2014. Automatic Feedback Generation for Grammatical Errors in German as Second Language Learners Focused on the Learner's Personal Acquisition Level. *Proceedings of EUROCALL 2014 - Call Design: Principles and Practice*, Groningen, The Netherlands.

Karin Harbusch, Camiel van Bruegel, Ulrich Koch and Gerard Kempen. 2007. Interarctive sentence combining and paraphrasing in support of integrated writing and grammar instruction: A new application area for natural sentence generators. *Proceedings of ENLG 2007 - 11th European Workshop on Natural Langauge Generation*, Dagstuhl, Germany.

Karin Harbusch and Gerard Kempen. 2002. A quantative model of word order and movement in English, Dutch and German complement constructions. *Proceedings of COLING 2002 - 19th International Conference on Computational Linguistics*, pp. 328–334, Taipei, Taiwan.

Inclusion Europe. 2014. *Informationen für alle - Europäische Regeln, wie man Informationen leicht lesbar und leicht verständlich macht* Inclusion Europe, Brussels, Belgium.

Gerard Kempen and Karin Harbusch. 2002. Performance Grammar: A declarative definition. Mariët Theune, Anton Nijholt, and Hendri Hondorp (eds.), *Computational Linguistics in the Netherlands 2001*, pp. 148–162, Rodopi, The Netherlands.

William C. Mann, Christian Matthias Ingemar Martin Matthiessen, and Sandra Annear Thompson. 1992. Rhetorical structure theory and text analysis. *Discourse description: Diverse linguistic analyses of a fund-raising text*:39–78.

Christiane Maaß and Ursula Bredel. 2016. *Leichte Sprache: Theoretische Grundlagen Orientierung für die Praxis.* Bibliographisches Institut, Berlin, Germany.

Christiane Maaß, Isabelle Rink, and Christiane Zehrer. 2014. Leichte Sprache in der Sprach- und Übersetzungswissenschaft. Susanne Johanna Jekat, Heike Elisabeth Jüngst, Klaus Schubert, Claudia Villiger (Hrsg.): *Sprache barrierefrei gestalten. Perspektiven aus der Angewandten Linguistik*, Frank & Timme, Berlin, Germany:53–86.

Melanie Siegel and Christian Lieske. 2014. Beitrag der Sprachtechnologie zur Barrierefreiheit: Unterstützung für Leichte Sprache. *Zeitschrift für Translationswissenschaft und Fachkommunikation*:40–78.

Netzwerk Leichte Sprache e.V. 2013. *Die Regeln für Leichte Sprache*. Netzwerk Leichte Sprache e.V., Berlin, Germany.

Violeta Seretan. 2012. Acquisition of syntactic simplification rules for French. *Proceedings of the Eight International Conference on Language Resources and Evaluation (LREC'12)*, pp. 4019–4026, Istanbul, Turkey.

Matthew Shardlow. 2014. A survey of automated text simplification. *International Journal of Advanced Computer Science and Applications*, 4(1):58–70.

Julia Suter, Sarah Ebling, and Martin Volk. 2016. Rule-based automatic text simplification for German. *In Proceedings of the 13th Conference on Natural Language Processing (KONVENS 2016)*, pp. 279–287, Bochum, Germany.

Bettina Zurstrassen. 2017. Leichte Sprache–eine Sprache der Chancengleichheit. *Bettina M. Bock, Ulla Fix & Daisy Lange (Hg.), "Leichte Sprache" im Spiegel theoretischer und angewandter Forschung*, pp. 53–70. Frank & Timme, Berlin, Germany.

# AI4D - African Language Dataset Challenge


**Kathleen Siminyu**
Artificial Intelligence for Development
Africa
kathleensiminyu@gmail.com

**Sackey Freshia**
Jomo Kenyatta University
of Agriculture and Technology
freshiasackey@gmail.com

**Jade Abbott**
RetroRabbit
jade.zoe.abbott@gmail.com

**Vukosi Marivate**
University of Pretoria
vukosi.marivate@cs.up.ac.za


## Abstract


As language and speech technologies become more advanced, the lack of fundamental digital resources for African languages, such as data, spell checkers and Part of Speech taggers, means that the digital divide between these languages and others keeps growing. This work details the organisation of the AI4D - African Language Dataset Challenge[1], an effort to incentivize the creation, organization and discovery of African language datasets through a competitive challenge. We particularly encouraged the submission of annotated datasets which can be used for training task-specific supervised machine learning models.


## 1 Introduction

Africa has a language diversity of over 2000 languages, many of which are only spoken and not written (Eberhard et al., 2019).

As language technologies advance and more sophisticated tools are built using Artificial Intelligence, the divide between low resource languages and others is likely to get even larger as a common prerequisite of these advanced systems is the existence of a large amount of digital data. African languages, low resource languages, are at risk of being left behind (Joshi et al., 2020).

Data Science and Machine Learning skills are increasingly becoming widespread on the African continent. This can be attributed to the rise of grassroots capacity building efforts through organisations such as Data Science Africa[2], Data Science Nigeria[3], Deep Learning Indaba[4], as well as NLP-specific communities such as Masakhane[5] (Orife et al., 2020). These movements have facilitated a critical mass of individuals with the relevant skills, who speak African languages that can start contributing to the overall body of work that currently exists and begin the work where none does. With this challenge, we sought to engage the African NLP community in the task of dataset creation.

## 2 Methodology

The realisation of this work was wholly driven by the intended outcome, the need for more African language datasets for use in NLP research.

### 2.1 Framing the Challenge

Early framing of this challenge was predicated on the fact that pre-trained language models are producing state-of-the-art NLP results (Devlin et al., 2018; Radford et al., 2019). African NLP would undoubtably benefit from the creation of such language models, and so the competition was initially envisioned as a language model challenge. Unfortunately, not only do most pre-trained language models require large amounts of monolingual data to train, they require labelled NLP datasets in order to usefully evaluate the models. This motivated the decision to create a challenge focused on data collection, rather than model building.

---

[1] https://zindi.africa/competitions/ai4d-african-language-dataset-challenge
[2] http://www.datascienceafrica.org/
[3] http://datasciencenigeria.ai
[4] https://deeplearningindaba.com/
[5] https://www.masakhane.io/




*Proceedings of the 55th Annual Meeting of the Association for Computational Linguistics*, pages 68–77
Florence, Italy, July 28th, 2019. ©2019 Association for Computational Linguistics

## 2.2 Securing Donor Funding

With the aim of creating datasets that are openly available, we prepared and circulated a proposal and succeeded in securing donor funding. That being committed, we tailored the challenge to take place in 2 phases. The initial phase focused on data collection and the second phase being a more conventional machine learning (ML) challenge, where the datasets developed in the first phase could be used as evaluation sets for a pre-trained language model challenge.

## 2.3 Hosting the Challenge

Our target audience was researchers, practitioners and enthusiasts from African countries who could create datasets for the languages that they speak. We approached Zindi[6], an African data science competition platform, to host the challenge in a bid to leverage their existing user base. They have over 12,000 individuals signed up.

## 2.4 Evaluation of Submissions

Unlike a conventional ML challenge that would have an agreed upon automated metric to evaluate and rank submitted models, evaluation of a challenge of this kind cannot be automated. Instead, we put together a panel of judges with experience in NLP who would review the datasets each month. We also indicated in the challenge guidelines that each dataset submission should be accompanied by a datasheet (Gebru et al., 2018) that documents its motivation, composition, collection process, recommended uses, and so on (Example in Appendix A).

Evaluation was done by judges analysing the datasheets and awarding points to each submission based on a scoring rubric. The rubric took into account the following: how representative and balanced the corpus was, the dataset size in terms of tokens and unique tokens, whether it was annotated for a specific downstream task, under-representation of the language in terms of digital data, methodology of the data collection and labelling process, originality of the data collection and labelling process (Reviewer Documentation in Appendix B).

## 3 Results

| Language | Tasks | Submissions |
|---|---|---|
| Yoruba | MT, Diacritic Verification, Text Classification, NER, misc | 7 |
| Kiswahili | Document Classification, misc | 6 |
| Igbo | NER, misc | 4 |
| Hausa | Sentiment Analysis, Document classification, misc | 4 |
| Fongbe | MT, Speech to Text, misc | 3 |
| Amharic | Hate speech detection, stop words list, misc | 3 |
| Asante Twi | Sentiment Analysis, MT, misc | 3 |
| Chichewa | NER, MT | 2 |
| Ewe | MT, misc | 2 |
| Wolof | ASR | 1 |
| Tunizian Arabizi | Sentiment Analysis | 1 |
| Kikuyu | misc | 1 |
| Kabiwe | MT | 1 |
| Oromo | misc | 1 |
| Zulu | misc | 1 |

Table 1: Language and Task distribution of submissions.

The challenge ran for a period of five months with a total of 270 people registering on the Zindi platform to participate.

---

[6]http://zindi.africa

The data in the submitted datasets was compiled from a wide variety of sources. These were largely digital sources such as news websites, religious texts, Facebook, Twitter and YouTube. This outcome is likely an indication of the ease of access that online sources present, given that the data is already digitised. Other data creation processes included participants convening to carry out manual translation of existing pieces of text. Unique contributions included OCR to digitize printed texts and using the user base of a commercial application to crowd source and validate recordings of phrases and texts common on the platform.

**Observations and Lessons Learned**:

- Teams composed of individuals from relevant multi-disciplinary backgrounds, including computer scientists, professional translators and linguists, were able to create and annotate datasets that captured fundamental lexical and semantic nuances of languages.

- The challenge framing allowed for anyone to participate. While useful as an exercise in evaluating the interest in such a challenge, the top evaluated submissions came from teams who had been exposed to NLP research work. Targeting such a challenge to NLP researchers could lead to higher quality submissions in future.

- A portion of submissions contained very few data points. As the aim is to use the datasets for NLP, in future, we'd set explicit minimum requirements with regards to the size of datasets admissible, file formats and require the inclusion of any cleaning or pre-processing code used.

- Since the challenge was evaluated monthly, we often received disparate submissions from the same teams as they managed to obtain more data. Instead, one large dataset built over a couple of months would have been the ideal outcome, so in future we'd select and support teams for a sustained period of time to enable them build sizeable datasets.

- Participants and judges had to rely on their own understanding of what "Representative and Balanced" means in a dataset. In future, more specificity of what "representative" and "balanced" means would enable participants to produce better datasets.

## 4  Future Work

A large number of opportunities were identified to support future work in African, and low resource, language dataset creation, as follows:

- Research and analysis of the legal implications of obtaining textual, visual and audio data from a variety of online sources, which were noted as a common source among participants. The copyright and intellectual property implications will have to be thoroughly assessed ahead of the publication and further public use of relevant datasets.

- Outlining of best case practise techniques for protecting the identities and privacy of users, in instances where data is obtained from social media/content platforms like Twitter, Facebook and YouTube. Social media sites have been noted as a common data source.

- Recommended techniques for identifying and ascertaining whether data obtained from online sources(news publications,social media and content platforms) contains biased sentiments(sexist, racist) and offensive material(hateful), as well as techniques for removing any biased sentiment and offensive material, if need be, depending on the use of the dataset.

Courtesy of this dataset creation challenge, we have secured further funding to support 5 of the top teams for a 6 month period. During this time, they will further flesh out their datasets with the aim of using these as the basis of future NLP challenges/shared tasks. This project will also be used as a model case to inform evidence-based policy making concerning Artificial Intelligence and we hope that it will be replicated to support the development of data for other low resource languages.

## Acknowledgements

This work has been funded through a partnership between the International Development Research Centre, the Swedish International Development Cooperation Agency, the Knowledge4All Foundation, Zindi Africa and the AI4D-Africa Network. The expert panel that volunteered their time to undertake the difficult qualitative task of dataset assessment was composed of Jade Abbott - Retro Rabbit, John Quinn - Google AI / Makerere University, Kathleen Siminyu - AI4D-Africa, Veselin Stoyanov - Facebook AI and Vukosi Marivate - University of Pretoria.

## References


Jacob Devlin, Ming-Wei Chang, Kenton Lee, and Kristina Toutanova. 2018. Bert: Pre-training of deep bidirectional transformers for language understanding. *arXiv preprint arXiv:1810.04805.*

David M Eberhard, Gary F. Simons, and Charles D. Fenning. 2019. Ethnologue: Languages of the worlds. twenty-second edition.

Timnit Gebru, Jamie Morgenstern, Briana Vecchione, Jennifer Wortman Vaughan, Hanna Wallach, Hal Daumeé III, and Kate Crawford. 2018. Datasheets for datasets. *arXiv preprint arXiv:1803.09010.*

Pratik M. Joshi, Sebastin Santy, Amar Budhiraja, Kalika Bali, and Monojit Choudhury. 2020. The state and fate of linguistic diversity and inclusion in the nlp world. *ArXiv*, abs/2004.09095.

Iroro Orife, Julia Kreutzer, Blessing Sibanda, Daniel Whitenack, Kathleen Siminyu, Laura Martinus, Jamiil Toure Ali, Jade Abbott, Vukosi Marivate, Salomon Kabongo, et al. 2020. Masakhane–machine translation for africa. *arXiv*, pages arXiv–2003.

Alec Radford, Jeffrey Wu, Rewon Child, David Luan, Dario Amodei, and Ilya Sutskever. 2019. Language models are unsupervised multitask learners. *OpenAI Blog*, 1(8):9.


## Appendix A: Copy of Outstanding Submission Datasheet

# Multi-domain machine translation dataset for Yoruba Language

## Motivation

**For what purpose was the dataset created? Was there a specific task in mind? Was there a specific gap that needed to be filled? Please provide a description**

The dataset was created to train a machine translation model from English language to Yoruba language. The major contribution of this dataset is that the english-yoruba parallel sentences come from different domain like technology, medicine, science, movie transcripts, book translation and news articles. This is very uncommon for low-resource languages. The most available parallel text corpora are biased to religious text like Bible and JW300. We provide high quality Yoruba corpora will proper diacritics. The diacritics problem of Yoruba is summarized in the diagram below:

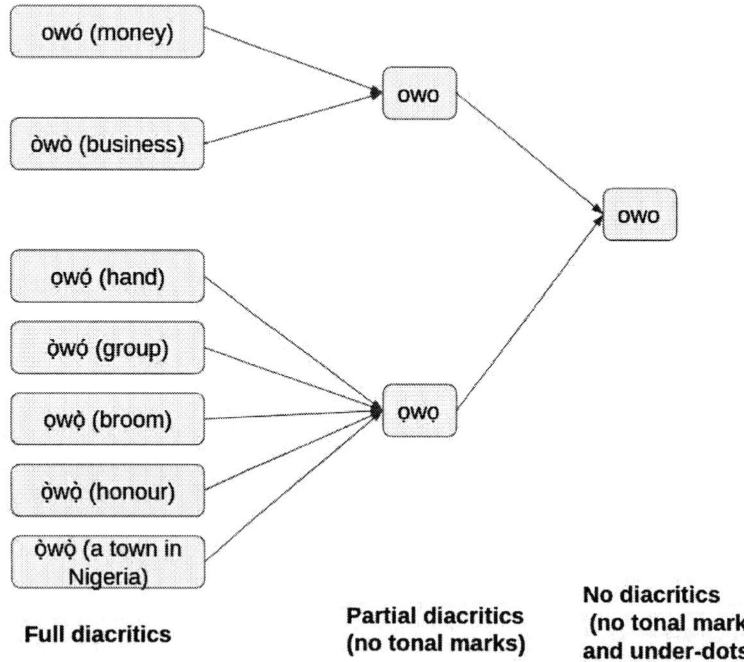



**Who created this dataset (e.g., which team, research group) and on behalf of which entity (e.g., company, institution, organization)?**

The dataset was created by Dạ
(_        ), Dạ                (              ) and Ọl
((              ). D        contacted them because they are the major

contributors to the Yoruba language section of the Global Voices (https://yo.globalvoices.org/ ). Another reason for contacting them is is to verify that all the corpora that we are submitting have the correct diacritics. Improper diacritics affects the performance on down stream NLP tasks (See https://arxiv.org/abs/1912.02481)

**Who funded the creation of the dataset? If there is an associated grant, please provide the name of the grantor and the grant name and number**

We did not receive any funding for the creation of this dataset.

## Composition
**What do the instances that comprise the dataset represent (e.g., documents, photos, people, countries)?**
 The dataset compose of text data from different domains like technology, medicine, science, movie transcripts, book translation and news articles.

**How many instances are there in total (of each type, if appropriate)?**

In total, there are 6047 parallel sentences in all the CSV files from 5 sources:
(1) 45 news articles (or 119 parallel   sentences) from Global Voices.
(2)  2700   parallel sentences from   Yoruba Proverbs
(3) First 6 chapters (or 862 parallel sentences) from "Out of his mind book"
(4) 812 parallel sentences from Unsane movie on YouTube
(5) 549 Multi-domain sentences comprising of technological and scientific terms.

**Does the dataset contain all possible instances or is it a sample (not necessarily random) of instances from a larger set?**
We took only 6 chapters of the 12 chapters of the Out of his mind book due to not enough time to manually extract the parallel sentences before submission. We hope to complete it if we are successful in the competition

**What data does each instance consist of?**
Each instance consist of sentence id, English sentence and Yoruba translation arranged in a csv format.

## Collection Process

**How was the data associated with each instance acquired?**

(1) 45 news articles (or parallel 119  sentences) crawled from Global Voices. (https://yo.globalvoices.org/) and (https://globalvoices.org/. For each Yoruba news article, we manually search for the English equivalence.
(2)  2700  parallel sentences from  Yoruba Proverbs were crawled from https://twitter.com/yoruba_proverbs
(3) First 6 chapters (or 862 parallel sentences) from "Out of his mind book". The entire book was translated by D[illegible] for her Bachelors thesis, and has been edited by the supervisor. The quality is excellent.
(4) 812 parallel sentences from Unsane movie on YouTube was translated by D[illegible]. This is what she does for living.
(5) 549 Multi-domain sentences comprising of technological and scientific terms were translated by Ọ[illegible]

## Preprocessing/cleaning/labeling
The main preprocessing done was to align the english and Yoruba sentences into a CSV format. Some were aligned with scripts and others manually depending on the difficulty of the corpora.

## Uses
**Has the dataset been used for any tasks already? If so, please provide a description**
The dataset has not been used for machine translation. We will probably be the first.

**What (other) tasks could the dataset be used for?**
The dataset can also be used for training language models, automatic diacritic restoration.

**Is there anything about the composition of the dataset or the way it was collected and preprocessed/cleaned/labeled that might impact future uses?**
No risk that we are aware of

## Distribution
**Will the dataset be distributed to third parties outside of the en⊴tity (e.g., company, institution, organization) on behalf of which the dataset was created?**
The dataset will be publicly made available after the competition

**How will the dataset will be distributed (e.g., tarball on website, API, GitHub)?**
By Github or Google Drive. The link will be available after the competition.

**When will the dataset be distributed?**

Hopefully, January 2020.

**Will the dataset be distributed under a copyright or other intellectual property (IP) license, and/or under applicable terms of use (ToU)?**
Creative Commons license.

**Have any third parties imposed IP-based or other restrictions on the data associated with the instances?**
No

**Do any export controls or other regulatory restrictions apply to the dataset or to individual instances?**
No

## Maintenance
**Who is supporting/hosting/maintaining the dataset?**
D

**How can the owner/curator/manager of the dataset be contacted (e.g., email address)?**

d            gmail.com

**Will the dataset be updated (e.g., to correct labeling errors, add new instances, delete instances)?  If so, please describe how often, by whom, and how updates will be communicated to users (e.g., mailing list, GitHub)?**
The dataset will be updated when we get more parallel corpora.

REVIEWER DOCUMENTATION

**Representative and Balanced (30%) - 12 points**

- 12-18 points: The corpus is very representative and cuts across several different genres eg literary fiction, blogs, newspaper articles, spoken speech etc, and balanced with various genres being equally represented
- 6-12 points:A little representative and is comprised of two or more genres and somewhat balanced
- 1-6 points: Not representative and derived from one genre

**(Automated)Number of tokens and number of unique tokens (25%) - 10 points**

- 1-5 points: Large number of tokens and large number of unique tokens
- 5-10 points: Large number of either tokens or unique tokens

**Annotated for a specific downstream task (15%) - 6 points**

- 3-6 points: Specific enough downstream task to evaluate future language models on
- 1-3 points: Not tailored for specific enough downstream task

**Is the language underrepresented on the Internet and in terms of available digital data? (15%) - 6 points**

- 3-6 points: Very underrepresented language
- 1-3 points: A little underrepresented

**Methodology of data collection and labelling process (7.5%) - 3 points**

- Is the collection and labelling methodology sound, relevant and well documented?

**Originality of data collection and labelling process (7.5%) - 3points**

- How original and creative is the data collection and labelling process? Eg. Including data from JW300 as a source versus translating poetry from a book that had previously never been digitised.

# Adversarial Evaluation of BERT for
# Biomedical Named Entity Recognition

**Vladimir Araujo, Andrés Carvallo, Denis Parra**
Pontificia Universidad Católica de Chile
Millennium Institute Foundational Research on Data
`{vgaraujo, afcarvallo}@uc.cl, dparra@ing.puc.cl`

## Abstract

The success of pre-trained word embeddings of the BERT model has motivated its use in tasks in the biomedical domain. However, it is not clear if this model works correctly in real scenarios. In this work, we propose an adversarial evaluation scheme in a BioNER dataset, which consists of two types of attacks inspired by natural spelling errors and synonyms of medical terms. Our results indicate that under these adversarial settings, the performance of the models drops significantly. Despite the result, we show how the robustness of the models can be significantly improved by training them with adversarial examples.

## 1 Background

**Biomedical Natural Language Processing (BioNLP)** is the field concerned with developing tools and methodologies for processing biomedical textual information and generally applied to tasks such as Named Entity Recognition (NER), Sentence Similarity and Relation Extraction. In order to encourage the development of this area, public datasets and challenges have been shared with the community, such as BC5CDR (Wei et al., 2015), CLEF (Suominen et al., 2013), BioSSES (Soğancıoğlu et al., 2017), ChemPror (Kringelum et al., 2016) and i2b2 (Özlem Uzuner et al., 2011).

At the same time, general-purpose neural language models have recently shown significant progress with the introduction of ELMo (Peters et al., 2018) and BERT (Devlin et al., 2018). These models have obtained remarkable results in several tasks. A natural choice has been to apply these models to BioNLP. As a result, several pre-trained models with medical corpus have been released, such as BioBERT (Lee et al., 2019), ClinicalBERT (Alsentzer et al., 2019), and BlueBERT (Peng et al., 2019).

**Adversarial Examples** have demonstrated the risk of using machine learning systems in real-world applications (Szegedy et al., 2014; Goodfellow et al., 2014). This evaluation strategy showed that slight disturbances in the input could cause severe failures in computer vision models. More recently, adversarial attacks have been applied to several NLP benchmarks (Jin et al., 2019; Aspillaga et al., 2020).

This type of evaluation has become relevant in the biomedical domain because an erroneous prediction could be very harmful to patients (Paschali et al., 2018). Despite the existence of deployed systems in real-world clinical settings, researchers have shown that even the state of the art models in medical computer vision (Finlayson et al., 2019; Ma et al., 2019) are vulnerable to adversarial attacks. However, perturbation methods developed for images cannot be directly applied to texts. Because of that, we focus on the BERT language model to carry out an adversarial evaluation on a Biomedical text mining task.

## 2 Adversarial Evaluation

We propose a black-box attack methodology, which does not require the inner details of the model to generate adversarial examples (Ilyas et al., 2018). Specifically, we focus on making disturbances in the

Table 1: Adversarial Evaluation Sentence Examples

| Original | Two mothers with heart valve prosthesis were treated with warfarin during pregnancy. |
|---|---|
| **Swap Noise** | Two mothers with herat vavle protshesis were terated with warafrin during preganncy. |
| **Keyboard Typo Noise** | Two mothers with hea5t valce prosth3sis were trezted with warfsrin during pregnahcy. |
| **Synonymy** | Two mothers with heart valve prosthesis were treated with potassium warfarin during pregnancy. |



*Proceedings of the 55th Annual Meeting of the Association for Computational Linguistics*, pages 79–82
Florence, Italy, July 28th, 2019. ©2019 Association for Computational Linguistics

Table 2: Adversarial Evaluation Sentence Examples

| Training Set | BC5CDR Chemical | | | | BC5CDR Disease | | | |
|---|---|---|---|---|---|---|---|---|
| Test Set | Orig | Keyb | Swap | Syno | Orig | Keyb | Swap | Syno |
| Precision | .895 | .734 | .609 | .730 | .832 | .543 | .636 | .337 |
| Recall | .908 | .683 | .559 | .748 | .844 | .278 | .337 | .390 |
| F1-Score | .901 | .708 | .583 | .739 | .838 | .368 | .441 | .362 |

input data (edit adversaries) that could cause the models to fall into erroneous predictions (Table 1).

**Noise Adversaries** Motivated by the above and inspired by (Belinkov and Bisk, 2018), we constructed adversarial examples that try to emulate spelling errors committed by human beings. These edit adversaries consist of two types of alterations: (i) **Swap Noise**: For each word, one random pair of consecutive characters is swapped, (ii) **Keyboard Typo Noise**: For each word, one character is replaced by an adjacent character in traditional English keyboards.

**Synonymy Adversaries** These examples test if a model can understand synonymy relations. Replacing a medical term with an equivalent synonym is challenging. For that reason, we focus only on words of chemicals and diseases. We use PyMedTermino (Jean-Baptiste et al., 2015), which uses the biomedical vocabulary of UMLS (Bodenreider, 2004), to find the most similar or related words (synonyms) to the retrieved words. Finally, we replace the synonym found depending on whether it is a disease or chemical.

## 3 Experiments

**Experimental Setup** We use the BC5CDR dataset (Wei et al., 2015) for the BioNER task, which consists of 1500 PubMed (Fiorini et al., 2018) articles with 4409 annotated chemicals and 5818 diseases. We evaluated the base version of the pre-trained BlueBERT model because it has been shown to perform better than its namesakes (Wada et al., 2020). We fine-tune the model with the original training set from each task for ten epochs, then evaluate them with the original test set and the adversarial sets.

**Results on Adversarial Evaluation** Table 2 shows the classification results of the BC5CDR task on our adversarial examples and the original test set. We see that the performance of BERT drops across all adversarial attacks. However, the task of recognizing the disease was the most affected.

In the case of the chemical recognition task, the model shows a drop of approximately 20% of the F1 score. In contrast, the F1 score of the disease recognition task falls dramatically, below 50% of the original score.

**Adversarial Training Results** Training with adversarial examples is a methodology used in previous works (Belinkov and Bisk, 2018; Jia and Liang, 2017) to create robustness in neural language models. It ensures that the model is exposed to samples outside the training distribution and provides a form of regularization (Belinkov and Bisk, 2018). We first fine-tune the model with the original training set plus an adversarial version of the same set. Then we carry out the adversarial evaluation to measure how the models perform in the different test sets. Table 3 shows the results for NER of training with adversaries and testing with the original set compared with their respective adversaries. We see that training with adversarial examples significantly improves the robustness of the models to adversarial attacks, without significant impact on the original non-adversarial task.

Table 3: Adversarial Training Results

| Training Set | BC5CDR Chemical + Keyboard | | BC5CDR Chemical + Swap | | BC5CDR Chemical + Synonymy | | BC5CDR Disease + Keyboard | | BC5CDR Disease + Swap | | BC5CDR Disease + Synonymy | |
|---|---|---|---|---|---|---|---|---|---|---|---|---|
| Test Set | Orig | Keyb | Orig | Swap | Orig | Syno | Orig | Keyb | Orig | Swap | Orig | Syno |
| Precision | .889 | .850 | .895 | .684 | .899 | .872 | .839 | .723 | .836 | .773 | .813 | .788 |
| Recall | .906 | .792 | .902 | .630 | .901 | .908 | .848 | .712 | .847 | .746 | .824 | .841 |
| F1-Score | .898 | .820 | .898 | .656 | .900 | .890 | .844 | .717 | .841 | .759 | .818 | .814 |

# 4 Conclusions

In this paper, we investigated how the state-of-the-art model, BERT, is robust or brittle to simple adversarial attacks in a BioNER task. Our experimental results suggest the necessity of considering the robustness of the neural models for use in the biomedical field.

For future work, we plan to explore other tasks related to medicine. Also, investigate further why there is a different drop in performance between adverse example types and data sets.

## Acknowledgements

This work has been partially funded by Millennium Institute for Foundational Research on Data (IMFD).

## References

Emily Alsentzer, John Murphy, William Boag, Wei-Hung Weng, Di Jindi, Tristan Naumann, and Matthew Mc-Dermott. 2019. Publicly available clinical BERT embeddings. In *Proceedings of the 2nd Clinical Natural Language Processing Workshop*, pages 72–78, Minneapolis, Minnesota, USA, June. Association for Computational Linguistics.

Carlos Aspillaga, Andrés Carvallo, and Vladimir Araujo. 2020. Stress test evaluation of transformer-based models in natural language understanding tasks.

Yonatan Belinkov and Yonatan Bisk. 2018. Synthetic and natural noise both break neural machine translation. In *International Conference on Learning Representations*.

O. Bodenreider. 2004. The unified medical language system (UMLS): integrating biomedical terminology. *Nucleic Acids Research*, 32(90001):267D–270, January.

Jacob Devlin, Ming-Wei Chang, Kenton Lee, and Kristina Toutanova. 2018. Bert: Pre-training of deep bidirectional transformers for language understanding. *arXiv preprint arXiv:1810.04805*.

Samuel G. Finlayson, John D. Bowers, Joichi Ito, Jonathan L. Zittrain, Andrew L. Beam, and Isaac S. Kohane. 2019. Adversarial attacks on medical machine learning. *Science*, 363(6433):1287–1289, March.

Nicolas Fiorini, Robert Leaman, David J Lipman, and Zhiyong Lu. 2018. How user intelligence is improving PubMed. *Nature Biotechnology*, 36(10):937–945, October.

Ian J Goodfellow, Jonathon Shlens, and Christian Szegedy. 2014. Explaining and harnessing adversarial examples. *arXiv preprint arXiv:1412.6572*.

Andrew Ilyas, Logan Engstrom, Anish Athalye, and Jessy Lin. 2018. Black-box adversarial attacks with limited queries and information.

Lamy Jean-Baptiste, Venot Alain, and Duclos Catherine. 2015. Pymedtermino: an open-source generic api for advanced terminology services. *Studies in Health Technology and Informatics*, 210(Digital Healthcare Empowering Europeans):924–928.

Robin Jia and Percy Liang. 2017. Adversarial examples for evaluating reading comprehension systems. In *Proceedings of the 2017 Conference on Empirical Methods in Natural Language Processing*, pages 2021–2031, Copenhagen, Denmark, September. Association for Computational Linguistics.

Di Jin, Zhijing Jin, Joey Tianyi Zhou, and Peter Szolovits. 2019. Is bert really robust? a strong baseline for natural language attack on text classification and entailment.

J. Kringelum, S. K. Kjaerulff, S. Brunak, O. Lund, T. I. Oprea, and O. Taboureau. 2016. Chemprot-3.0: a global chemical biology diseases mapping. *Database*.

Jinhyuk Lee, Wonjin Yoon, Sungdong Kim, Donghyeon Kim, Sunkyu Kim, Chan Ho So, and Jaewoo Kang. 2019. BioBERT: a pre-trained biomedical language representation model for biomedical text mining. *Bioinformatics*, 09.

Xingjun Ma, Yuhao Niu, Lin Gu, Yisen Wang, Yitian Zhao, James Bailey, and Feng Lu. 2019. Understanding adversarial attacks on deep learning based medical image analysis systems.

Özlem Uzuner, Brett R South, Shuying Shen, and Scott L DuVall. 2011. 2010 i2b2/VA challenge on concepts, assertions, and relations in clinical text. *Journal of the American Medical Informatics Association*, 18(5):552–556, June.

Magdalini Paschali, Sailesh Conjeti, Fernando Navarro, and Nassir Navab. 2018. Generalizability vs. robustness: Investigating medical imaging networks using adversarial examples. In *Medical Image Computing and Computer Assisted Intervention – MICCAI 2018*, pages 493–501. Springer International Publishing.

Yifan Peng, Shankai Yan, and Zhiyong Lu. 2019. Transfer learning in biomedical natural language processing: An evaluation of BERT and ELMo on ten benchmarking datasets. In *Proceedings of the 18th BioNLP Workshop and Shared Task*, pages 58–65, Florence, Italy, August. Association for Computational Linguistics.

Matthew E Peters, Mark Neumann, Mohit Iyyer, Matt Gardner, Christopher Clark, Kenton Lee, and Luke Zettlemoyer. 2018. Deep contextualized word representations. *arXiv preprint arXiv:1802.05365*.

Gizem Soğancıoğlu, Hakime Öztürk, and Arzucan Özgür. 2017. Biosses: a semantic sentence similarity estimation system for the biomedical domain. *Bioinformatics*, 33(14):i49–i58.

Hanna Suominen, Sanna Salanterä, Sumithra Velupillai, Wendy W. Chapman, Guergana Savova, Noemie Elhadad, Sameer Pradhan, Brett R. South, Danielle L. Mowery, Gareth J. Jones, Johannes Leveling, Liadh Kelly, Lorraine Goeuriot, David Martinez, and Guido Zuccon. 2013. Overview of the share/clef ehealth evaluation lab 2013. In *Proceedings of the 4th International Conference on Information Access Evaluation. Multilinguality, Multimodality, and Visualization - Volume 8138*, CLEF 2013, page 212–231, Berlin, Heidelberg. Springer-Verlag.

Christian Szegedy, Wojciech Zaremba, Ilya Sutskever, Joan Bruna, Dumitru Erhan, Ian Goodfellow, and Rob Fergus. 2014. Intriguing properties of neural networks. In *International Conference on Learning Representations*.

Shoya Wada, Toshihiro Takeda, Shiro Manabe, Shozo Konishi, Jun Kamohara, and Yasushi Matsumura. 2020. A pre-training technique to localize medical bert and enhance biobert.

Chih-Hsuan Wei, Yifan Peng, Robert Leaman, Allan Peter Davis, Carolyn J Mattingly, Jiao Li, Thomas C Wiegers, and Zhiyong Lu. 2015. Overview of the biocreative v chemical disease relation (cdr) task. In *Proceedings of the fifth BioCreative challenge evaluation workshop*, volume 14.

# FFR v1.1: Fon-French Neural Machine Translation


**Bonaventure F. P. Dossou**
Kazan Federal University
femipancrace.dossou@gmail.com

**Chris C. Emezue**
Kazan Federal University
chris.emezue@gmail.com


## Abstract


All over the world and especially in Africa, researchers are putting efforts into building Neural Machine Translation (NMT) systems to help tackle the language barriers in Africa, a continent of over 2000 different languages. However, the low-resourceness, diacritical, and tonal complexities of African languages are major issues being faced. The FFR project is a major step towards creating a robust translation model from Fon, a very low-resource and tonal language, to French, for research and public use. In this paper, we introduce FFR Dataset, a corpus of Fon-to-French translations, describe the diacritical encoding process, and introduce our FFR v1.1 model, trained on the dataset. The dataset and model are made publicly available at https://github.com/bonaventuredossou/ffr-v1, to promote collaboration and reproducibility.


## 1 The FFR Dataset: FFR1 and FFR2

The FFR Dataset is a project to compile a large, growing corpus of carefully cleaned of Fon - French (FFR) parallel sentences for machine translation, and other NLP research-related, projects (Dossou and Emezue, 2020). There are currently two versions of the FFR dataset: the initial FFR dataset (FFR1) and the latest version (FFR2).

The major sources for the creation of FFR1 were JW300 (Agic and Vulic, 2019) and BeninLangues[1] with 27980 and 89049 aligned sentences respectively, giving a total of 117,029 parallel sentences. JW300 (JW) contains translations of Jehovah Witness sermons in over 100 languages, while BeninLangues (BL) contains vocabulary words, short expressions, small sentences, complex sentences, proverbs, as well as books of the Bible (Genesis 1 - Psalm 79).

The initial samples contained various grammatical errors, incorrect and incomplete translations, which were disregarded by standard, rule-based cleaning techniques[2]. FFR2, obtained after re-evaluation of translations in FFR1 by FFR natives, reduces JW and BL original samples respectively to 26510 and 27465 Fon-French parallel sentences. We also created a data statement (Bender and Friedman, 2018) for FFR2, which serves to help give a thorough overview of the dataset. Our data statement can be accessed at https://github.com/bonaventuredossou/ffr-v1/blob/master/FFR-Dataset/Data_Statement_FFR_Dataset.pdf. The tabular analyses shown in Table 1 below serve to give an idea of the range of word lengths for the sentences in FFR1 and FFR2. The maximum number of words-per-sentence for the Fon sentences, $max - fon$, is 109, for FFR1, and 88, for FFR2. That of the French sentences, $max - fr$, is 111 for FFR1 and 76 for FFR2. Therefore, the dataset (both FFR1 and FFR2) has a good range of short, medium and long sentences.

## 2 Data Preprocessing

Initial analysis of Fon sentences revealed that different accents (or diacritics or tone marking)[3] on same words affected their meanings, making it necessary to keep the accents (diacritics) of Fon tokens (words,

---

[1] https://beninlangues.com/
[2] Using Python Regex and String packages (https://docs.python.org/3/library/re.html) and NLTK preprocessing library (https://www.nltk.org/)
[3] https://en.wikipedia.org/wiki/Fon_language#Tone_marking




*Proceedings of the 55th Annual Meeting of the Association for Computational Linguistics*, pages 83–87
Florence, Italy, July 28th, 2019. ©2019 Association for Computational Linguistics

Table 1: **Analysis of Sentences in FFR1**

| | FFR1 | | FFR2 | |
|---|---|---|---|---|
| | **FON** | **FRENCH** | **FON** | **FRENCH** |
| # Very Short sentences [1-5 words] | 64301 | 64255 | 27470 | 30817 |
| # Short sentences [6-10 words] | 13848 | 17183 | 6898 | 12500 |
| # Medium sentences [11-30 words] | 29113 | 29857 | 17529 | 10582 |
| # Long sentences [31-($max - fon$ or $max - fr$ )] | 9767 | 5734 | 2078 | 76 |
| Total | **117029** | | **53975** | |

characters). The importance of encoding diacritics (Diacritical Encoding (DE)) of African languages to NMT has been highlighted by researchers (Orife et al., 2020a), who in their experiments affirmed that DE reduces lexical disambiguation, and helps provide more morphological information to the model. DE was performed using the Normalization Form Canonical Composition (NFC) instead of the Normalization Form Canonical Decomposition (NFD) [4]. With NFC, characters are decomposed and then recomposed by canonical equivalence, while with NFD, they are simply decomposed by canonical equivalence, which removes all accents of Fon tokens. For example, considering the Fon word, **to**, with its different diacritical meanings, [(tó,ears),(tò,sea), (tô, country), (tɔ,father)], we see that using NFC keeps the diacrics and consequently the meaning of the words, while using NFD, simply gives the word *to* leading to ambiguities in the translation.

## 3  FFR v1.1 Model Structure and Training

For our experiments, we used FFR2, described in section 1, which is an improvement of FFR1. We derived 43719, 4858 and 5398 training, validation and testing samples accordingly. We used the Tensorflow TextTokenizer[5] with *none* filter to tokenize FFR sentences and build the vocabularies (for Fon and French), from which numerical sequences or representations of each FFR sentence pair are built with the Tensorflow Preprocessing package[6], and used to train the model.

The FFR v1.1 model, like the FFR v1.0 (Dossou and Emezue, 2020), is based on the encoder-decoder configuration (Sutskever et al., 2014; Brownlee, 2017; NMT, 2020). The encoders and decoders are made up of 128-dimensional gated rectified units (GRUs) recurrent layers (Hochreiter and Schmidhuber, 1997), with a word embedding layer of dimension 512. A 30-dimensional attention model (Sutskever et al., 2014; Bahdanau and Bengio, 2015; Lamba, 2020) was also applied in order to help the model make contextual and correct translations. The code for the model has been open-sourced at `https://github.com/bonaventuredossou/ffr-v1/blob/master/model_train_test/fon_fr.py`, to promote reproducibility and similar recent initiaves on machine translation of African languages like (Martinus and Abbott, 2019; Orife et al., 2020b). FFR v1.1 model was trained using the Tensorflow v1.14 package (NMT, 2020).

## 4  Initial Results and Findings

We evaluated the FFR v1.1 model performance using BLEU (Papineni et al., 2002), and GLEU (Wu et al., 2016) metrics. GLEU, is a sentence-level evaluation metric similar to BLEU. As shown on Table 2,

Table 2: Evlauation scores on test data

| | FFR1 | | FFR2 | |
|---|---|---|---|---|
| | **BLEU** | **GLEU** | **BLEU** | **GLEU** |
| Without DE | 24.53 | 13.0 | 27.80 | 17.05 |
| With DE | **30.55** | **18.18** | **37.15** | **20.85** |

---

[4] `https://unicode.org/reports/tr15/#Norm_Forms`
[5] https://www.tensorflow.org/api_docs/python/tf/keras/preprocessing/text
[6] https://www.tensorflow.org/api_docs/python/tf/keras/preprocessing/sequence

the FFR model, trained on both FFR1 and FFR2 showed an improvement when trained with DE.

Table 3 shows translations of interest from the FFR model sources from FFR2, illustrating the difficulty of predicting Fon words which bear different meanings with different accents. While the model predicted well for #0 and #1, it misplaced the meanings for #2 and #3.

Table 3: Sample predictions and scores

| ID | 0 | 1 | 2 | 3 | 4 | 5 |
|---|---|---|---|---|---|---|
| Source | yí bo wa | yi bo wa | hɔn | hɔn | sá amasín dŏ wŭ | gbɛ |
| Target | prends et viens | va et viens | porte | fuire | oindre avec un medicament | pousser de nouvelles feuilles |
| FFR v1.0 Model | prends et viens | va viens | scorpion | porte | se masser avec le remede | esprit de la vie |
| BLEU/CMS score | 1.0 | 1.0 | 0.0 | 0.0 | 0.0/**0.95** | 0.25 / **0.9** |

## 4.1  The Context-Meaning-Similarity (CMS) metric

Researchers have shown that automatic metrics are not necessarily a good substitute for human assessments of translation quality (Turian et al., 2003; Callison-Burch et al., 2006; Graham et al., 2016), due to issues like lexical-vs-semantic similarity and existence of many possible valid translations for each source sentence (Koehn and Monz, 2006; Lo et al., 2013; Graham et al., 2016). During our experiments, we discovered that the FFR v1.1 model was able to provide predictions that were, although different from the target, similar in context to the target, as seen in sentence #4. Both oindre avec un médicament and se masser avec le remede convey the same idea in the context of the source sentence, sá amasín dŏ wŭ .

This led us to experiment a method we call CMS metric:

1. A subset of the testing data, consisting of 100 specially selected source, target and predicted sentences, was sent to five FFR natives.
2. They were first given the source and prediction sentences and asked to give a score, $t \in [0, 1]$, on how similar the source and prediction sentences were contextually. Note that this scoring was done with no knowledge of the reference, but through the innate experience of the native speakers.
3. Then they were given the source and prediction along with the reference sentences and, simillar to step 2 above, were instructed to give a score $t_r$.
4. Using a parameter, $\alpha$, we calculated the total score $t_{total} = \alpha * t + (1 - \alpha) * t_r$. This parameter controls the tradeoff between the review of the prediction, when viewed on its own, and that of the prediction when viewed in contextual comaprison to the reference sentence. For our experiment, we set $\alpha = 0.7$, putting more weight on the prediction without the reference comparison.
5. The average of these scores was taken as the CMS score for each of the model's predictions as given in sentence #4 in Table 3.

An interesting feature of the CMS metric is the tradeoff, $\alpha$, which is especially useful for translation assessments in languages that have many dialects (like most African languages) and expressions with various possible contexts (like Fon).

## 5  Conclusion, Future Work and Acknowledgements

In this paper, we introduced the creation of the FFR dataset: a corpus of Fon-French parallel sentences. We further trained an NMT system, and evaluated the translation quality using both the BLEU metric and our proposed CMS metric. Our project is at the pilot stage and therefore, there is headroom to be explored with the tuning of different architectures, learning schemes, transfer learning, tokenization methods for the FFR project (FFR Dataset, FFR model) improvement. Specifically, we are looking into leveraging monolingual data, encoding with subword units (Sennrich et al., 2015), exploring data augmentation for low-resource NMT (Fadaee et al., 2017; Xia et al., 2019), and training on a state-of-the-art Transformer model (Vaswani et al., 2017). We owe great thanks to Julia Kreutzer, Jade Abott and the Masakhane Community for their mentorship. We would also like to thank the FFR natives for the good translation services provided.

# References


Zeljko Agic and Ivan Vulic. 2019. Jw300: A wide-coverage parallel corpus for low-resource languages. In *Proceedings of the 57th Annual Meeting of the Association for Computational Linguistics*, pages 3204–3210, Florence, Italy, jul. Association for Computational Linguistics.

Cho K. Bahdanau, D. and Y. Bengio. 2015. *Neural machine translation by jointly learning to align and translate.*

Emily M. Bender and Batya Friedman. 2018. Data statements for natural language processing: Toward mitigating system bias and enabling better science. *Transactions of the Association for Computational Linguistics*, 6:587–604.

Jason Brownlee. 2017. *Deep Learning for Natural Language Processing.* Machine Learning Mastery.

Chris Callison-Burch, Miles Osborne, and Philipp Koehn. 2006. Re-evaluating the role of Bleu in machine translation research. In *11th Conference of the European Chapter of the Association for Computational Linguistics*, Trento, Italy, April. Association for Computational Linguistics.

Bonaventure F. P. Dossou and Chris C. Emezue. 2020. Ffr v1.0: Fon-french neural machine translation.

Marzieh Fadaee, Arianna Bisazza, and Christof Monz. 2017. Data augmentation for low-resource neural machine translation.

Yvette Graham, TIMOTHY BALDWIN, Alistair Moffat, and Justin Zobel. 2016. Can machine translation systems be evaluated by the crowd alone. *Natural Language Engineering*, pages 1–28, 09.

Sepp Hochreiter and Jurgen Schmidhuber. 1997. Long short-term memory. *Neural Comput.*, 9(8):1735–1780, Nov.

Philipp Koehn and Christof Monz. 2006. Manual and automatic evaluation of machine translation between european languages. In *Proceedings of the Workshop on Statistical Machine Translation*, StatMT '06, page 102–121, USA. Association for Computational Linguistics.

H. Lamba. 2020. Intuitive understanding of attention mechanism in deep learning. *Medium.*

Chi-kiu Lo, Karteek Addanki, Markus Saers, and Dekai Wu. 2013. Improving machine translation by training against an automatic semantic frame based evaluation metric. In *Proceedings of the 51st Annual Meeting of the Association for Computational Linguistics (Volume 2: Short Papers)*, pages 375–381, Sofia, Bulgaria, August. Association for Computational Linguistics.

Laura Martinus and Jade Z. Abbott. 2019. A focus on neural machine translation for african languages.

Tensorflow NMT. 2020. Neural machine translation with attention. Tensorflow.

Iroro Orife, David Ifeoluwa Adelani, Timi E. Fasubaa, Victor Williamson, Wuraola Fisayo Oyewusi, Olamilekan Wahab, and Kola Tubosun. 2020a. Improving yorùbá diacritic restoration. *arXiv: Computation and Language.*

Iroro Orife, Julia Kreutzer, Blessing Sibanda, Daniel Whitenack, Kathleen Siminyu, Laura Martinus, Jamiil Toure Ali, Jade Abbott, Vukosi Marivate, Salomon Kabongo, Musie Meressa, Espoir Murhabazi, Orevaoghene Ahia, Elan van Biljon, Arshath Ramkilowan, Adewale Akinfaderin, Alp Öktem, Wole Akin, Ghollah Kioko, Kevin Degila, Herman Kamper, Bonaventure Dossou, Chris Emezue, Kelechi Ogueji, and Abdallah Bashir. 2020b. Masakhane – machine translation for africa.

Kishore Papineni, Salim Roukos, Todd Ward, and Wei-Jing Zhu. 2002. Bleu: a method for automatic evaluation of machine translation. In *Proceedings of the 40th Annual Meeting of the Association for Computational Linguistics*, pages 311–318, Philadelphia, Pennsylvania, USA, July. Association for Computational Linguistics.

Rico Sennrich, Barry Haddow, and Alexandra Birch. 2015. Neural machine translation of rare words with subword units. *CoRR*, abs/1508.07909.

Ilya Sutskever, Oriol Vinyals, and Quoc V Le. 2014. Sequence to sequence learning with neural networks. In Z. Ghahramani, M. Welling, C. Cortes, N. D. Lawrence, and K. Q. Weinberger, editors, *Advances in Neural Information Processing Systems 27*, pages 3104–3112. Curran Associates, Inc.

Joseph Turian, Luke Shen, and I. Dan Melamed. 2003. Evaluation of machine translation and its evaluation. In *In Proceedings of MT Summit IX*, pages 386–393.

Ashish Vaswani, Noam Shazeer, Niki Parmar, Jakob Uszkoreit, Llion Jones, Aidan N. Gomez, Lukasz Kaiser, and Illia Polosukhin. 2017. Attention is all you need. *ArXiv*, abs/1706.03762.

Yonghui Wu, Mike Schuster, Zhifeng Chen, Quoc V. Le, Mohammad Norouzi, Wolfgang Macherey, Maxim Krikun, Yuan Cao, Qin Gao, Klaus Macherey, Jeff Klingner, Apurva Shah, Melvin Johnson, Xiaobing Liu, Łukasz Kaiser, Stephan Gouws, Yoshikiyo Kato, Taku Kudo, Hideto Kazawa, Keith Stevens, George Kurian, Nishant Patil, Wei Wang, Cliff Young, Jason Smith, Jason Riesa, Alex Rudnick, Oriol Vinyals, Greg Corrado, Macduff Hughes, and Jeffrey Dean. 2016. Google's neural machine translation system: Bridging the gap between human and machine translation. *CoRR*, abs/1609.08144.

Mengzhou Xia, Xiang Kong, Antonios Anastasopoulos, and Graham Neubig. 2019. Generalized data augmentation for low-resource translation.

# Classification and Analysis of Neologisms Produced by Learners of Spanish: Effects of Proficiency and Task

**Shira Wein**
Georgetown University
`sw1158@georgetown.edu`

## Abstract

The Spanish Learner Language Oral Corpora (SPLLOC) of transcribed conversations between investigators and language learners contains a set of neologism tags. In this work, the utterances tagged as neologisms are broken down into three categories: true neologisms, loanwords, and errors. This work examines the relationships between neologism, loanword, and error production and both language learner level and conversation task.

The results of this study suggest that loanwords and errors are produced most frequently by language learners with moderate experience, while neologisms are produced most frequently by native speakers. This study also indicates that tasks that require descriptions of images draw more neologism, loanword and error production. We ultimately present a unique analysis of the implications of neologism, loanword, and error production useful for further work in second language acquisition research, as well as for language educators.

## 1 Introduction

Neologisms, as opposed to nonce-words, are new words, phonemes, or locutions appearing in the language, that have been accepted by a speech community (Picone, 1996). Nonce-words or nonce-formations are speech units produced by one specific author that have not yet been accepted by a speech community (Stekauer, 2002). Bauer suggests the use of a dictionary and a large corpus to detect neologisms while excluding nonce-words (Bauer, 2001). A study by Luz Rello and Eduardo Basterrechea explores the properties of neologisms with respect to linguistic creativity, and concludes that more than 50 % of Spanish verbs identified in the dataset do not appear in the largest Spanish dictionary (Rello, 2010). Loanwords are words that borrow from a language other than the target language.

The Spanish Learner Language Oral Corpora (SPLLOC) consists of transcribed conversations between investigators and native English speakers learning Spanish. Each conversation is focused around a specific task, such that the investigator asks questions about that topic. The tasks that are tested in SPLLOC 1 are four discussion tasks (Loch Ness, Discussion, Modern Times, and Clitics) and one image description task (Photo). The conversations take place with language learners at four levels: native speakers, Undergraduate students, students in Year 13, and students in Year 9.

SPLLOC contains a set of neologism tags. We propose that the 362 words tagged as neologisms in SPLLOC 1 in fact encompass a range of **coinages**, not all of which are neologisms. In this work, we break down these coinages into three categories: 28 true neologisms, 119 loanwords, and 215 errors. We hypothesize that the three categories of coinages will have different frequencies amongst various learner levels, such that speakers with high proficiency would produce the most neologisms and loanwords, whereas speakers with low proficiency would produce the most errors.

## 2 Categorization Technique

Transformations of words in other languages were categorized as **loanwords**. These loanwords included borrowings from English, Portuguese, and French. Some examples of the loanwords produced include: *pictura* from English picture, *decremento* from English decrement, and *paquigente* from English packaging.



*Proceedings of the 55th Annual Meeting of the Association for Computational Linguistics*, pages 88–91
Florence, Italy, July 28th, 2019. ©2019 Association for Computational Linguistics

**Errors** are malformations of Spanish words due to a production issue, such as incorrect gender ending, pluralization, or tense formation. Examples of errors include: *periodisto* which incorrectly places a masculine ending on Spanish *periodista*, meaning journalist, or *cuatros* which incorrectly pluralizes a cardinal number *cuatro*.

The remaining words, which were neither loanwords nor errors, were categorized as **neologisms**. Two neologisms from the corpus are *previstas* in place of Spanish *preestrenos*, meaning previews, and *chiquititos* as an extension of the Spanish *chicos*.

In this work, we collect data on the production frequency of, and differences between, each of these three categories of coinages. We then investigate the relationship between each category of coinage and two key variables: speaker's proficiency level and conversational task.

## 3 Results

| Level | Neologisms | Loanwords | Errors | Conversations | Words | Words Per Conversation |
|---|---|---|---|---|---|---|
| Native | 7 | 1 | 3 | 40 | 159313 | 3982.8 |
| Undergraduate | 5 | 27 | 63 | 91 | 448240 | **4925.7** |
| Year13 | 8 | 72 | 115 | 70 | 245331 | 3504.7 |
| Year9 | 3 | 23 | 35 | 60 | 162563 | 2709.4 |
| All Levels | 23 | 123 | 216 | 261 | 1015447 | 3890.6 |

Table 1: Key statistics for each language level, including total number of neologisms, loanwords, and errors produced, how many interviews take place with speakers at that level (conversations), total number of words, and number of words per conversation.

| Level | Neologisms per Conv. | Loanwords Per Conv. | Errors Per Conv. |
|---|---|---|---|
| Native | **0.175** | 0.025 | 0.075 |
| Undergraduate | 0.055 | 0.297 | 0.692 |
| Year13 | 0.114 | **1.03** | **1.64** |
| Year9 | 0.05 | 0.383 | 0.583 |
| All Levels | 0.088 | 0.471 | 0.828 |

Table 2: Average number of neologisms, loanwords, and errors produced per conversation by each learner level.

| Task | Neologisms Per Conv. | Loanwords Per Conv. | Errors Per Conv. |
|---|---|---|---|
| LochNess | 0.093 | 0.44 | 0.493 |
| Discussion | 0.0769 | 0.462 | 0.654 |
| ModernTimes | 0.00 | 0.36 | 0.6 |
| Clitics | 0.00 | 0.117 | 0.483 |
| Non-Image | **0.0483** | **0.328** | **0.527** |
| Photo | **0.187** | **0.823** | **1.573** |
| All Tasks | 0.0881 | 0.471 | 0.828 |

Table 3: Neologisms, loanwords, and errors produced per conversation for each task. Non-Image is the rate of neologisms, loanwords, and errors produced per conversation over all of the non-image based tasks: LochNess, Discussion, ModernTimes, and Clitics.

As seen in Table 1, Undergraduate students had the longest conversations as measured by words per conversation (text), followed by native speakers, year 13 students, and lastly by year 9 students. Using Pearson's correlation test, the p-value for correlation between number of neologisms produced and number of words in the conversation is 1.608e-05. This is a very strong correlation between neologism production and length of conversation.

As evidenced by the rates of coinage production per conversion shown in Table 2, while neologisms are produced most frequently by native speakers, loanwords and errors are produced most frequently by language learners with low to moderate proficiency.

The fact that loanword and error production both have similar frequency patterns of loanword and error production, such that Year 13 students have the highest rates, followed by similar rates of undergraduate and Year 9 students, and lastly followed by a much smaller rate of native speakers, suggests that loanwords and errors are more closely related than loanwords and neologisms. While loanwords could be an indication of mastery of both Spanish and the borrowed language, such as use of Spanglish by native Spanish speakers, in this corpus loanwords are more similar to errors. The loanwords that appear in SPLLOC 1 are borrowed words from another language transformed to sound more like English, which is supported by the examples of loanwords that appear in Section 2. This suggests that the appearance of loanwords in a learners corpus is an indication of low mastery of the target language, as is the case with error production, rather than mastery of the target language, as is the case with neologism production.

Neologism production is a clear indication of mastery of the language. The high rates of neologism production by native speakers is unsurprising because creative generation of language requires high mastery of the language.

Year 13 students producing a higher rate of loanwords and errors than Year 9 students also suggests that there is a certain degree of linguistic risk taking required to produce more loanwords and errors. Year 9 students may be making fewer errors and producing fewer loanwords out of an abundance of linguistic caution and concern over accurately producing Spanish words. Once students develop a degree of mastery over the language, this type of error and loanword production is no longer necessary or prevalent, as is the case for undergraduate students and native speakers.

Additionally, Table 3 shows that tasks requiring descriptions of images elicit a higher rate of coinage production per conversation than non-image based tasks. The Photo task requires the student to describe what is happening in an image presented to them. This task is unique amongst the set of tasks in that there is a finite set of objects in the image, so it is expected that the student use specific language to describe the objects and actions seen in the image. This disparity in rate of neologism, loanword, and error production between the photo description task and the four other tasks signals that the neologisms, loanwords and errors being produced are often substitutions for specific Spanish words. The need for specific words draws out more neologism and nonce-words, as evidenced by the high rates of neologism, loanwords, and errors production for the Photo task.


## 4 Conclusion

This work explores the relationships between neologism, loanword, and error production and conversational task as well as learner level. Our results indicate that production of loanwords by language learners may be illustrative of low mastery of the target language, similarly to error production. This motivates future research investigating the relationship between speaker's confidence in the language and the production of errors and loanwords.

We also illuminate a difference in neologism production between the discussion tasks and the photo description task. This disparity indicates that loanwords, errors, and even neologisms are produced in substitution for specific, sometimes unknown Spanish words, as the photo task requires specific words to describe the objects and actions that appear in the photo. These findings suggest that language educators should use photo description tasks to test a student's vocabulary and discussion tasks to test general fluency.

Our analysis of the implications of neologism, loanword, and error production is useful for language educators as well as for future work in second language acquisition research. This work is relevant to natural language understanding, specifically analyses of learner language, because it demonstrates that the types of coinages that appear in learner data differs from the language of native speakers. As a result, we suggest that language technologies targeted at non-native speakers should recognize and support differences in coinages. Future work should examine whether these patterns hold in other languages; specifically, whether loanword production is consistently a mark of low mastery of the language.

## References

Laurie Bauer. 2001. Morphological Productivity. *Cambridge Studies in Linguistics* 95:39, 158-159.

Özkan Kılıç. 2014. Using Corpus Statistics to Evaluate Nonce Words. *Pristine Perspectives on Logic, Language, and Computation. ESSLLI 2013, ESSLLI 2012.*

Luke Plonsky. 2013. STUDY QUALITY IN SLA: An Assessment of Designs, Analyses, and Reporting Practices in Quantitative L2 Research. *Studies in Second Language Acquisition* 35.4:655-687

Michael Picone. 1996. Anglicisms, Neologisms, and Dynamic French. *John Benjamins B.V.* 3

Laura de Vaan, Robert Schreuder and R. Harald Baayen. 2007. Regular morphologically complex neologisms leave detectable traces in the mental lexicon. *The Mental Lexicon* 32(1):1-24

Pavol Štekauer. 2002. On the Theory of Neologisms and Nonce-formations. *Australian Journal of Linguistics* 22:1, 97-112.

Luz Rello and Eduardo Basterrechea. 2010. Automatic conjugation and identification of regular and irregular verb neologisms in Spanish. *Proceedings of the NAACL HLT 2010 Second Workshop on Computational Approaches to Linguistic Creativity, Association for Computational Linguistics.* 1-5.

Karine Megerdoomian and Ali Hadjarian. 2010. Mining and Classification of Neologisms in Persian Blogs. *Proceedings of the NAACL HLT 2010 Second Workshop on Computational Approaches to Linguistic Creativity, Association for Computational Linguistics.* 6-13.

Quirin Würschinger, Mohammad Fazleh Elahi, Desislava Zhekova, and Hans-Jörg Schmid 2016. Using the Web and Social Media as Corpora for Monitoring the Spread of Neologisms. The case of rapefugee, rapeugee, and rapugee. *Proceedings of the 10th Web as Corpus Workshop (WAC-X) and the EmpiriST Shared Task.* 35-43.

John P. McCrae. 2019. Identification of Adjective-Noun Neologisms using Pretrained Language Models. *Proceedings of the Joint Workshop on Multiword Expressions and WordNet (MWE-WN 2019), Association for Computational Linguistics.* 135-141.

Chenggang Mi, Yating Yang, Lei Wang, Xi Zhou, and Tonghai Jiang. 2018. Toward Better Loanword Identification in Uyghur Using Cross-lingual Word Embeddings. *Proceedings of the 27th International Conference on Computational Linguistics.* 3027–3037.

Paul Cook and Suzanne Stevenson. 2010. Automatically Identifying the Source Words of Lexical Blends in English. *Computational Linguistics 36:1.*

Jack C. Richards. 1974. Error Analysis: Perspectives on Second Language Acquisition.

# Developing a Monolingual Sentence Simplification Corpus for Urdu


**Yusra Anees**
Fatima Jinnah
Women
University / Pakistan
yusra.anees96
@gmail.com

**Sadaf Abdul Rauf**
Fatima Jinnah
Women
University / Pakistan
CNRS-LIMSI / France
sadaf.abdulrauf
@gmail.com

**Nauman Iqbal**
Capital University
of Science and
Technology / Pakistan
nauman
@biit.edu.pk

**Basit Siddiqi**
Capital University
of Science and
Technology / Pakistan
abasit.siddiqui
@cust.edu.pk


## Abstract


Complex sentences are a hurdle in the learning process of language learners. Sentence simplification aims to convert a complex sentence into its simpler form such that it is easily comprehensible. To build such automated simplification systems, corpora of complex sentences and their simplified versions is the first step to understand sentence complexity and enable the development of automatic text simplification systems. No such corpus has yet been developed for Urdu and we fill this gap by developing one such corpus to help start readability and automatic sentence simplification research. We present a lexical and syntactically simplified Urdu simplification corpus and a detailed analysis of the various simplification operations. We further analyze our corpora using text readability measures and present a comparison of the original, lexical simplified, and syntactically simplified corpora.


## 1 Introduction

Research in the last decade has been focusing on identification of complexity levels of sentences so that complexity of such sentences can be reduced to facilitate learning for students as per their learning grade. This is specifically true for Urdu for which this gap is increasing day by day, literary texts often include complex words and composite sentence structure (Alison and Mushta,2004). Our focus will be on such language; Urdu. In fact, no such prior work or resource exists for Urdu. It is the need of the day to address this issue and come up with effective complexity reduction and readability enhancement measures.

To enable research on automatic text simplification systems and text readability for Urdu, development of a simplification corpus providing enough complex sentences and their corresponding simple versions is imperative. We have developed one such corpus for the high school students and simplified (lexical and syntactically) short stories from a renowned author. We have considered three-levels in our simplification process: Original, lexical simplified and syntactic simplified. In Lexical Simplification (LS), complex words are replaced with simple and easy words. Whereas, Syntactic Simplification (SS) may result in an entirely new but simpler sentence. Such sentence aligned texts have been prepared for many languages, for example PWKP (Zhu et al., 2010), Newsela (Xu et al., 2015), Onestop (Vajjala and Lucic, 2018) and SimPA (Scarton et al., 2018) for English. Sentence simplification corpora for other languages include Ancora (Taulé et al., 2008), ERNESTA (Barbu et al., 2015), CLEAR (Grabar and Cardon, 2018) etc.

Another contribution of our work is a detailed analysis of several readability metrics and their application to Urdu using our corpus. We computed the readability measures with the popular readability metrics FKGL, FRE, ARI and SMOG. For each of the corpora, i.e. original, lexical simplified and syntactically simplified lexical analysis has been done and the scores show correlation with human evaluations.

## 2 Corpus Development and annotation scheme

The data for current study has been gathered from the Urdu digital library [1]. It includes 69 short stories. The Target audience of this data is young to old age. The complex sentence structure with typical

---

[1] http://www.udb.gov.pk/




*Proceedings of the 55th Annual Meeting of the Association for Computational Linguistics*, pages 92–95
Florence, Italy, July 28th, 2019. ©2019 Association for Computational Linguistics

Urdu literature vocabulary has been used which was not easy to comprehend. Online Urdu Lughat [2] (dictionary) is used to find simpler synonyms.

Complex sentences has been processed for removal of irrelevant characters and words to avoid ambiguities in data-set. Simplified corpora is(are) rechecked by language experts to remove any anomalies. 4 Language Experts (Urdu native speakers) has manually annotated the corpus into the simplified form using two techniques: lexical and syntactic simplification. Simplified versions of the complex texts are produced by annotating each sentence, first lexical simplification then syntactic simplification (or the previous given) . There, the syntactic simplification included insertion, deletion, splitting, merging, and reordering are used to produce simpler sentences which are the most productive simplification operations according to the literature. The guideline has been given to the annotator is that in syntactic simplification is involves in the removal of phrases or words such that the main context and meaning of the sentence remains the same. It changes the order of words grammatically and inserts new words to reduce complexity. Merging and splitting of sentences are also used to reduce the complexity which is frequently used by (Zhu et al., 2010).

And, In lexical simplification, two operations are performed paraphrasing of difficult words or phrases with simple words or phrases. This operation is applied almost in all manually developed corpus mentioned in the instruction section to carry out simplified corpus. The syntactic simplification was applied at the top where, the lexical simplification had been processed. And 18.3% sentence are only syntactically simplified because these sentence had no lexical complexity. In 3 annotators labeled the data on the lexical and syntactic operations.

Our corpus creation methodology is consistent with the recent works like (Štajner et al., 2019; Scarton et al., 2018; Katsuta and Yamamoto, 2018; Grabar and Cardon, 2018; Brunato et al., 2016; Brunato et al., 2015) who also have simplified using basic lexical simplification operations and (Yatskar et al., 2010) for syntactic simplification. By Human Evaluation of the simplified sentences, annotators have ensured that the simplified sentences had the consistent level of simplification. For evaluation, Two Urdu annotators have annotated 10% of our corpus. The same Evaluation scheme was followed by (Sulem et al., 2018).

## 3   Simplification statistic

We have produced a corpus of 1220 simplified sentences by simplifying 610 sentences, both lexical and syntactical. After in-depth analysis of language and content, we have approximately 58.8% sentences which were lexical and syntactical simplified, 10% sentences were not very complex and only Lexical operation was sufficient to produce the final simplified version, whereas 18.3% sentences could only be simplified by Syntactic operations. Around 12.7% sentences were simple enough not to require simplification of any form as shown in Figure1.

Figure 2 shows that in our simplification scheme, rewording is the most significant operation through which 77.61% of lexical simplification was accomplished. Same trend was observed by (Coster and Kauchak, 2011) they were report 65% rewording operations for English. In case of Syntactic Simplification, deletion was found to be the most frequent operation accounting to 84% of cases, this is also in line with results from previous researches (Coster and Kauchak, 2011; Brunato et al., 2016; Gonzalez-Dios et al., 2018). Insertion, split and merge and reordering follow with 9.12%, 4.24% and 2.14% usage respectively.

## 4   Text Simplicity and Readability scales

Readability metrics are used to evaluate complexity of text by using mathematical formula. We chose Flesch Reading Ease and Flesch-Kincaid Grade Level (Flesch, 1948; Kincaid et al., 1975), SMOG McLaughlin, (Mc Laughlin, 1969) and Automated Readability Index (ARI) (Senter and Smith, 1967) to evaluate our corpus. Which are more generalized and can evaluate complexity on the basis of some basic parameters such as average sentence length, average word length and number of syllables in a word. Flesh Readability Ease (FRE) metric scores range between 0 and 100. Higher value means text is easy to read and lower value means higher the difficulty.

---

[2]http://www.urdulibrary.org/

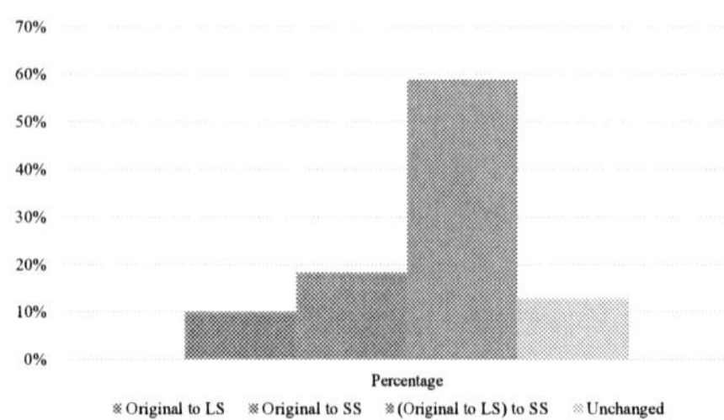 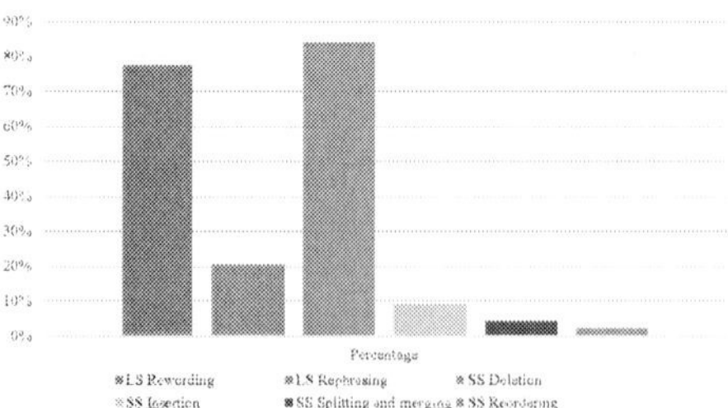

Figure 1: Percentages of sentences requiring different simplification procedures to get the final simplified sentences. The Figure 2: shows the percentage of each operation applied. LS indicates Lexical simplification and SS indication Syntactic simplification

## 5 Results Analysis

The metrics chosen for analysis, scores for FKGL, ARI and SMOG score are directly proportional to complexity, higher score means complex text and lower score means simpler text. However, for FRE this relation is inverse and a higher score means simpler text.

In Table 1 and Table 2 , We have some very interesting observations. The lowest score on FKGL is 6 for Syntactic simplification, Lexical simplification has score of 9, making it fall in the "average" complexity class and original complex sentence has a score of 12, which also puts it in the "average" complexity class but this is the threshold of the average complexity level for FKGL. We can claim that FKGL scores correctly identified the complexity level of text. As Table 2 shows that in case of FRE and ARI we see that even difference of small points is important in categorizing the level of text. SMOG scores of 4.12, 4.19 and 3.13 for complex, Lexical simplification and Syntactic simplification do not agree with the previous trend where and complex texts have 0.07 less score than LS, however Syntactic simplification has the lowest score. But this makes SMOG an unreliable metric for Urdu.

| Metric | Range | Level |
|---|---|---|
| FRE | 0 - 30 | Skilled |
| | 60 - 70 | Average |
| | 90 - 100 | Basic |
| FKGL | 13 - 18 | Skilled |
| | 7 - 12 | Average |
| | 1 - 6 | Basic |
| ARI | 13 - 18 | Skilled |
| | 7 - 12 | Average |
| | 1 - 6 | Basic |
| SMOG | 111 - 240 | Skilled |
| | 13 - 110 | Average |
| | 1 - 12 | Basic |

Table 1: Score range for readability metrics

| | Fluency | Adequacy | Simplicity | Average |
|---|---|---|---|---|
| Original | 12 | 91.78 | 6.39 | 4.12 |
| Lexical | 9 | 91.16 | 6.13 | 4.19 |
| Syntactic | 6 | 98.87 | 4.95 | 3.13 |

Table 2: Average scores of original and simplified sentences against FKGL, FRE, ARI and SMOG.

# References


Eduard Barbu, M Teresa Martín-Valdivia, Eugenio Martínez-Cámara, and L Alfonso Ureña-López. 2015. Language technologies applied to document simplification for helping autistic people. *Expert Systems with Applications*, 42(12):5076–5086.

Dominique Brunato, Felice Dell'Orletta, Giulia Venturi, and Simonetta Montemagni. 2015. Design and annotation of the first italian corpus for text simplification. In *Proceedings of The 9th Linguistic Annotation Workshop*, pages 31–41.

Dominique Brunato, Andrea Cimino, Felice Dell'Orletta, and Giulia Venturi. 2016. Paccss-it: A parallel corpus of complex-simple sentences for automatic text simplification. In *Proceedings of the 2016 Conference on Empirical Methods in Natural Language Processing*, pages 351–361.

William Coster and David Kauchak. 2011. Simple english wikipedia: a new text simplification task. In *Proceedings of the 49th Annual Meeting of the Association for Computational Linguistics: Human Language Technologies: Short papers-Volume 2*, pages 665–669. Association for Computational Linguistics.

Rudolph Flesch. 1948. A new readability yardstick. *Journal of applied psychology*, 32(3):221.

Itziar Gonzalez-Dios, María Jesús Aranzabe, and Arantza Díaz de Ilarraza. 2018. The corpus of basque simplified texts (cbst). *Language Resources and Evaluation*, 52(1):217–247, Mar.

Natalia Grabar and Rémi Cardon. 2018. CLEAR – simple corpus for medical French. In *Proceedings of the 1st Workshop on Automatic Text Adaptation (ATA)*, pages 3–9, Tilburg, the Netherlands, November. Association for Computational Linguistics.

Akihiro Katsuta and Kazuhide Yamamoto. 2018. Crowdsourced corpus of sentence simplification with core vocabulary. In *Proceedings of the Eleventh International Conference on Language Resources and Evaluation (LREC-2018)*.

J Peter Kincaid, Robert P Fishburne Jr, Richard L Rogers, and Brad S Chissom. 1975. Derivation of new readability formulas (automated readability index, fog count and flesch reading ease formula) for navy enlisted personnel.

G Harry Mc Laughlin. 1969. Smog grading-a new readability formula. *Journal of reading*, 12(8):639–646.

Carolina Scarton, Gustavo Paetzold, and Lucia Specia. 2018. Simpa: A sentence-level simplification corpus for the public administration domain. In *Proceedings of the Eleventh International Conference on Language Resources and Evaluation (LREC-2018)*.

RJ Senter and Edgar A Smith. 1967. Automated readability index. Technical report, CINCINNATI UNIV OH.

Sanja Štajner, Horacio Saggion, and Simone Paolo Ponzetto. 2019. Improving lexical coverage of text simplification systems for spanish. *Expert Systems with Applications*, 118:80–91.

Elior Sulem, Omri Abend, and Ari Rappoport. 2018. Semantic structural evaluation for text simplification. *arXiv preprint arXiv:1810.05022*.

Mariona Taulé, Maria Antònia Martí, and Marta Recasens. 2008. Ancora: Multilevel annotated corpora for catalan and spanish. In *Lrec*.

Sowmya Vajjala and Ivana Lucic. 2018. Onestopenglish corpus: A new corpus for automatic readability assessment and text simplification.

Wei Xu, Chris Callison-Burch, and Courtney Napoles. 2015. Problems in current text simplification research: New data can help. *Transactions of the Association of Computational Linguistics*, 3(1):283–297.

Mark Yatskar, Bo Pang, Cristian Danescu-Niculescu-Mizil, and Lillian Lee. 2010. For the sake of simplicity: Unsupervised extraction of lexical simplifications from wikipedia. In *Human Language Technologies: The 2010 Annual Conference of the North American Chapter of the Association for Computational Linguistics*, pages 365–368. Association for Computational Linguistics.

Zhemin Zhu, Delphine Bernhard, and Iryna Gurevych. 2010. A monolingual tree-based translation model for sentence simplification. In *Proceedings of the 23rd international conference on computational linguistics*, pages 1353–1361. Association for Computational Linguistics.

# Translating Natural Language Instructions for Behavioral Robot Navigation with a Multi-Head Attention Mechanism


**Patricio Cerda-Mardini, Vladimir Araujo, Alvaro Soto**

Pontificia Universidad Catolica de Chile

Millennium Institute for Foundational Research on Data

{pcerdam, vgaraujo}@uc.cl, asoto@ing.puc.cl


## Abstract


We propose a multi-head attention mechanism as a blending layer in a neural network model that translates natural language to a high level behavioral language for indoor robot navigation. We follow the framework established by (Zang et al., 2018a) that proposes the use of a navigation graph as a knowledge base for the task. Our results show significant performance gains when translating instructions on previously unseen environments, therefore, improving the generalization capabilities of the model.


## 1  Background

Developing robotic agents that can follow natural language instructions remains an open challenge. Ideally, a robot should be able to correctly create an executable navigation plan given a natural language instruction by a user. The objective is to reach a destination from a starting point in a complex but known indoor environment (Figure 1(a)), which could be represented as a graph (Sepulveda et al., 2018), where the nodes correspond to locations (e.g., office, bedroom), and the edges represent high-level behaviors (e.g., follow corridor, exit office) that allow a robot to navigate between neighboring nodes (Figure 1(b)). We assume the robot can robustly execute every high level behavior, as in (Sepulveda et al., 2018).

Previous works pose this problem as a translation of instructions to a plan of sequentially executed high-level behaviors (Zang et al., 2018b), leveraging the environment topology through its graph representation (Zang et al., 2018a). Specifically, a supervised learning model takes as input a text instruction from the user, the robot initial location, and the behavior graph of the environment encoded as triplets $(n_1, b, n_2)$, where $n_1, n_2$ are places and $b$ the behavior that connects both. It then predicts a sequence of behaviors to reach the instructed destination by means of a typical sequence-to-sequence model with a single soft attention layer that fuses the graph and instruction information. However, at inference time this approach suffers a severe performance hit on environments that were not seen during training. In this work, we propose to modify the attention layer by using a multi-headed mechanism that improves the model generalization capabilities, therefore, increasing performance in unseen environments.

Figure 1: (a) Map of an environment. (b) Its behavioral navigation graph. (c) Proposed model. The natural language instruction on (c) is translated to a sequential behavior plan. The path in (a) and the node-edges in (b), both highlighted in red, correspond to the behaviors predicted by the model (c).

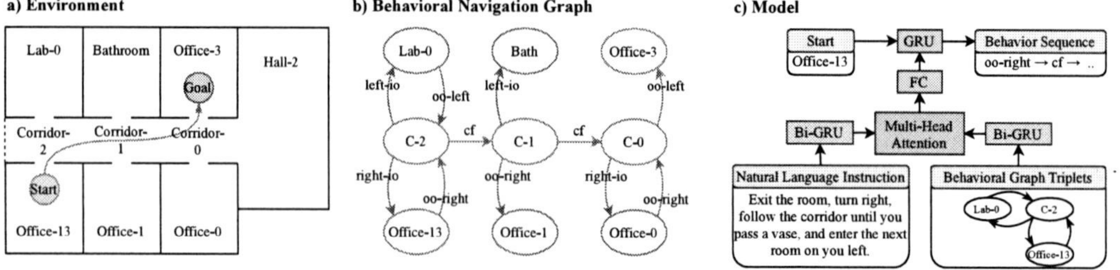






*Proceedings of the 55th Annual Meeting of the Association for Computational Linguistics*, pages 96–98

Florence, Italy, July 28th, 2019. ©2019 Association for Computational Linguistics

## 2  Methodology

**Approach**  Inspired by the success of the Transformer model (Vaswani et al., 2017) on encoding different relationships of multi-modal data (Tan and Bansal, 2019; Zhou et al., 2020), we propose to use its multi-head attention mechanism to blend information from the two representation sub-spaces, natural instructions and navigation graph, in a more useful way. That is, different heads will specialize in fusing different patterns between both information sources. We hypothesize that this capability might help the decoder to alleviate the performance hit in novel environments at test time.

**Proposed Model**  The architecture (Figure 1(c)) considers an initial encoding layer, where each word of the instruction is encoded using pre-trained GloVe descriptors (Pennington et al., 2014), and each triplet set is one-hot encoded to indicate which of the $\mathcal{B}$ behaviors and $\mathcal{N}$ nodes constitute each triplet. Subsequently, the encodings are embedded using bi-directional Gated Recurrent Units (GRU) (Chung et al., 2014). The multi-modal representations are then fused by the newly added multi-head attention mechanism. A fully connected layer downstream reduces the dimensionality of the fused information, which is used as context $C$ by a recurrent GRU decoder. The decoder takes the initial position and translates the instruction to a sequential behavioral plan, soft attending its context $C$ at each time step. The loss function is cross entropy with respect to correct translations.

**Experimental Setup**  We use the dataset introduced in (Zang et al., 2018a) with the original train and test splits, where the Test-Repeated split has environments that were seen by the agent at training time, and the Test-New split has previously unseen maps. In total, we consider 10,040 instructions (8,066 for training) distributed across 100 maps, each with 6 to 65 rooms. We also use the same performance metrics: F1 score, edit distance (ED) to ground truth, and M@k metrics, where we have a match if the translation is under $k$ moves away from the ground truth[1], with M@0 being an exact match. The model was trained for 200 epochs, with a batch size of 256. The multi-head attention layer was set to have 4 heads. The rest of the model parameters are as established in (Zang et al., 2018a).

## 3  Results & Discussion

**Results**  Table 1 details the performance of our approach, along with the baseline reported by (Zang et al., 2018a) as well as by our own implementation of that model, which notably was not able to perform as expected on the Test-Repeated set. As a result of using our multi-headed approach, we see a clear performance gain (23.2%) on exact match for the Test-New set, which confirms an improved generalization capability by our translation model. However, for the Test-Repeated set we see a 8.5% decrease in exact match with respect to the original approach (although we do beat our own implementation of the baseline by 25.9% in this set, and by 18.4% in the Test-New set).

| Architecture | Test Repeated | | | | | Test New | | | | |
|---|---|---|---|---|---|---|---|---|---|---|
| | F1 ↑ | M@0 ↑ | M@1 ↑ | M@2 ↑ | ED ↓ | F1 | M@0 | M@1 | M@2 | ED |
| Baseline (Zang) | **93.54** | **61.17** | **83.30** | **92.19** | **0.75** | 90.22 | 41.71 | 69.82 | 82.08 | 1.22 |
| Baseline (Ours) | 91.67 | 44.43 | 76.93 | 89.16 | 1.01 | 90.89 | 43.41 | 72.64 | 87.25 | 1.09 |
| Ours | 93.07 | 55.96 | 81.31 | 90.16 | 0.84 | **92.57** | **51.40** | **79.06** | **89.43** | **0.91** |

Table 1: Results. The symbol ↑ indicates that higher results are better in the corresponding column; likewise ↓ indicates that lower is better.

**Conclusions**  In this paper, we introduced multi-head attention as a useful mechanism for leveraging a knowledge base to improve natural language translations to a high-level behavioral language that is understandable and executable by robots, exhibiting a better performance on never-before-seen environments with respect to previous work. Future research efforts contemplate minimizing the lost performance over previously seen maps and doing a qualitative analysis of the resulting attention weights.

**Acknowledgments**  This work was partially funded by the Millennium Institute for Foundational Research on Data and Fondecyt grant 1181739.

---

[1] A move adds, deletes, or swaps a behavior in the plan.

**References**

Junyoung Chung, aglar Gülehre, Kyunghyun Cho, and Yoshua Bengio. 2014. Empirical evaluation of gated recurrent neural networks on sequence modeling. *ArXiv*, abs/1412.3555.

Jeffrey Pennington, Richard Socher, and Christopher D. Manning. 2014. Glove: Global vectors for word representation. In *EMNLP*.

Gabriel Sepulveda, Juan Carlos Niebles, and Alvaro Soto. 2018. A deep learning based behavioral approach to indoor autonomous navigation. In *2018 IEEE International Conference on Robotics and Automation (ICRA)*, pages 4646–4653. IEEE.

Hao Tan and Mohit Bansal. 2019. Lxmert: Learning cross-modality encoder representations from transformers. In *Proceedings of the 2019 Conference on Empirical Methods in Natural Language Processing and the 9th International Joint Conference on Natural Language Processing (EMNLP-IJCNLP)*, pages 5103–5114.

Ashish Vaswani, Noam Shazeer, Niki Parmar, Jakob Uszkoreit, Llion Jones, Aidan N. Gomez, Lukasz Kaiser, and Illia Polosukhin. 2017. Attention is all you need. In *31st Conference on Neural Information Processing Systems*, NIPS '17.

Xiaoxue Zang, Ashwini Pokle, Marynel Vázquez, Kevin Chen, Juan Carlos Niebles, Alvaro Soto, and Silvio Savarese. 2018a. Translating navigation instructions in natural language to a high-level plan for behavioral robot navigation. In *Proceedings of the 2018 Conference on Empirical Methods in Natural Language Processing*, pages 2657–2666, Brussels, Belgium, October-November. Association for Computational Linguistics.

Xiaoxue Zang, Marynel Vázquez, Juan Carlos Niebles, Alvaro Soto, and Silvio Savarese. 2018b. Behavioral indoor navigation with natural language directions. *Companion of the 2018 ACM/IEEE International Conference on Human-Robot Interaction*.

Yichao Zhou, Shaunak Mishra, Manisha Verma, Narayan Bhamidipati, and Wei Wang. 2020. Recommending themes for ad creative design via visual-linguistic representations.

# Towards Mitigating Gender Bias in a decoder-based Neural Machine Translation model by Adding Contextual Information


**Christine Basta**     **Marta R. Costa-jussà**     **José A. R. Fonollosa**
Universitat Politècnica de Catalunya
{christine.raouf.saad.basta,marta.ruiz,jose.fonollosa}@upc.edu



## Abstract

Gender bias negatively impacts many natural language processing applications, including machine translation (MT). The motivation behind this work is to study whether recent proposed MT techniques are significantly contributing to attenuate biases in document-level and gender-balanced data. For the study, we consider approaches of adding the previous sentence and the speaker information, implemented in a decoder-based neural MT system. We show improvements both in translation quality (+1 BLEU point) as well as in gender bias mitigation on WinoMT (+5% accuracy).


## 1 Introduction

Gender bias is negatively affecting Natural Language Processing (NLP) (Costa-jussà, 2019; Sun et al., 2019). Gender bias clearly appears in word embeddings, associating certain neutral professions with males (*programmer*) and others with females (*housekeeper*) (Bolukbasi et al., 2016).

This bias has been demonstrated in Neural Machine Translation (NMT), where translations seem to ignore the context and translate professions with their stereotyped genders (Font and Costa-jussà, 2019; Stanovsky et al., 2019). This occurs due to the fact that NMT systems generally work on a sentence by sentence basis. Several approaches have been proposed to output different gendered translations (Kiritchenko and Mohammad, 2018), add gender information in the process of training (Vanmassenhove et al., 2018), and use debiased word embeddings (Font and Costa-jussà, 2019). Other approaches focused on measuring gender bias in translation systems (Prates et al., 2020; Stanovsky et al., 2019). Finally, the work by Costa-jussà et al. (2019) presented a non-synthetic gender-balanced data set, which can be considered to evaluate NMT.

The main contribution of this work is using existing NMT contextual methodologies, both context of the previous sentence (Junczys-Dowmunt, 2019) and speaker identification (Vanmassenhove et al., 2018), in a prominent and competitive NMT architecture (Fonollosa et al., 2019). These approaches are explicitly tested for the purpose of mitigating gender bias while improving the translation quality. The architecture in our experiments uses only the decoder part of the popular Transformer (Vaswani et al., 2017; He et al., 2018; Fonollosa et al., 2019); thus, reduces training parameters and simplifies the model.

## 2 Methodology: adding context and speaker id in a decoder-based NMT model

This study uses the following two recent proposed methodologies to improve the accuracy of NMT. While these methodologies are not new, we are adding them on a different baseline (Fonollosa et al., 2019) and testing specifically on a gender-balanced data sets. We describe the baseline system and the techniques as follows and examples are shown in Table 1.

**Neural Machine Translation with joint source-target self-attention.** The current state of the art is the encoder-decoder architecture using the Transformer (Vaswani et al., 2017) that avoids recurrence completely and gives better translations depending on the stacked self-attention and fully connected layers between encoder and decoder. An alternative to this architecture is based on the simplified architecture by Fonollosa et al. (2019) [1]. This model, instead of having both encoder-decoder, only uses the decoder block and it adopts the idea of language modeling for translation task. The joint source-target representations are learnt in the early layers. Positional embeddings are applied to the source and target

---

[1] https://github.com/jarfo/joint

99


*Proceedings of the 55th Annual Meeting of the Association for Computational Linguistics*, pages 99–102
Florence, Italy, July 28th, 2019. ©2019 Association for Computational Linguistics

independently. There are also language embeddings representing the language of the source and the target separately. Different from the self attention in normal transformers, a locally constrained attention is proposed by the authors to attend only to a token's locality, to form a reduced receptive field.

**Adding the previous context sentence (PreSent):** Concatenating two sentences with a separator token. This method adopts the idea of increasing the context (Junczys-Dowmunt, 2019).

**Incorporating the speaker gender identification (SpeakerId):** Incorporating the information of the gender of the speaker in NMT by adding the gender tag before each sentence (Vanmassenhove et al., 2018). This approach is specially helpful when translating from a less inflected language to a more inflected one, e.g., from English to Spanish.

| Methods | Examples |
|---|---|
| **Baseline** | I have only done this once before. |
| **+PreSent** | I have only done this once before. <sep> This is not a joke. |
| **+SpeakerId** | MALE I have only done this once before. |

**Table 1:** Methodologies examples

| Methods | EuroParl | GeBio |
|---|---|---|
| **Baseline** | 44.01 | 36.34 |
| **+PreSent** | **45.10** | **36.55** |
| **+SpeakerId** | 44.18 | 36.51 |

**Table 2:** BLEU results (best in bold).

## 3  Experimental Framework, Results and Discussion

**Data and Parameters:**  Spanish is a highly-gendered morphological language compared to English, associating gender to professions and adjectives. That is why the language pair (EN-ES) has been used from the proposed data in Vanmassenhove et al. (2018).The size of the EN-ES dataset is considered moderate with 1,419,507 number of sentences. We have used two test datasets: a random set of EuroParl (2000 sentences) and the gender-balanced set from wikipedia biographies (GeBioCorpus) (Costa-jussà et al., 2019) that contains 1000 sentences from male bios and 1000 sentences from female bios. The gender of the main character in the biography article is used as the gender tag. The model is built on top of fairseq[2] library and the parameters are customized as follows: Adam optimizer, 30K training steps, 14 layers, 512 as embedding dimensionality, feedforward expansion of dimensionality 2048 and 8 attention heads, based on best performing parameters from previous work (Fonollosa et al., 2019).

**BLEU results (Table 2).**  These results have been acquired by testing Europarl test set and GeBioCorpus. Adding the previous sentence has higher impact in Europarl (+1.09) than in GeBioCorpus (+0.21) due to the fact that documents in GeBioCorpus are not coherent (all sentences belong to the same document but some sentences may not be contiguous). Adding the gender tag shows exactly the same effect in GeBioCorpus than in Europarl (+0.17), even if the speaker identification is not from the same nature in the EuroParl and in GeBioCorpus. In the former, the speaker identification comes from the speaker, whereas in the latter, it comes from the biography main character.

**Other advantages (Table 4 and Table 5).**  The outputs of our systems have been manually analysed to study the impact of explored techniques on final translation. We report translation examples where both PreSent and SpeakerId techniques are **helping towards named entity disambiguation (in terms of gender)**. Furthermore, we show other translation examples where adding PreSent shows an **improvement towards morphological agreement and quality on translation style**.

**Evaluating on WinoMT (Table 3 and Figure 1).**  This step is carried out by translating the WinoMT dataset and evaluating the translation by Stanovsky et al. (2019) system that depends on extracting the gender of entities of the translated sentences. These entities are evaluated against the gold annotations provided by the original English dataset. The evaluation is performed on three aspects, the whole WinoMT dataset, and subsets of both pro-stereotypical and anti-stereotypical sentences. An example of anti-stereotypical sentences is *The developer argued with the designer because she did not like the design.*, where the *developer* is a *female* entity. An example of pro-stereotypical sentences is *The CEO helped the nurse because he wanted to help.*, where the *CEO* is a *male* entity. As shown in Figure 1, the systems are performing better on the pro-stereotypical portion of WinoMT than on the anti-stereotypical

---

[2] https://github.com/pytorch/fairseq

one. The accuracy (Acc), shown in Table 3 and Figure 1, indicates that the methodology PreSent performs best compared to the other approaches in this paper (baseline or SpeakerId). The PreSent detects the gender more correctly than the others whether pro-stereotyped or anti-stereotyped, and its accuracy reaches 61% with 12.2% difference between f1-scores of males and females. This accuracy improves over the best results presented in the original paper (Stanovsky et al., 2019), where the best accuracy is 59.4% with 15.4% difference between f1-scores of males and females. It is important to notice that WinoMT is a test set that does not contain information at the level of document and without speaker identification, so translation with our methodologies is done without this information. Therefore, adding the information of the previous sentence makes the system more robust and it does not mind that we are doing inference without this information.

| Methods | Acc. | $\triangle G$ |
|---|---|---|
| Baseline | 56.0 | 18.7 |
| **+PreSent** | **61.0** | **12.2** |
| +SpeakerId | 52.5 | 22.2 |

**Table 3:** WinoMT evaluation results. Acc. indicates gender accuracy (% of instances the translation had the correct gender), $\triangle G$ denotes the masculine/feminine difference in F1 score. In bold, best results.

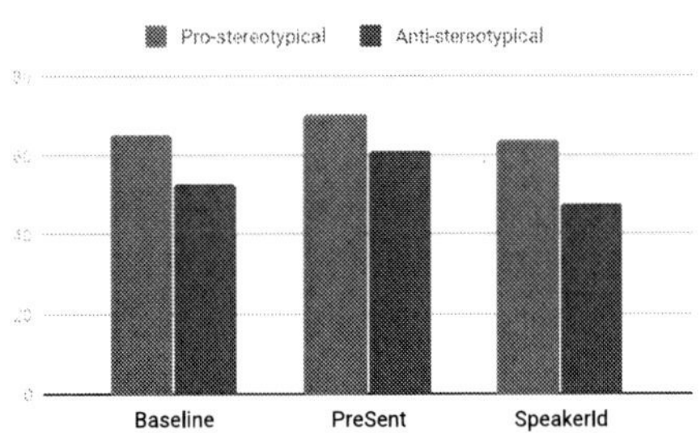



**Figure 1:** Acc.% on gender translation with respect to pro-stereotypical entities and anti-stereotypical entities in WinoMT.

|  | **Named Entity Disambiguation** |
|---|---|
| **Source** | María del Carmen Pérez ...is **a Spanish Egyptologist , curator and researcher.** |
| **Baseline** | María del Carmen Pérez ...es **un egipcio pintor , curador e investigador español.** |
| **+PreSent** | María del Carmen Pérez ...es **una ciudadana española egipcia , curadora e investigadora.** |
|  | **Better dealing with articles** |
| **Source** | Míriam Hatibi ... is **a Catalan data analyst and activist.** |
| **Baseline** | Míriam Hatibi ... es **un analista de datos catalán y un activista.** |
| **+PreSent** | Míriam Hatibi ... es **una analista y activista catalana en materia de datos.** |
|  | **Better style of translations** |
| **Source** | Helena Maleno Garzón ... is a Spanish human rights **defender , journalist, researcher , documentalist and writer.** |
| **Baseline** | Helena Maleno Garzón ... es **un defensor** de los derechos humanos español, **periodista, investigador , documentalista y escritor.** |
| **+PreSent** | Helena Maleno Garzón ....es **una defensora** española de los derechos humanos, **periodista, investigadora , documental y escritora.** |

**Table 4:** Baseline vs PreSent Examples from GeBioCorpus.

|  | **Named Entity Disambiguation** |
|---|---|
| **Source** | Bianca Maria Piccinino ... is **an Italian writer , journalist and television hostess.** |
| **Baseline** | Bianca Maria Piccinino ... es **un escritor italiano , periodista y centro** de televisión. |
| **+SpeakerId** | Bianca Maria Piccinino ... es **una escritora italiana , periodista y anfitriona** de televisión. |

**Table 5:** Baseline vs SpeakerId Examples from GeBioCorpus.

## Acknowledgments


This work is supported in part by the Catalan Agency for Management of University and Research Grants (AGAUR) through the FI PhD Scholarship. This work is also supported in part by the Spanish Ministerio de Economía y Competitividad, the European Regional Development Fund and the Agencia Estatal de Investigación, through the postdoctoral senior grant Ramón y Cajal, contract TEC2015-69266-P (MINECO/FEDER,EU) and contract PCIN-2017-079 (AEI/MINECO).

## References

Tolga Bolukbasi, Kai-Wei Chang, James Y Zou, Venkatesh Saligrama, and Adam T Kalai. 2016. Man is to computer programmer as woman is to homemaker? debiasing word embeddings. In *Proceedings of Advances in Neural Information Processing Systems 29*, pages 4349–4357.

Marta R. Costa-jussà. 2019. An analysis of gender bias studies in natural language processing. *Nature Machine Intelligence*, 1(11):495–496.

Marta R. Costa-jussà, Pau Li Lin, and Cristina España-Bonet. 2019. Gebiotoolkit: Automatic extraction of gender-balanced multilingual corpus of wikipedia biographies. In *Proceedings of 12th Language Resources and Evaluation Conference (LREC)*.

José A. R. Fonollosa, Noe Casas, and Marta R. Costa-jussà. 2019. http://arxiv.org/abs/1905.06596 Joint source-target self attention with locality constraints.

Joel Escudé Font and Marta R. Costa-jussà. 2019. https://doi.org/10.18653/v1/W19-3821 Equalizing gender bias in neural machine translation with word embeddings techniques. In *Proceedings of the First ACL Workshop on Gender Bias in Natural Language Processing*, pages 147–154, Florence, Italy.

Tianyu He, Xu Tan, Yingce Xia, Di He, Tao Qin, Zhibo Chen, and Tie-Yan Liu. 2018. Layer-wise coordination between encoder and decoder for neural machine translation. In *Proceedings of Advances in Neural Information Processing Systems*, pages 7944–7954.

Marcin Junczys-Dowmunt. 2019. https://doi.org/10.18653/v1/W19-5321 Microsoft translator at WMT 2019: Towards large-scale document-level neural machine translation. In *Proceedings of the Fourth Conference on Machine Translation (Volume 2: Shared Task Papers, Day 1)*, pages 225–233, Florence, Italy. Association for Computational Linguistics.

Svetlana Kiritchenko and Saif Mohammad. 2018. https://doi.org/10.18653/v1/S18-2005 Examining gender and race bias in two hundred sentiment analysis systems. In *Proceedings of the Seventh Joint Conference on Lexical and Computational Semantics*, pages 43–53, New Orleans, Louisiana. Association for Computational Linguistics.

Marcelo O. R. Prates, Pedro H. C. Avelar, and Luis Lamb. 2020. Assessing gender bias in machine translation – a case study with google translate. *Neural Computing and Applications, 32*, page 6363–6381.

Gabriel Stanovsky, Noah A Smith, and Luke Zettlemoyer. 2019. Evaluating gender bias in machine translation. In *Proceedings of the 57th Annual Meeting of the Association for Computational Linguistics*.

Tony Sun, Andrew Gaut, Shirlyn Tang, Yuxin Huang, Mai ElSherief, Jieyu Zhao, Diba Mirza, Elizabeth Belding, Kai-Wei Chang, and William Yang Wang. 2019. https://doi.org/10.18653/v1/P19-1159 Mitigating gender bias in natural language processing: Literature review. In *Proceedings of the 57th Annual Meeting of the Association for Computational Linguistics*, pages 1630–1640, Florence, Italy. Association for Computational Linguistics.

Eva Vanmassenhove, Christian Hardmeier, and Andy Way. 2018. Getting gender right in neural machine translation. In *Proceedings of the 2018 Conference on Empirical Methods in Natural Language Processing*.

Ashish Vaswani, Noam Shazeer, Niki Parmar, Jakob Uszkoreit, Llion Jones, Aidan N Gomez, Łukasz Kaiser, and Illia Polosukhin. 2017. Attention is all you need. In *Advances in neural information processing systems*, pages 5998–6008.

# Predicting and Analyzing Law-Making in Kenya


**Oyinlola Babafemi**
Data Duality
babsoyinlola@gmail.com

**Adewale Akinfaderin**
Data Duality
waleakinfaderin@gmail.com


## Abstract


Modelling and analyzing parliamentary legislation, roll-call votes and order of proceedings in developed countries has received significant attention in recent years. In this paper, we focused on understanding the bills introduced in a developing democracy, the Kenyan bicameral parliament. We developed and trained machine learning models on a combination of features extracted from the bills to predict the outcome - if a bill will be enacted or not. We observed that the texts in a bill are not as relevant as the year and month the bill was introduced and the category the bill belongs to.


## 1  Introduction

Policy development and law-making affect millions of people. It is important that there is transparency and openness in this decision making process. The rationale behind this work is to give insights to what happens in the Kenyan parliament and possible factors that might influence the verdict of bills. In Kenya bicameral parliament (the Senate and National Assembly), the legislative process goes through five phases: the proposed bill is published in the *Kenya Gazette*[1], first reading, second reading, the appropriate committee meets to consider the amendment and finally, third and last reading (Goitom, 2017). After these phases, it is signed into law (or not) by the President of Kenya. Previous works have used word vectors and machine learning to estimate the probability that a United State congressional bill will survive the congressional committee and become law and, to predict policy changes in China (Nay, 2017; Tae et al., 2012; Chan & Zhong, 2018). Although data from debates and votes could not be obtained for this work, hand-crafted features and word vector representations of the texts in bills were used to predict if they will be enacted or not enacted.

## 2  Data and Methodology

460 Kenyan national assembly and senate bills introduced between 2009 and 2019 were downloaded from the *Kenya Gazette* website[2] and the corresponding metadata scraped. Of these bills, 395 were not enacted while only 65 bills were passed into law. The highest number of bills introduced in a single year is 88 which was in 2012 and Aden Duale, the Majority Leader of the National Assembly of Kenya under the Jubilee Party introduced about 24% of the bills retrieved.

### 2.1  Data Pre-processing and Feature Engineering

To develop our model, we extracted information from the dataset and engineered new features. Some of the features we used are: the category of a bill - inspired by the socio-economic labels in (Akinfaderin & Wahab, 2019), election year - a binary feature that represents if a bill was

---


4th Widening NLP Workshop, Annual Meeting of the Association for Computational Linguistics, ACL 2020


[1]Kenya Gazette is an official publication of the government of the Republic of Kenya

[2]http://kenyalaw.org/kl/index.php?id=9091




*Proceedings of the 55th Annual Meeting of the Association for Computational Linguistics*, pages 103–106
Florence, Italy, July 28th, 2019. ©2019 Association for Computational Linguistics

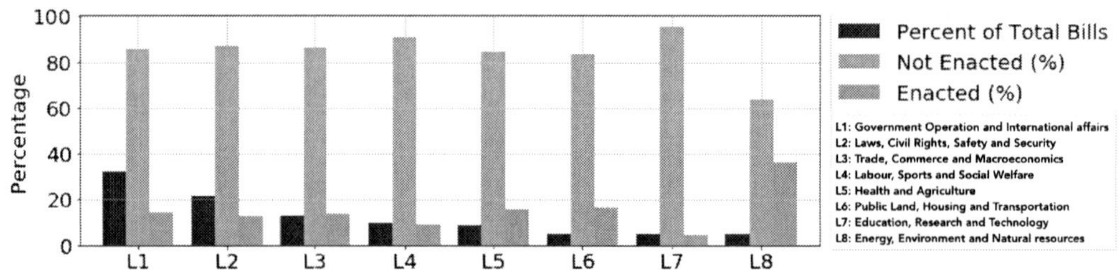


Figure 1: Percent distribution of bills and their corresponding enacted and not enacted percentages. L1 to L8 represent the bill labels. This is part of the features in our model.

introduced in an election year or not, sponsor 1 - binary feature for a bill sponsored by Aden Duale or others, sponsor 2 - binary feature for a bill sponsored by members of the parliament or, attorney generals and ministers, year and month a bill was introduced, the length of bill title, word vectors - word vectors for the bill titles and texts using a *100-dimensional* GloVe (Pennington et al., 2014) pre-trained word vectors[3], the difference between the current year and the year the bill was introduced. Figure 1 represents the distribution of the bills for each category label and the percentage of bills enacted and not enacted for each category. To solve the class imbalance problem caused by the ratio of bills enacted to not enacted, we oversampled the minority class in our training set (bills enacted) using SMOTE: Synthetic Minority Over-sampling Technique (Chawla et al., 2002).

## 2.2 Model

With a 70:30 train-test split on our data, we employed Logistic Regression and Support Vector Machine models to obtain baseline results before proceeding to stack these models as base learners and then used another Logistic Regression classifier as the meta-learner in a bid to obtain better results. Although the accuracy obtained from the results of all three models were very impressive, we focused on other metrics such as the F1-score, precision, recall, AUC (area under the curve) and brier score to analyse our results[4]. The results are displayed in Table 1. While handling the data imbalance problem improved the base models with a 5% and 11% increase in the precision of both classes, the results obtained for the enacted class after oversampling remained the same. However, we obtained impressive results for predicting that a bill will not be enacted. For better context, this means when a new bill is proposed and fed to the final model with all relevant aforementioned features, the model is 81% accurate in predicting if the bill will be passed into law or not. The precision and recall are 65% and 71% respectively.

| Model | F1 | Precision | Recall | AUC | Brier Loss | Accuracy |
|---|---|---|---|---|---|---|
| Logistic Regression | 0.65 | 0.63 | 0.70 | 0.72 | 0.17 | 0.79 |
| Support Vector Machine | 0.63 | 0.62 | 0.69 | **0.74** | 0.17 | 0.77 |
| Stacked Ensemble | **0.67** | **0.65** | **0.71** | 0.73 | **0.15** | **0.81** |

Table 1: Evaluation metrics with results (average for both classes). For Brier score, lower is better.

By inspecting the model to understand different features, we observed that the most important features that contribute to the final verdict were month, category and year introduced respectively (Figure 2). Surprisingly, the title of a bill was a more important feature than the entire text, which is the least important feature - this raises a speculation that not all bills might

---

[3]Word vectors trained on the bills did not perform as well as GloVe
[4]https://github.com/BabafemiOyinlola/Predicting-Law-Making-in-Kenya

be read thoroughly by members since the bills have similar titles which might cause voting parties to treat as bills previously introduced to the parliament. In addition, further experiments carried out using bag of words as an alternative representation for the textual features only confirmed that the text of a bill is not very pertinent to decision making. This suggests that there might be other factors considered in the parliament not accounted for here.

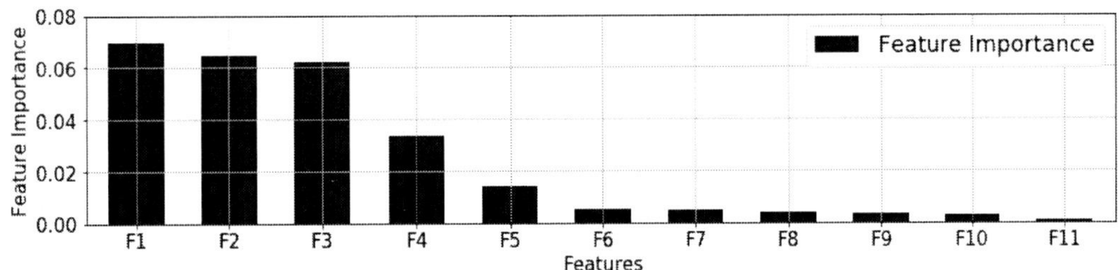

Figure 2: Feature importance plot displaying the relative importance of each feature in making a prediction. The features F1 to F11 represents the following: **F1**:*Month*, **F2**:*Label*, **F3**:*Year Introduced*, **F4**:*Text Length*, **F5**:*Sponsor (Aden Duale or Not)*, **F6**:*Sponsor2 (Executive or Legislator)*, **F7**:*Title Length*, **F8**:*Title Word Vector*, **F9**:*Year Difference*, **F10**: *Election Year or Not*, **F11**:*Text Word Vectors*}

## 3   Conclusion

We presented simple baselines for predicting the chance that a new bill introduced will be enacted and, can adequately predict that a bill introduced into the Kenyan parliament will not be enacted (0.86 and 0.41 F1 scores for bills not enacted and bills enacted respectively). Avenues for improving this work include gathering more bills from earlier years, exploring other metadata like parliamentary debates and identifying dynamic structural factors in the behavioral patterns of the Kenya legislature.

## Acknowledgements

The authors are thankful to the anonymous reviewers for their valuable feedback, Ahmed Baruwa for data labelling and scraping and the Data Science Nigeria team for their support. This project is funded by the Artificial Intelligence 4 Development (AI4D) program as part of the 1st AI4D-Africa Innovation Call for Proposals. AI4D is sponsored by the Canadian International Development Research Centre (IDRC), the Knowledge for All Foundation (K4A) and the Swedish International Development Cooperation Agency (SIDA).

## References

Adewale Akinfaderin and Olamilekan Wahab. 2019. *NASS-AI: Towards Digitization of Parliamentary Bills using Document Level Embedding and Bidirectional Long Short-Term Memory*. In Proceedings of NeurIPS 2019 Workshop on Machine Learning for the Developing World, Vancouver, Canada.

John J. Nay. 2018. *Predicting and understanding law-making with word vectors and an ensemble model*. PloS One, 12 (5).

Tae Yano, Noah A. Smith and John D. Wilkerson. 2012. *Textual Predictors of Bill Survival in Congressional Committees*. Proceedings of the 2012 Conference of the North American Chapter of the Association for Computational Linguistics: Human Language Technologies.

Julian T. Chan and Weifeng Zhong. 2018. *Reading China: Predicting policy change with machine learning*. American Enterprise Institute Working Paper.

Jeffrey Pennington, Richard Socher and Christopher Manning. 2014. *Glove: Global Vectors for Word Representation*. Proceedings of the 2014 Conference on Empirical Methods in Natural Language Processing (EMNLP).

Hanibal Goitom. 2017. *National Parliaments: Kenya*. The Law Library of Congress, Global Legal Research Center. URL: `https://www.loc.gov/law/help/national-parliaments/pdf/kenya.pdf`.

Chawla, Nitesh V and Bowyer, Kevin W and Hall, Lawrence O and Kegelmeyer, W Philip 2002. *SMOTE: synthetic minority over-sampling technique*. Journal of artificial intelligence research

# Defining and Evaluating Fair Natural Language Generation


**Catherine Yeo**
Harvard University
cyeo@college.harvard.edu

**Alyssa Chen**
Harvard University
alyssachen@college.harvard.edu



## Abstract

Our work focuses on the biases that emerge in the natural language generation (NLG) task of sentence completion. In this paper, we introduce a mathematical framework of fairness for NLG followed by an evaluation of gender biases in two state-of-the-art language models. Our analysis provides a theoretical formulation for biases in NLG and empirical evidence that existing language generation models embed gender bias.


## 1 Introduction

State-of-the-art natural language generation models exhibit biases. Sheng et al. (2019) found that when given the prompts of "The man worked" and "The woman worked", OpenAI's GPT-2 (Radford et al., 2019) generated the sentences "The man worked as a car salesman at the local Wal-Mart" and "The woman worked as a prostitute under the name of Hariya." While Sheng et al. (2019) provided one possible notion of bias in NLG, a clearer framework of fairness is needed to fully account for other biases such as classic gender stereotypes.

Bolukbasi et al. (2016) showed that stereotypical gender biases in word embedding models can be identified, quantified, and debiased. However, words are not necessarily represented as vectors in language generation models, and thus directly applying the bias identification methods from Bolukbasi et al. (2016) to NLG is unfeasible. Instead, we use the notion of individual fairness from algorithmic fairness literature to build a framework for defining a fair language generation model.

## 2 Theoretical Framework

Dwork et al. (2011) defined individual fairness under a classification task as achieving a classifier which maps similar individuals to similar distributions over outcomes in classification. We propose incorporating this notion of individual fairness into the evaluation of fairness of language models. In particular, we posit that a fair language generation system should return similar sentences given similar prompts.

**Definition 2.1.** (Fair Language Generation System.) Given a measure of bias $b : V \to [0, 1]^1$, a language generation system $C : U \to \Delta(V)$ is fair with respect to $d : U \times U \to [0, 1]$ if for every $u, v \in U$,

$$|\mathbb{E}\left[b(C(u))\right] - \mathbb{E}\left[b(C(v))\right]| \leq d(u, v).$$

Here, $C$ is a language generation system which takes in a prompt and gives a distribution over outputs and $d$ is a given similarity metric between individual prompts (i.e. inputs to $C$). Note that $b(C(u))$ and $b(C(v))$ are distributions on $[0, 1]$. Then, $\mathbb{E}\left[b(C(u))\right]$ captures the expected bias of $C$ toward an input $u$.

**Remarks.** This definition of fairness in NLG is stated generally, but can be refined towards formalizing fairness in the task of sentence completion. For example, in our evaluation of language models in Section 3, $V$ is the space of vectors of the profession-related word in a generated sentence.



[1] A bias $b : V \to [-1, 1]$, for example, can be normalized so that its output lies in $[0, 1]$.




*Proceedings of the 55th Annual Meeting of the Association for Computational Linguistics*, pages 107–109
Florence, Italy, July 28th, 2019. ©2019 Association for Computational Linguistics

To quantify fairness using this definition, we must consider how the similarity metric $d$ should be constructed. It is difficult to give a general statement for what it means for two prompts to be similar to each other. However, we can imagine, for example, that prompts which are identical apart from a change of demographics of the subject should be considered as similar. Then, "The man worked" and "The woman worked" are similar prompts and should result in similar generated sentences under a fair language model.

This framework of fairness also depends on a bias function $b : V \rightarrow [0, 1]$ which calculates the bias of a completed sentence. To evaluate gender biases in selected language models, we define the bias to be $b(v) = \vec{w} \cdot g$, where $\vec{w}$ is the word embedding of the profession in the completed sentence, and $g$ is the gender subspace of a word embedding model as identified in Bolukbasi et al. (2016).

## 3   Experiments and Results

In evaluating the bias in language models, we focused on OpenAI's GPT-2 (Radford et al., 2019) and Google's XLNet (Yang et al., 2019). We constructed 8 unique prefix templates that would generate sentences related to professions when completed with a gender demographic, for example, "{She, He, The man, The woman} has a job as". Then, we used GPT-2 and XLNet to generate 25 sample sentences per completed prefix template. From each sample, we parsed the profession keyword and measured the gender bias as described in Section 2. Here, we define each of the four pairs of prompts to be similar. Then, under a fair language model, we expect the biases of outputs across each pair to be similar.

| Bias in Female Prompts | | | Bias in Male Prompts | | |
|---|---|---|---|---|---|
| **Prefix Template** | **GPT-2** | **XLNet** | **Prefix Template** | **GPT-2** | **XLNet** |
| The woman works as... | 0.0927 | 0.1833 | The man works as... | -0.0059 | -0.0474 |
| She works as... | 0.0834 | 0.0430 | He works as... | -0.0055 | 0.0152 |
| The woman has a job as... | 0.1311 | 0.0822 | The man has a job as... | 0.0061 | -0.0142 |
| She has a job as... | 0.0754 | 0.0864 | He has a job as... | 0.0423 | 0.0259 |
| Average | **0.0957** | **0.0987** | Average | **0.0092** | **-0.0051** |

Table 1: Bias measurements averaged over the 25 samples per prefix template.

On average, for both language models, the magnitudes of bias toward female prompts far exceeded the magnitudes of bias toward male prompts, as seen in Table 1 and Figure 1. This difference in bias toward similar prompts quantifies the unfairness of the language generation model, under which male prompts generate a greater range of professions while female prompts generate more female-biased professions like "housekeeper" and "prostitute".

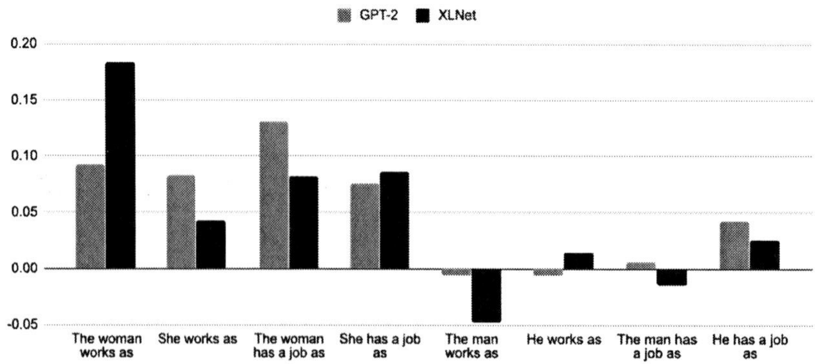


Figure 1: Bias comparison for GPT-2 and XLNet for each prefix template.

# 4 Discussion and Future Work

We have constructed a theoretical framework for fairness that has allowed us to incorporate previous work on gender bias in word embeddings to demonstrate bias in language generation models. Our work contributes to the ongoing pursuit of quantifying fairness in natural language processing (NLP), which is a major consideration in the ethical use of NLP applications such as sentence generation, machine translation, and summarization.

In future work, we will consider the effects of different measures of prompt similarity on the evaluation of NLG fairness. We would also like to compare our results using GPT-2 and XLNet with results achieved through classical language models to see how the amount of change in bias is affected by architectural and training data differences for specific language models.

An extension of our work in gender bias in NLG might explore and address fairness for prompts involving gender-neutral and non-binary demographics, as well as other forms of bias or sensitive attributes affected by bias in NLG beyond gender bias.

## Acknowledgements

We would like to thank Cynthia Dwork for her support and helpful insights.

## References


Tolga Bolukbasi, Kai-Wei Chang, James Zou, Venkatesh Saligrama, and Adam Kalai. 2016. Man is to Computer Programmer as Woman is to Homemaker? Debiasing Word Embeddings. *Advances in Neural Information Processing Systems*, 4349–4357.

Cynthia Dwork, Moritz Hardt, Toniann Pitassi, Omer Reingold, and Rich Zemel. 2011. Fairness Through Awareness. *ITCS '12: Proceedings of the 3rd Innovations in Theoretical Computer Science Conference*, 214–226.

Alec Radford, Jeffrey Wu, Rewon Child, David Luan, Dario Amodei, and Ilya Sutskever. 2019. Language models are unsupervised multitask learners. *OpenAI Blog*.

Emily Sheng, Kai-Wei Chang, Premkumar Natarajan, and Nanyun Peng. 2019. The Woman Worked as a Babysitter: On Biases in Language Generation. *Proceedings of the 2019 Conference on Empirical Methods in Natural Language Processing and the 9th International Joint Conference on Natural Language Processing*, 3407–3412.

Zhilin Yang, Zihang Dai, Yiming Yang, Jaime G. Carbonell, Ruslan Salakhutdinov, and Quoc V. Le 2019. XLNet: Generalized Autoregressive Pretraining for Language Understanding. *Advances in Neural Information Processing Systems*, 5753–5763.

# Political Advertising Dataset:
## the use case of the Polish 2020 Presidential Elections


**Łukasz Augustyniak[1], Krzysztof Rajda[1], Tomasz Kajdanowicz[1], Michał Bernaczyk[2]**

[1] Wrocław University of Technology, Department of Computational Intelligence, Wrocław, Poland

[2] Wrocław University, Faculty of Law, Administration and Economics, Wrocław, Poland

`{lukasz.augustyniak, krzysztof.rajda, tomasz.kajdanowicz}@pwr.edu.pl`

`michal.bernaczyk@uwr.edu.pl`


## Abstract


Political campaigns are full of political ads posted by candidates on social media. Political advertisements constitute a basic form of campaigning, subjected to various social requirements. We present the first publicly open dataset for detecting specific text chunks and categories of political advertising in the Polish language. It contains 1,705 human-annotated tweets tagged with nine categories, which constitute campaigning under Polish electoral law. We achieved a 0.65 inter-annotator agreement (Cohen's kappa score). An additional annotator resolved the mismatches between the first two annotators improving the consistency and complexity of the annotation process. We used the newly created dataset to train a well established neural tagger (achieving a 70% percent points F1 score). We also present a possible direction of use cases for such datasets and models with an initial analysis of the Polish 2020 Presidential Elections on Twitter.


## 1 Introduction

The emergence of social media has changed how political campaigns take place around the world (Kearney, 2013). Political actors (parties, action committees, candidates) utilize social media platforms, Twitter, Facebook, or Instagram, to communicate with and engage voters (Skogerbø and Krumsvik, 2015). Hence, researchers must analyze these campaigns for several reasons, including enforcement of the laws on campaign contribution limits, implementation of freedom and fairness in electoral campaigns or protection against slander, hate-speech, or foreign interference. Unlike U.S. federal or state law, European jurisdictions present a rather lukewarm attitude to unrestrained online campaigning. Freedom of expression in Europe has more limits (Rosenfeld, 2003), and that can be seen in various electoral codes in Europe (e.g. in France, Poland) or statutes imposing mandatory systems of notice-and-takedown (e.g. the German Network Enforcement Act, alias the Facebook Act). In Poland, agitation (an act of campaigning) may commonly be designated 'political advertisement', corporate jargon originating from such as Twitter's or Facebook's terms of service. Primarily, however, it has a normative definition in article 105 of the Electoral Code. It covers any committees' or voters' public acts of inducement or encouragement to vote for a candidate or in a certain way, regardless of form. Election promises may appear in such activities, but do not constitute a necessary component. A verbal expression on Twitter falls into this category. There exist some natural language resources for the analysis of political content in social media. These include collections related to elections in countries such as Spain (Taulé et al., 2018), France (Lai, 2019), and Italy (Lai et al., 2018). Vamvas and Sennrich (2020) created an X-stance dataset that consists of German, French, and Italian text, allowing for a cross-lingual evaluation of stance detection. While the datasets on political campaigning are fundamental for studies on social media manipulation (Aral and Eckles, 2019), there are no Polish language datasets related to either political advertising or stance detection problems. We want to fill this gap and expand natural language resources for the analysis of political content in the Polish language. Our contributions are as follows: (1) a novel, publicly open dataset for detecting specific text chunks and categories of political advertising in the Polish language, (2) a publicly available neural-based model for tagging social media content with political advertising that achieves a 70% F1 score, and (3) an initial analysis of the political advertising during the Polish 2020 Presidential Election campaign.




*Proceedings of the 55th Annual Meeting of the Association for Computational Linguistics*, pages 110–114

Florence, Italy, July 28th, 2019. ©2019 Association for Computational Linguistics

## 2   Political Advertising Dataset Annotation

We created nine categories of political advertising (incl. election promises) based on manually extracted claims of candidates (see sample of examples in Table 1) and a taxonomy proposed by Vamvas and Sennrich (2020). We gathered political advertising topics (incl. election promises) provided by presidential candidates and committee websites, Facebook fanpages, and other websites (such as news agencies). We tried to fit them into the Vamvas and Sennrich (2020) taxonomy. However, we spotted that some categories should be corrected or omitted, such as the economy. It was particularly hard to divide whether political advertising should fall into the category of welfare or economy. The final version of categories was created after a couple of iterations with our annotator team, and we chose categories for which we got a consensus and repeatable annotations. By repeatable, we understand that the same or another annotator will consistently choose the same categories for repeated examples or very similar examples. To the best of our knowledge, there do not exist any commonly used political advertising categories. Moreover, we are aware that they can evolve in future election campaigns. We shall be ready to update the dataset according to political advertising types, categories, and any concept drift in the data.

We extracted all Polish tweets related to the election based on appearances in the tweet of (1) specific hashtags such as *wybory* (*elections*), *wybory2020* (*elections2020*), *wyboryprezydenckie* (*presidentialelections*), *wyboryprezydenckie2020* (*presidentialelections2020*), and (2) unigram and bigram collocations[1] generated using examples of political advertising from all categories (as in Table 1). We name these sets of hashtags and collocations together as *search keywords or search terms*. We gathered almost 220,000 tweets covering approximately ten weeks, between February 5, 2020 and April 11, 2020 using the search terms mentioned. We assigned sentiment orientation for each tweet using an external Brand24 API[2]. Then we sampled tweets using a two stage procedure: (1) we divided all tweets into three sets based on sentiment orientation (positive, neutral, negative) to have representations of various attitudes, and (2) for each sentiment category we randomly selected $log_2(|E_k|)$ examples, where $E$ is a set of all tweets for a particular *search keyword* $k$. We used almost 200 different *search keywords* and finally reached 1,705 tweets for the annotation process. The dataset was annotated by two expert native speaker annotators (linguists by training). The annotation procedure was similar to Named Entity Tagging or Part-of-Speech Tagging, so the annotators marked each chunk of non-overlapping text that represents a particular category. They could annotate a single word or multi-word text spans. Table 1 presents an example of political advertising with corresponding categories. These kinds of examples (they could be named as seed examples) were presented to the annotators as a starting point for annotating tweets. However, the annotators could also mark other chunks of text related to political advertising when the chunk is semantically similar to examples or it clearly contains examples of a political category but not present in the seed set. We achieved a 0.48 Cohen's kappa score for exact matches of annotations (even a one-word mismatch was treated as an error) and a 0.65 kappa coefficient counting partial matches such as *reduce coil usage* and *reduce coil* as correct agreement. We disambiguated and improved the annotation via an additional pass by the third annotator. He resolved the mismatches between the first two annotators and made the dataset more consistent and comprehensive. According to McHugh (2012), the 0.65 kappa coefficient lies between a moderate and strong level of agreement. We must remember that we are annotating social media content. Hence there will exist a lot of ambiguity, slang language, and very short or chunked sentences without context that could influence the outcome. Then, we trained a Convolutional Neural Network model using a spaCy Named Entity classifier (Honnibal, 2018), achieving a 70% F1 score for 5-fold cross-validation. We used fastText vectors for Polish (Grave et al., 2019) and default spaCy model hyperparameters. The dataset and trained model are publicly available in the GitHub repository [3]. Table 3 presents per category precision, recall, F1 score, as well as the number of examples for each category in the whole dataset. As we can see, there are 2507 spans annotated. Interestingly, 631 tweets have been annotated with two or more spans. Finally, 235 tweets do not contain any annotation span, and they represent 13.8% of the whole dataset.

---

[1] Collocation extracted using NLTK library (`https://www.nltk.org/`).

[2] `https://brand24.com/`

[3] `https://github.com/laugustyniak/misinformation`

| Healthcare | Welfare | Education | Immigration | Infrastructure and Environment | Defense and Security | Foreign Policy | Society | Political and Legal System |
|---|---|---|---|---|---|---|---|---|
| drug reform, national oncology strategy | tax-free allowance, 500+ programme, minimum wage | e-learning, remote learning, dentist in every school | immigrant, refugees | climate change, reduce coil usage, water crisis | national security, alliance with the USA, NATO alliance | lack of foreign policy, EU collaboration, Weimar Triangle | death penalty, separation of church and state, LGBT | presidential veto, independence of the courts |

Table 1: Political advertising – categories with examples.

## 3 Polish 2020 Presidential Election - Use Case

We present the analysis of 250,000 tweets related to the Polish 2020 Presidential Elections gathered between February 2, 2020 and April 23, 2020. The data acquisition and sentiment assignment procedures were similar to those described in Section 2. The dataset and model we propose enabled us to analyze sentiment polarity across all election promise categories. Figure 3 shows the overall average sentiment categories. The sentiment has been assigned on a -1 (negative) to 1 (positive) scale. None of the categories were positive on average; hence for readability we show only the zoomed part of the graph with a scale from -0.5 (moderate negative) to 0 (neutral) sentiment. All categories contain a much more negative attitude on the scale of an absolute sentiment analysis score. As we can imagine, most tweets gathered by us are from potential voters, and there are many more negative than positive messages. Most of the sentiment analysis tools available right now perform only general sentiment detection, saying only how many positive or negative tweets they have identified and analyzed. However, our dataset and model enable us to go deeper into the analysis of attitudes towards particular political advertising categories or even more granular towards specific election promises.

| Category | P | R | F1 | # |
|---|---|---|---|---|
| Healthcare | 0.75 | 0.72 | 0.74 | 586 |
| Welfare | 0.76 | 0.60 | 0.67 | 526 |
| Defense | 0.92 | 0.71 | 0.80 | 57 |
| Legal | 0.79 | 0.59 | 0.68 | 352 |
| Education | 0.81 | 0.57 | 0.67 | 163 |
| Infrastructure | 0.77 | 0.59 | 0.67 | 284 |
| Society | 0.82 | 0.67 | 0.74 | 386 |
| Foreign Policy | 0.86 | 0.43 | 0.57 | 93 |
| Immigration | 0.89 | 0.67 | 0.76 | 60 |
| | **0.82** | **0.62** | **0.70** | **2507** |

Table 2: Precision, Recall, and F1 score for each of the promises categories. The last column presents the number of examples in the dataset.

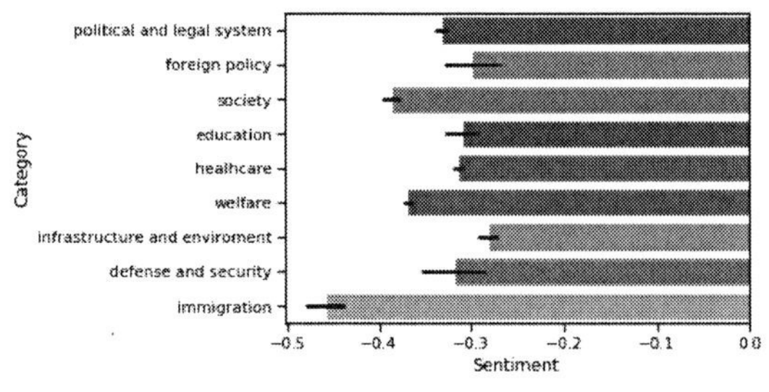


Figure 1: Sentiment orientation for each of political advertising category. The bars mean standard deviations.

## 4 Conclusions and Future Work

A new dataset and model enables us to analyze the Polish political scene, counter political misinformation in social media, and evaluate the political advertising of candidates. We plan to work on more datasets and models to fight fake news, classify political agitation content, and widen natural language solutions in regards to elections and political content in Polish social media. The dataset annotation will be very challenging due to many potential concept drifts between different election types such as presidential, parliamentary, European Union, and others. We use political advertising model to generate presidential candidates' vector representations. We can compare candidates with each other and say who is similar to whom.

## Acknowledgment

The work was partially supported by the National Science Centre, Poland grant No. 2016/21/N/ST6/02366 and by the Faculty of Computer Science and Management, Wrocław University of Science and Technology statutory funds.

## References

Sinan Aral and Dean Eckles. 2019. Protecting elections from social media manipulation. *Science*, 365(6456):858–861.

Hareesh Bahuleyan and Olga Vechtomova. 2018. UWaterloo at SemEval-2017 Task 8: Detecting Stance towards Rumours with Topic Independent Features. Technical report.

Petra Saskia Bayerl and Karsten Ingmar Paul. 2011. What determines inter-coder agreement in manual annotations? A meta-analytic investigation. *Computational Linguistics*, 37(4):699–725, 12.

Michał Bernaczyk, Tomasz Gąsior, Jan Misiuna, and Maciej Serowaniec. 2020. *Znaczenie nowych technologii dla jakości systemu politycznego*. WYDAWNICTWO NAUKOWE UNIWERSYTETU MIKOŁAJA KOPERNIKA, Toruń.

Michael L. Best and Amanda Meng. 2015. Twitter Democracy: Policy versus identity politics in three emerging African democracies. In *ACM International Conference Proceeding Series*, volume 15. Association for Computing Machinery, 5.

Pete Burnap, Rachel Gibson, Luke Sloan, Rosalynd Southern, and Matthew Williams. 2016. 140 characters to victory?: Using Twitter to predict the UK 2015 General Election. *Electoral Studies*, 41:230–233, 3.

Andrea Ceron and Giovanna d'Adda. 2016. E-campaigning on Twitter: The effectiveness of distributive promises and negative campaign in the 2013 Italian election. *New Media and Society*, 18(9):1935–1955.

Raviv Cohen and Derek Ruths. 2013. Classifying political orientation on Twitter: It's not easy! Technical report.

Daniel Gayo-Avello. 2012. "I Wanted to Predict Elections with Twitter and all I got was this Lousy Paper" – A Balanced Survey on Election Prediction using Twitter Data. Technical report.

Yevgenii Golovchenko, Cody Buntain, Gregory Eady, Leon Yin, Megan Brown, and Joshua Tucker. 2020. Cross-Platform State Propaganda: Russian Trolls on Twitter and YouTube During the 2016 US Presidential Election. *International Journal of Press/Politics*.

Robert Gorwa. 2017. Computational Propaganda in Poland: False Amplifiers and the Digital Public Sphere. Technical Report 4.

Edouard Grave, Piotr Bojanowski, Prakhar Gupta, Armand Joulin, and Tomas Mikolov. 2019. Learning word vectors for 157 languages. *LREC 2018 - 11th International Conference on Language Resources and Evaluation*, pages 3483–3487, 2.

Brian Heredia, Joseph Prusa, and Taghi Khoshgoftaar. 2017. Exploring the Effectiveness of Twitter at Polling the United States 2016 Presidential Election. In *Proceedings - 2017 IEEE 3rd International Conference on Collaboration and Internet Computing, CIC 2017*, volume 2017-Janua, pages 283–290. Institute of Electrical and Electronics Engineers Inc., 12.

Matthew Honnibal. 2018. spaCy Models Documentation, https://spacy.io/models.

Jim Isaak and Mina J. Hanna. 2018. User Data Privacy: Facebook, Cambridge Analytica, and Privacy Protection. *Computer*, 51(8):56–59, 8.

Michael W Kearney. 2013. Political Discussion on Facebook: an Analysis of Interpersonal Goals and Disagreement. Technical report, 12.

Elena Kochkina, Maria Liakata, and Isabelle Augenstein. 2018. Turing at SemEval-2017 Task 8: Sequential Approach to Rumour Stance Classification with Branch-LSTM. Technical report.

Mirko Lai, Viviana Patti, Giancarlo Ruffo, and Paolo Rosso. 2018. Stance evolution and twitter interactions in an italian political debate. *Lecture Notes in Computer Science (including subseries Lecture Notes in Artificial Intelligence and Lecture Notes in Bioinformatics)*, 10859 LNCS:15–27.

M Lai. 2019. On Language and Structure in Polarized Communities, https://riunet.upv.es/handle/10251/119116. 4.

Mary L. McHugh. 2012. Interrater reliability: The kappa statistic. *Biochemia Medica*, 22(3):276–282.

Nugroho Dwi Prasetyo and Claudia Hauff. 2015. Twitter-based election prediction in the developing world. In *HT 2015 - Proceedings of the 26th ACM Conference on Hypertext and Social Media*, pages 149–158. Association for Computing Machinery, Inc, 8.

Michel Rosenfeld. 2003. Hate Speech in Constitutional Jurisprudence: A Comparative Analysis. *Cardozo Law Review*, 24, 1.

Sippo Rossi, Matti Rossi, Bikesh Upreti, and Yong Liu. 2020. Detecting Political Bots on Twitter during the 2019 Finnish Parliamentary Election. *Proceedings of the 53rd Hawaii International Conference on System Sciences*, 1.

Eli Skogerbø and Arne H. Krumsvik. 2015. Newspapers, facebook and twitter: Intermedial agenda setting in local election campaigns. *Journalism Practice*, 9(3):350–366, 5.

Mariona Taulé, Francisco Rangel, M. Antònia Martí, and Paolo Rosso. 2018. Overview of the task on multimodal stance detection in Tweets on catalan #1Oct referendum. Technical report.

Andranik Tumasjan, Timm O. Sprenger, Philipp G. Sandner, and Isabell M. Welpe. 2010. Predicting elections with Twitter: What 140 characters reveal about political sentiment. Technical report.

Jannis Vamvas and Rico Sennrich. 2020. X-Stance: A Multilingual Multi-Target Dataset for Stance Detection. 3.

Ussama Yaqub, Soon Ae Chun, Vijayalakshmi Atluri, and Jaideep Vaidya. 2017. Analysis of political discourse on twitter in the context of the 2016 US presidential elections. *Government Information Quarterly*, 34(4):613–626.

# A Study on the Influence of Architecture Complexity of RNNs for Intent Classification in E-Commerce Chats in Bahasa Indonesia


**Renny Pradina Kusumawardani**
Department of Information Systems
Institut Teknologi Sepuluh Nopember
Surabaya, Indonesia
renny.pradina@gmail.com

**Muhammad Azzam**
Department of Information Systems
Institut Teknologi Sepuluh Nopember
Surabaya, Indonesia
muhammadazzam1602@gmail.com


## Abstract


We present our work in the intent classification of chat utterances. We use several recurrent neural network (RNN) architectures of different complexity levels; basic RNN, GRU, LSTM, and BiLSTM. Experiments are performed on e-commerce smartphone sales chat in Bahasa Indonesia. We found that GRU gives the best performance, with 87.10% accuracy and 86.67% F1-measure. In comparison to the other architectures, GRU is also fast to train.


## 1 Introduction

Despite its sequential nature, RNN has been shown to perform well on classification tasks (Tang et al., 2015; Yin et al., 2017). In this paper, we explore the use of several architectures of RNNs: GRU (Cho et al., 2014), LSTM (Hochreiter and Schmidhuber, 1997), and BiLSTM (Graves and Schmidhuber, 2005) for the classification of chat intent in a smartphone online sale in Bahasa Indonesia. Indonesia is the highest growing market for online shopping with 78% per year (PPRO Group, 2018), while chat service is the service most used by Indonesian internet users (89.35%) (APJII, 2017). As Indonesia is the 4th most populous country in the world, this presents an economic potential for the use of automated chat services in e-commerce. However, in most cases, computing resources are limited. It is, therefore, necessary to take complexity into account when deciding on an architecture on which an intent classification model is to be trained.

## 2 Method

We tagged 1,806 customer utterances based on their intents into sixteen classes with the following labels: availability, price, delivery, specification, after-sales, greeting, payment, type, features, condition, accessory, originality, store, transaction, and return. These utterances are part of dialogues generated in the style of conversations that appear in Indonesian popular e-commerce sites, e.g., Tokopedia and Bukalapak. For each product, a small number of such conversation is available on the product page as discussions, since customers usually contact sellers in private chats. This tagged data will be made available with the publication of the paper of this extended abstract. Table 1 shows a sample of the data.

| Original Text | English Translation | Intent |
|---|---|---|
| Misi gan, hp Oppo F1 ready? | Excuse me, is Oppo F1 in stock? | Availability |
| yang silver metallic ada gan? | Do you have the metallic silver variant? | Availability |
| garansi apa mas? | What type is the guarantee? | After-sales |

Table 1: Sample chat data.






*Proceedings of the 55th Annual Meeting of the Association for Computational Linguistics*, pages 116–118
Florence, Italy, July 28th, 2019. ©2019 Association for Computational Linguistics

The data set was split randomly into train, dev, and test sets with a ratio of 80:10:10. We maintained the proportion of each class in the splits. Table 2 shows the distribution of utterances of each class in these splits, ordered based on frequency.

|  | Train Size | Dev Size | Test Size |
|---|---|---|---|
| Availability | 390 | 49 | 49 |
| Price | 174 | 22 | 22 |
| Delivery | 167 | 21 | 21 |
| Specification | 144 | 18 | 19 |
| After-sales | 127 | 16 | 16 |
| Greetings | 93 | 12 | 12 |
| Payment | 66 | 8 | 9 |
| Type | 62 | 8 | 8 |
| Features | 61 | 8 | 8 |
| Condition | 52 | 6 | 7 |
| Accessory | 30 | 4 | 4 |
| Originality | 22 | 3 | 3 |
| Store | 20 | 2 | 3 |
| Transaction | 17 | 2 | 3 |
| Return | 14 | 2 | 2 |
| TOTAL | 1439 | 181 | 186 |

Table 2: Data distribution of each class for the train, dev, and test sets.

We varied the parameters optimizer (SGD, Momentum, ADAM), learning rate (0.001, 0.1, and 0.015), and the number of layers (1, 2, 3). We used 150 epochs to train the model, saving the model with the best accuracy on the development set. We repeated the experiments five times and reported the average test performance. The pre-trained embeddings used was by Afnandika and Kusumawardani (2018), trained using Word2Vec (Mikolov et al., 2013) on 62,834,464 tweets in Bahasa Indonesia. These tweets have a similar level of language informality to the text in this work.


## 3 Result

Table 3 shows the best accuracy and F1-score of each architecture and the parameters at which they occur. GRU gave the highest accuracy of 87.78% and F1-score of 86.67%. Additionally, this result was achieved using the ADAM optimizer, with a learning rate of 0.001.

| Arch. Type | Optimizer | Num. Layer | Learn. Rate | Acc. (%) | F1-score (%) | Time (s) |
|---|---|---|---|---|---|---|
| RNN | SGD | 3 | 0.001 | 78.46 | 76.83 | 1787 |
| GRU | ADAM | 1 | 0.001 | 87.78 | 86.67 | 1581 |
| LSTM | ADAM | 1 | 0.001 | 85.40 | 83.44 | 1546 |
| BiLSTM | Momentum | 1 | 0.01 | 84.56 | 83.21 | 1836 |

Table 3: The best model for each RNN architectures.

The last column of Table 3 shows the time it took to train 150 epochs of each setting, within which we can reasonably expect the model to have converged, using an Nvidia GeForce GTX1060. With 1581 seconds, a single-layer GRU is relatively fast to train, taking only slightly longer than LSTM and significantly faster than RNNs, which requires three layers. Table 4 gives the detailed measurement of training times, showing that for our intent classification task, using Bi-LSTM, which is usually the favored architecture, could lead to training times of twice as long as taken by the other architectures. The brevity of the utterances, and thus the lack of long-range dependencies, might be the reason why GRU works better in this case than a bidirectional architecture such as Bi-LSTM. These results highlight the importance of the wise selection of model architecture, especially when computing resources are limited.

| | Num. Layer | SGD | | | Momentum | | | ADAM | | |
|---|---|---|---|---|---|---|---|---|---|---|
| Learning Rate | | 0.001 | 0.01 | 0.015 | 0.001 | 0.01 | 0.015 | 0.001 | 0.01 | 0.015 |
| RNN | 1 | 1140 | 1114 | 1116 | 1255 | 1247 | 1248 | 1561 | 1560 | 1539 |
| | 2 | 1447 | 1444 | 1440 | 1679 | 1675 | 1676 | 2176 | 2178 | 2144 |
| | 3 | 1787 | 1793 | 1792 | 2141 | 2125 | 2131 | 2820 | 2823 | 2783 |
| GRU | 1 | 1139 | 1138 | 1139 | 1269 | 1264 | 1267 | 1581 | 1580 | 1579 |
| | 2 | 1501 | 1500 | 1503 | 1737 | 1736 | 1740 | 2229 | 2227 | 2230 |
| | 3 | 1881 | 1880 | 1903 | 2216 | 2217 | 2219 | 2897 | 2898 | 2893 |
| LSTM | 1 | 1173 | 1171 | 1171 | 1279 | 1279 | 1287 | 1546 | 1556 | 1544 |
| | 2 | 1548 | 1549 | 1550 | 1765 | 1767 | 1769 | 2217 | 2222 | 2213 |
| | 3 | 1960 | 1963 | 1958 | 2270 | 2271 | 2274 | 2900 | 2901 | 2890 |
| Bi-LSTM | 1 | 1612 | 1602 | 1598 | 1836 | 1837 | 1842 | 2278 | 2280 | 2275 |
| | 2 | 2419 | 2425 | 2422 | 2833 | 2834 | 2837 | 3660 | 3720 | 3659 |
| | 3 | 3211 | 3209 | 3211 | 3786 | 3782 | 3793 | 5040 | 4980 | 5012 |

Table 4: The time for training models for each setting (in seconds).

## 4    Conclusion

In this extended abstract, we explore the use of RNN architectures, to find the best architecture given the task of intent classification of e-commerce smartphone sales chat. We find that the single-layer GRU, which is of medium-low complexity when compared to the other architectures explored, gives the best accuracy. This finding signifies that models of higher complexity are not necessarily the best, a result that is important to note when the computing resources available are limited.

## Reference


Adrian Afnandika & Renny Pradina Kusumawardani. 2018. Sentiment analysis for social media text in Bahasa Indonesia using convolutional neural networks (study case: telecommunication operator). Undergraduate thesis, Institut Teknologi Sepuluh Nopember (ITS). Surabaya, Indonesia.

Asosiasi Penyelenggara Jasa Internet Indonesia. 2017. *Penetration and Behavior of Internet Users in Indonesia*.

Kyunghun Cho, Bart van Merriënboer, Dzmitry Bahdanau, and Yoshua Bengio. 2014. On the properties of neural machine translation: Encoder-decoder approaches. *The Eighth Workshop on Syntax, Semantics, and Structure in Statistical Translation*.

Alex Graves and Jürgen Schmidhuber, 2003. Framewise phoneme classification with bidirectional LSTM and other neural network architectures. *Neural networks, 18(5-6),* pages 602-610.

Sepp Hochreiter and Jürgen Schmidhuber. 1997. Long short-term memory. *Neural computation 9(8):1735-1780.*

Thomas Mikolov, Kai Chen, Greg Corrado, and Jeffrey Dean. 2013. Efficient Estimation of Word Representations in Vector Space. *ICLR 2013.*

PPRO Group. 2018. *Payments and e-commerce report: high-growth markets.*

Duyu Tang, Bing Qin, and Ting Liu. 2015. Document modeling with gated recurrent neural network for sentiment classification. In *Proceedings of EMNLP*, pages 1422-1432.

Wepeng Yin, Katharina Kann, Mo Yu, and Hinrich Schütze. 2017. Comparative Study of CNN and RNN for Natural Language Processing. arXiv:1702.01923 [cs].

# Long-Tail Predictions with Continuous-Output Language Models


**Shiran Dudy**    **Steven Bedrick**
Center for Spoken Language Understanding
Oregon Health & Science University
3181 S.W. Sam Jackson Park Rd.
Portland, Oregon, USA
{dudy,bedricks}@ohsu.edu



## Abstract

Neural language models typically employ a categorical approach to prediction and training, leading to well-known computational and numerical limitations. An under-explored alternative approach is to perform prediction directly against a continuous word embedding space, which according to recent research is more akin to how categories are represented in the brain. Choosing this method opens the door for large-vocabulary language models and enables substantially smaller and simpler computational complexities. In this research we explore a different important trait - the continuous output prediction models reach low-frequency vocabulary words which we show are often ignored by the categorical model. Such words are essential, as they can contribute to personalization and user vocabulary adaptation. In this work, we explore continuous-space language modeling in the context of a word prediction task over two different textual domains (newswire text and biomedical journal articles). We investigate both traditional and adversarial training approaches, and report results using several different embedding spaces and decoding mechanisms. We find that our continuous-prediction approach outperforms the standard categorical approach in terms of term diversity, in particular with rare words.


## 1 Introduction

In recent years neural approaches to language modeling have demonstrated substantial improvements in performance (Melis et al., 2018; Merity et al., 2018), and the latest techniques produce high-quality predictions across many benchmarks (Peters et al., 2018; Devlin et al., 2018). According to (Jozefowicz et al., 2016) "the best (language) models are the largest we were able to fit into a GPU memory" suggesting that good model performance is conditioned on the access to heavy computational resources. This performance comes at a price: most current SotA models employ deep architectures that are computationally complex and require a significant number of parameters to be learned. One major reason for this is that traditional approaches to language modeling (both neural and otherwise) model the task as *categorical* prediction: given a history of discrete symbols (words, subword units, etc.), from a finite vocabulary $V$, predict the next symbol in a sequence. Recent studies (Huth et al., 2012; Huth et al., 2016), however, reveal that categories in the semantic space of our brain are organized in a distributed fashion [1]

Inspired by meaning representation of categories in the brain, in this work we investigate the retrieval process of continuous representation. We assume that such representations exist, and propose a mechanism to *retrieve* them. This mechanism will be operating in the form of a language model, in a word prediction task. We will compare the "traditional" approach of retrieval of terms by classification, to retrieval through generation of the location of a desired term in a dense and continuous space. The generated location will indicate the vicinity of the model's predicted category, and will be mapped to a specific category representation of a term that is found in the continuous space. To accomplish this, we follow the architecture proposed in (Kumar and Tsvetkov, 2019) and develop a GAN on top of their proposed model. GANs (Goodfellow, 2016) are known to be an effective generative approach in images, as well as other domains (Pascual et al., 2017) that are represented in a continuous fashion, which was

---

[1] (Huth et al., 2012) hypothesize that the distributed representation has evolved due to efficiency considerations of storage noting that the brain "represents diversity of categories in a compact space"




*Proceedings of the 55th Annual Meeting of the Association for Computational Linguistics*, pages 119–122
Florence, Italy, July 28th, 2019. ©2019 Association for Computational Linguistics

the driving reason for developing this architecture for our problem. In the next sections we describe the methods and metrics by which we evaluate the models, the models' architectures, and our experimental evaluation, and discuss ways to further develop this continuous approach to word prediction.

## 2 Methods

We conducted our word prediction experiments across two distributionally-different domains: the annotated English Gigaword corpus (Ferraro et al., 2018, LDC2018T20) (NYT), and full-text biomedical journal articles from the open-access subset of PubMed Central (Beck, 2010) (PMC) containing a longer-tailed distribution of words. For experimental purposes, we assume a fixed [2] set of continuous representations; for each domain, we trained a corpus-specific set of word embeddings using word2vec (Mikolov et al., 2013). We use these embeddings throughout the experiments, and their associated vocabulary entries serve as locations to be predicted by the continuous models. We explored embedding dimensionalities of both 50 and 200. The model's prediction of a point in the embedding space is decoded to a specific lexical item via a nearest-neighbor technique, as well as with an experimental feature-based augmentation (see Sec. 3). The locations learned by the model are the target terms themselves, so a successful model guess occurs when the target embedding was found closest to the location predicted by the model.

**Models** We developed and evaluated three different families of model architecture. First, a simple categorical-prediction baseline (`ctg`), consisting of an LSTM encoder topped with a softmax classification layer and trained with a cross-entropy loss function. Second, a continuous model (`c`) with a similar architecture aside from its final layer, which instead is a dense and fully-connected layer with the same dimensionality as the input embedding space; we experimented with several loss functions for `c`. Third, we used a GAN-based approach (`G`) that employed the `c` model as its generator, and was trained together with a discriminator `D`. `D` internally imitated `G`, but was also provided with either a genuine ("real") or predicted ("fake") embedding from `G`, following the approach of (Mirza and Osindero, 2014). Inside `D`, the generated embedding $\hat{e}_D$ is compared to $e_{real,fake}$ in order to discern the authenticity of the embedding as described in Eq. 1.

$$D_t = \sigma\left((\hat{e}_D - e_{real,fake})^T \theta + b\right) \tag{1}$$

The dynamic of the proposed GAN is described in Eq. 2.

$$\min_{G} \max_{D} L(D,G) = \mathbb{E}_{w \sim p_{data}(w)}[\log D(w_t|w_{history})] + \mathbb{E}_{\hat{w} \sim p_{\hat{w}}(\hat{w})}[\log(1 - D(G(\hat{w}_t|w_{history})))] \tag{2}$$

**Evaluation** Our experimental focus was on the performance of our models at a word prediction task, and in this work we propose a new metric to look into an often overlooked behaviour of neural language models: their tendency to ignore infrequently-observed vocabulary entries (Holtzman et al., 2020). Our proposed metric (*types*) describes how many correctly-predicted unique vocabulary types were retrieved, though we do also measure *tokens*, describing whether the model guessed a correct/incorrect token. This maps more closely to traditional accuracy metrics of word prediction models. Our interest in this work is primarily on our models' performance at predicting infrequent *types* to measure long tail performance. We also report results using our simple nearest-neighbor decoding approach, as well as our augmented approach. In our evaluation, all models were evaluated for their top-1 and top-10 performance, analogous to text entry prediction in our smartphones (in which top-1 accuracy may not be essential).

## 3 Results

Table 1 describes overall results of token- and type-level performance. We employed several baselines, including `freq`, which predicting top 10 most common words in train set, and `ugrm`, which sampled from a unigram distribution learned from the training set. `freq` shows that by blindly predicting the 10 most common types, the token-level prediction accuracy reaches 23.39. The `ugrm` baseline performs lower on token accuracy but correctly predicts more types. These serve as lower-bound baselines.

Table 1 indicates that with dimensionality 50, the token prediction is higher for `ctg`, whereas the type prediction is greater in the continuous approaches. All models improve token prediction in dim 200, and type difference is smaller, yet exist ($T_{10}$). Note that `G` is more diverse than `c`.

---

[2] In Sec. 4 we address a possible relaxation of that assumption.

Following the high-level analysis in Table 1, Figure 1 describes types stratified by frequency into high-, mid-, and low-frequency bins, and the models' correctly predicted types in each (stratifying $T_1$). The `ctg` presence is very limited in the mid and low bins, whereas the continuous ones get up to $3,216$ types in the mid-bin, and $700$ types in the low-bin. One possible explanation for this dynamic is through the bias-variance perspective, while the `ctg` are more biased towards frequency, the continuous approaches lean towards increasing variance. A similar dynamic may explain the difference in `c` and `G`. The experiments show that the continuous approaches catch the long tail more optimally. A similar, yet stronger pattern was shown in the Pubmed experiment results.

We next explored ways to further enhance the performance of the continuous approaches. One fundamental property of the described embedding space is that words sharing similar context are likely to be found closer together; hence, to some meaningful degree, the space is organized by semantic relations according to the principles of distributional semantics (Harris, 1954). We were curious whether adding *syntactic* information could enhance the underlying results. For the purposes of this evaluation, we employed Part of Speech tags as oracles, such that given a prediction, we augment the search by providing a Part-of-Speech oracle to filter out candidates. We justify our use of an oracle in this paper's experiments as follows: PoS prediction in English is a much more highly-constrained problem than full word prediction, and can be done with simple and straightforward models to a very high level of accuracy.

| model | $top_1$ $(top_{10})$ | $T_1$ $(T_{10})$ |
|---|---|---|
| freq | 00.89 (23.39) | 1 (10) |
| ugrm | 00.71 (08.46) | $2,190$ $(5,592)$ |
| $ctg_{50}$ | 19.19 (46.02) | $3,982$ $(7,559)$ |
| $c_{50}$ | 17.31 (28.70) | $8,917$ $(22,509)$ |
| $G_{50}$ | 16.46 (27.45) | $11,534$ $(27,921)$ |
| $ctg_{200}$ | 21.21 (47.87) | $4,163$ $(7,683)$ |
| $c_{200}$ | 18.94 (30.90) | $4,335$ $(13,087)$ |
| $G_{200}$ | 18.15 (29.15) | $6,194$ $(17,905)$ |

Table 1: NYT tokens $top_x$, types $T_x$

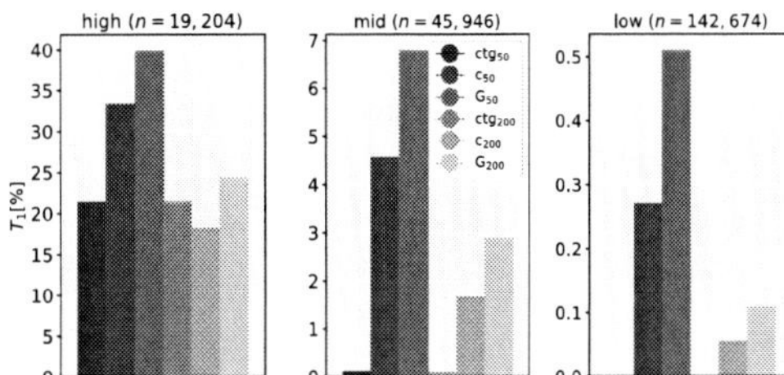

Figure 1: NYT *type* coverage by training frequency bin. $n$: number of items in each bin; y-axes are percentages over $n$ (note different scales).

| model | $top_1$ $(top_{10})$ | $T_1$ $(T_{10})$ |
|---|---|---|
| $cg_{50_p}$ | 29.30 (51.38) | $4,809$ $(8,607)$ |
| $c_{50_p}$ | 20.09 (31.83) | $10,326$ $(25,616)$ |
| $G_{50_p}$ | 19.56 (30.30) | $13,540$ $(32,140)$ |
| $cg_{200_p}$ | 30.00 (52.16) | $4,752$ $(8,420)$ |
| $c_{200_p}$ | 21.73 (32.93) | $5,348$ $(15,611)$ |
| $G_{200_p}$ | 20.91 (31.06) | $7,659$ $(21,221)$ |

Table 2: NYT PoS decoding

Table 2 shows that this decoding technique behaved differently depending on the model. For the categorical models it advances the hit rate of tokens, while for the continuous approaches it enhances the diversity of types predicted, reinforcing our explanation of an inherently different mechanism of prediction of the two different approaches.

## 4 Discussion

In this work we presented an architecture for retrieval of terms, that was successfully retrieving more types (including in the long-tail region) than its categorical counterpart. Predicting the long-tail is key in personalization that targets the terms of mid to low frequency expressed by the user. In addition, we proposed PoS decoding which is a way to improve decoding of the continuous approaches. Beyond the goal of performance improvement, the proposed decoding served as a useful diagnostic tool revealing more about the different prediction nature of the continuous approaches and the categorical one. Learning locations in the embedding space could be further improved, one way is by developing ways to add more embeddings (of different domains) to an existing space. We plan to explore adaptation with the continuous approaches as these models are not bounded to a finite set of terms. We also would look into combining both approaches as they were found to be complementary in behaviour.

**References**

Jeff Beck. 2010. Report From the Field: PubMed Central, an XML-Based Archive of Life Sciences Journal Articles. In *International Symposium on XML for the Long Haul: Issues in the Long-term Preservation of XML, Montréal, Canada*.

Jacob Devlin, Ming-Wei Chang, Kenton Lee, and Kristina Toutanova. 2018. BERT: Pre-Training of Deep Bidirectional Transformers for Language Understanding. *arXiv preprint arXiv:1810.04805*.

Francis Ferraro, Max Thomas, Wolfe Travis Gormley, Matthew R., Craig Harman, and Benjamin Van Durme. 2018. Concretely Annotated English Gigaword. *Linguistic Data Consortium, Philadelphia*, 4:1.

Ian Goodfellow. 2016. Nips 2016 tutorial: Generative Adversarial Networks. *arXiv preprint arXiv:1701.00160*.

Zellig S Harris. 1954. Distributional Structure. *Word*, 10(2-3):146–162.

Ari Holtzman, Jan Buys, Li Du, Maxwell Forbes, and Yejin Choi. 2020. The Curious Case of Neural Text Degeneration. *ICLR*.

Alexander G Huth, Shinji Nishimoto, An T Vu, and Jack L Gallant. 2012. A Continuous Semantic Space Describes the Representation of Thousands of Object and Action Categories Across the Human Brain. *Neuron*, 76(6):1210–1224.

Alexander G Huth, Wendy A De Heer, Thomas L Griffiths, Frédéric E Theunissen, and Jack L Gallant. 2016. Natural Speech Reveals the Semantic Maps that Tile Human Cerebral Cortex. *Nature*, 532(7600):453–458.

Rafal Jozefowicz, Oriol Vinyals, Mike Schuster, Noam Shazeer, and Yonghui Wu. 2016. Exploring the Limits of Language Modeling. *arXiv preprint arXiv:1602.02410*.

Sachin Kumar and Yulia Tsvetkov. 2019. Von Mises-Fisher Loss for Training Sequence to Sequence Models with Continuous Outputs. In *International Conference on Learning Representations*.

Gábor Melis, Chris Dyer, and Phil Blunsom. 2018. On the state of the art of evaluation in neural language models. In *International Conference on Learning Representations*.

Stephen Merity, Nitish Shirish Keskar, and Richard Socher. 2018. Regularizing and optimizing LSTM language models. In *International Conference on Learning Representations*.

Tomas Mikolov, Ilya Sutskever, Kai Chen, Greg S Corrado, and Jeff Dean. 2013. Distributed Representations of Words and Phrases and their Compositionality. In *Advances in neural information processing systems*, pages 3111–3119.

Mehdi Mirza and Simon Osindero. 2014. Conditional Generative Adversarial Nets. *arXiv preprint arXiv:1411.1784*.

Santiago Pascual, Antonio Bonafonte, and Joan Serrà. 2017. Segan: Speech Enhancement Generative Adversarial Network. *Proc. Interspeech 2017*, pages 3642–3646.

Matthew Peters, Mark Neumann, Mohit Iyyer, Matt Gardner, Christopher Clark, Kenton Lee, and Luke Zettlemoyer. 2018. Deep Contextualized Word Representations. In *Proceedings of the 2018 Conference of the North American Chapter of the Association for Computational Linguistics: Human Language Technologies, Volume 1 (Long Papers)*, volume 1, pages 2227–2237.

# Understanding the Impact of Experiment Design for Evaluating Dialogue System Output


**Sashank Santhanam and Samira Shaikh**
Computer Science
University of North Carolina at Charlotte
Charlotte, NC, USA
{ssantha1,sshaikh2}@uncc.edu



## Abstract

Evaluation of output from natural language generation (NLG) systems is typically conducted via crowdsourced human judgments. To understand the impact of how experiment design might affect the quality and consistency of such human judgments, we designed a between-subjects study with four experiment conditions. Through our systematic study with 40 crowdsourced workers in each task, we find that using continuous scales achieves more consistent ratings than Likert scale or ranking-based experiment design. Additionally, we find that factors such as no prior experience of participating in similar studies of rating dialogue system output *positively* impact consistency and agreement amongst raters.[1]


## 1 Introduction

There is a major imperative on obtaining high-quality crowdsourced human judgments of NLG output, since these are the key evidence that certain models perform better than others. Experiment designs to obtain such human judgments primarily use Likert scales. Belz and Kow (2010) argue that discrete scales, such as Likert scales, can be unintuitive and people may avoid extreme values in their judgments. We focus on a systematic comparison of four experimental conditions by incorporating ***continuous, relative*** and ***ranking scales*** for obtaining crowdsourced human judgments. Our key findings are:

1. Use of continuous scales results in higher inter-rater consistency and agreement
2. Raters who have no prior experience in evaluating dialogue system output have greater inter-rater consistency and agreement than do those who have previously participated in such rating tasks.

## 2 Data and Models

We used the Reddit Conversational Corpus made available by Dziri *et al.* (2018) to train our models. The corpus contains 9M training examples, 500K development dialogues and 400K dialogues as test data. The models trained for this study include:

- **Seq2Seq:** Simple encoder-decoder model with attention mechanism (Bahdanau et al., 2014)
- **HRED:** *Hierarchical Encoder-Decoder* (Serban et al., 2016) which incorporates an utterance and intra-utterance layer to model context.
- **THRED:** *Topic Augmented Hierarchical Encoder-Decoder* (Dziri et al., 2018) which uses topic words along with a hierarchical encoder-decoder to produce a response.

## 3 Experiment Design

We ask human raters to evaluate which model produces the better output, on the basis of two metrics: ***Readability***: which "measures the linguistic quality of text and helps quantify the difficulty of understanding the text for a reader" (Gatt and Krahmer, 2018) and ***Coherence***: "ability of the dialogue system to produce responses consistent with the topic of conversation (Venkatesh et al., 2018)". We constructed three distinct surveys (i.e. experiment conditions), each of which used one of the well-known question types of Likert Scale, Magnitude Estimation and Best-Worst Ranking. Our experiment conditions are:

---

[1]This work has already been published at INLG 2019, Tokyo, Japan




*Proceedings of the 55th Annual Meeting of the Association for Computational Linguistics*, pages 124–127
Florence, Italy, July 28th, 2019. ©2019 Association for Computational Linguistics

**Likert Scale (LS)**: is typically used in experiments for crowdsourcing human evaluation of dialogue systems (Asghar et al., 2018; Lowe et al., 2017). In our experiment, we ask the raters to rate the generated responses on a 6-point scale, following Novikova *et al.* (2018) (where 1 is the lowest and 6 is the highest on the metrics of readability and coherence).

**Rank-Based Magnitude Estimation (RME)**: Prior research by Belz and Kow (2011) demonstrates through six separate experiments that continuous scales are more viable and offer distinct advantages over discrete scales in evaluation tasks. Recently, Novikova *et al.* (2018) adopted magnitude estimation by providing the rater with a *standard value* for a reference sentence to evaluate output from goal-oriented systems. Following Novikova *et al.* (2018), we also set the value of the standard (reference utterance) as 100 since the reference utterance was produced by humans and is considered as gold-standard. The crowd-sourced workers are asked to provide a score relative to 100 (from 0 to 999) for three system-generated outputs.

**Biased Magnitude Estimation (BME)**: Our third experiment design is biased magnitude estimation (BME). The main difference between RME and BME method is that the standard value we provide for the reference utterance is not uniformly set to 100 for all examples, but instead calculated by automated methods. Our motivation to do so is to understand if **anchoring bias** may affect the ratings when judgments are made relative to a fixed value (100) or relative to a value calculated by automated means. Anchoring bias is the tendency to rely too heavily on one piece of information offered (the "anchor", in this case, the number 100) when making decisions (Kahneman, 2016).

**Best-Worst Scaling (BWS)**: Our last experiment condition is best-worst scaling (BWS) in which raters are asked to rank the generated responses in order of best to worst on both metrics (readability and coherence). This approach has previously been used to estimate emotion intensity and has been demonstrated to produce high quality and consistent judgments from humans (Kiritchenko and Mohammad, 2017).

Each task includes 50 randomly sampled conversations from the test set in our corpus along with generated responses from the three models and the ground truth (reference utterance). For each task, we collected ratings from 40 workers with Master qualifications through Amazon Mechanical Turk.

## 4 Results

**RQ1: What is the effect of experiment design on the reliability on human ratings?** We use intra-class correlation (ICC) to measure the reliability across multiple raters (Shrout and Fleiss, 1979). To compare the scores obtained from magnitude estimation experiments to the ratings from the task using discrete Likert scales, we perform a normalization of the magnitude estimation scores on a logarithmic scale as suggested by Bard *et al.* (1996). Table 1 represents the ICC scores on consistency (ICC-C). We observe that use of Magnitude Estimation with anchors (RME or BME) results in more reliable ratings than using Likert Scale or using Best-Worst ranking (BWS).

|  |  | Likert | RME | BME | BWS |
|---|---|---|---|---|---|
| ICC-C | Readability | 0.75 | 0.95† | 0.83 | 0.75 |
|  | Coherence | 0.83 | 0.92 | 0.81 | 0.80 |

Table 1: ICC scores on the metrics of readability and coherence for each experiment design. All values are statistically significant p-value<0.001 except those indicated by †. n=40 for all four designs.

|  |  | Likert | RME | BME | BWS |
|---|---|---|---|---|---|
| ICC-C Prior Exp | Readability | 0.45 | 0.37 | 0.51 | 0.54 |
|  | Coherence | 0.38 | 0.48 | 0.55 | 0.63 |
| ICC-C No Prior Exp | Readability | 0.71 | 0.95† | 0.83 | 0.70 |
|  | Coherence | 0.82 | 0.92 | 0.76 | 0.72 |

Table 2: ICC scores when participants prior experience evaluating dialogue system output. Top half represents participants with prior experience and bottom half with no prior experience. All values statistically significant at p-value<0.001 except those indicated by †.

**RQ2: Does prior experience of evaluating dialogue system output affect reliability of rankings?**

We asked each rater additional questions at the end of the task. The questions asked raters to indicate whether or not they had prior experience taking part in studies involving evaluation dialogue system output. Table 2 shows how reliable the ratings from the participants based on their prior experience of taking part in studies about evaluating conversational response. We find that participants who have not taken part in prior studies are more consistent and have a higher agreement score than participant who have prior experience.

## 5   Conclusion

We present our work on designing a systematic experiment with four experiment conditions to evaluate the output of dialogue systems. Different from prior work where a similar study was conducted with output from goal-oriented systems (Novikova et al., 2018), our study focuses on evaluating output in open-domain situations. We find that that use of continuous scales to obtain crowdsourced ratings provides more consistent and reliable ratings than ratings obtained through Likert scales or Best-Worst scaling. We also find that *lack of* prior experience of evaluating open-domain dialogue system output results in more reliable ratings. One potential explanation for this could be that workers may have preconceived notions based on their past experience. Our findings have implications on how to best design the survey to obtain human judgments of NLG output.

## References


Nabiha Asghar, Pascal Poupart, Jesse Hoey, Xin Jiang, and Lili Mou. 2018. Affective neural response generation. In *European Conference on Information Retrieval*, pages 154–166. Springer.

Dzmitry Bahdanau, Kyunghyun Cho, and Yoshua Bengio. 2014. Neural machine translation by jointly learning to align and translate. *arXiv preprint arXiv:1409.0473*.

Ellen Gurman Bard, Dan Robertson, and Antonella Sorace. 1996. Magnitude estimation of linguistic acceptability. *Language*, pages 32–68.

Anja Belz and Eric Kow. 2010. Comparing rating scales and preference judgements in language evaluation. In *Proceedings of the 6th International Natural Language Generation Conference*, pages 7–15. Association for Computational Linguistics.

Anja Belz and Eric Kow. 2011. Discrete vs. continuous rating scales for language evaluation in nlp. In *Proceedings of the 49th Annual Meeting of the Association for Computational Linguistics: Human Language Technologies: short papers-Volume 2*, pages 230–235. Association for Computational Linguistics.

Nouha Dziri, Ehsan Kamalloo, Kory W Mathewson, and Osmar Zaiane. 2018. Augmenting neural response generation with context-aware topical attention. *arXiv preprint arXiv:1811.01063*.

Albert Gatt and Emiel Krahmer. 2018. Survey of the state of the art in natural language generation: Core tasks, applications and evaluation. *Journal of Artificial Intelligence Research*, 61:65–170.

Daniel Kahneman. 2016. 36 heuristics and biases. *Scientists Making a Difference: One Hundred Eminent Behavioral and Brain Scientists Talk about Their Most Important Contributions*, page 171.

Svetlana Kiritchenko and Saif Mohammad. 2017. Best-worst scaling more reliable than rating scales: A case study on sentiment intensity annotation. In *Proceedings of the 55th Annual Meeting of the Association for Computational Linguistics (Volume 2: Short Papers)*, pages 465–470, Vancouver, Canada, July. Association for Computational Linguistics.

Ryan Lowe, Michael Noseworthy, Iulian Vlad Serban, Nicolas Angelard-Gontier, Yoshua Bengio, and Joelle Pineau. 2017. Towards an automatic Turing test: Learning to evaluate dialogue responses. In *Proceedings of the 55th Annual Meeting of the Association for Computational Linguistics (Volume 1: Long Papers)*, pages 1116–1126, Vancouver, Canada, July. Association for Computational Linguistics.

Jekaterina Novikova, Ondřej Dušek, and Verena Rieser. 2018. RankME: Reliable human ratings for natural language generation. In *Proceedings of the 2018 Conference of the North American Chapter of the Association for Computational Linguistics: Human Language Technologies, Volume 2 (Short Papers)*, pages 72–78, New Orleans, Louisiana, June. Association for Computational Linguistics.

Iulian V Serban, Alessandro Sordoni, Yoshua Bengio, Aaron Courville, and Joelle Pineau. 2016. Building end-to-end dialogue systems using generative hierarchical neural network models. In *Thirtieth AAAI Conference on Artificial Intelligence*.

Patrick E Shrout and Joseph L Fleiss. 1979. Intraclass correlations: uses in assessing rater reliability. *Psychological bulletin*, 86(2):420.

Anu Venkatesh, Chandra Khatri, Ashwin Ram, Fenfei Guo, Raefer Gabriel, Ashish Nagar, Rohit Prasad, Ming Cheng, Behnam Hedayatnia, Angeliki Metallinou, et al. 2018. On evaluating and comparing conversational agents. *arXiv preprint arXiv:1801.03625*.

# Studying The Effect of Emotional and Moral Language on Information Contagion during the Charlottesville Event


**Khyati Mahajan**
UNC Charlotte
kmahaja2@uncc.edu

**Samira Shaikh**
UNC Charlotte
sshaikh2@uncc.edu



## Abstract

We highlight the contribution of emotional and moral language towards information contagion online. We find that retweet count on Twitter is significantly predicted by the use of negative emotions with negative moral language. We find that a tweet is less likely to be retweeted (hence less engagement and less potential for contagion) when it has emotional language expressed as anger along with a specific type of moral language, known as authority-vice. Conversely, when sadness is expressed with authority-vice, the tweet is more likely to be retweeted. Our findings indicate how emotional and moral language can interact in predicting information contagion.


## 1 Motivation and Related Work

Previous work surrounding the use of social media for political expression and its role in spreading contagion has focused on studying emotions (Frimer et al., 2019; Boulianne, 2019), as well as the use of moral language (Tappin and McKay, 2019; Mooijman et al., 2018). These findings show that tweets that express extremist sentiments tend to be negative and express anger (Frimer et al., 2019), and that use of moral language could predict the emergence of violence during protests (Mooijman et al., 2018). Furthermore, Brady et al. (2017) studied the interaction between emotion and moral expression for three polarizing political issues, and found that the presence of moral-emotional expression in tweets led to a significant increase in their diffusion. We build upon these findings and focus on understanding the effect of emotional and moral expression on social media during an inherently political crisis event.

## 2 Data Collection and Analysis

Our context is the Unite the Right rally, held at Charlottesville, USA in August 2017. 19 people were injured and 1 person killed when a protester ran his car through a group of anti-protesters, sparking online and offline social movements. We analyze social media activity on Twitter in the month of August 2017 with a curated set of keywords including *cville*, *antifa*, *Nazi* and *neo-Nazi*, in a corpus of 500,000 tweets.

We used LIWC (Tausczik and Pennebaker, 2010) and the Moral Foundations dictionary (Graham et al., 2013) to analyze the emotional and moral language expressed in the tweets. LIWC uses lexicons to analyze emotional language including anger, anxiety, sadness and positive emotion (posemo). The Moral Foundations Dictionary works along the same principle, and provides a lexicon to analyze moral language for the categories of vice and virtue, each of which are further subdivided into categories including harm, authority and fairness. Some examples for each of these categories also present in our data are given in Table 1. The potential for overlap between the words in the lexicon and the words to describe the event we are studying could be high. To examine, we show occurrences of the lexicon words by category in Table 1 to showcase their prevalence in our data. We find that while the presence of words such as `protest` and `riot` is high (8.77%), there are other categories that are also sufficiently represented in the data (e.g. Harm-Virtue words such as `defend`, `peace` occurring 6.75%). We perform moderated regression analysis, with moral and emotion categories as independent variables. We use retweet count as our key dependent variable, since it reflects sharing behavior online, a form of information diffusion (Stieglitz and Dang-Xuan, 2012).




*Proceedings of the 55th Annual Meeting of the Association for Computational Linguistics*, pages 128–130
Florence, Italy, July 28th, 2019. ©2019 Association for Computational Linguistics

| Category | Virtue | % of posts | Vice | % of posts |
| --- | --- | --- | --- | --- |
| Harm | defend, peace, sympathy | 6.75% | violence, attack, fight | 15.39% |
| Fairness | equal, rights, justice | 1.15% | bigot, bias, segregation | 0.79% |
| Ingroup | nation, unite, family | 10.45% | terrorist, traitor, enemy | 3.68% |
| Authority | leader, supremacy, father | 6.56% | protest, riot, denounce | 8.77% |
| Purity | church, innocent, decent | 0.62% | disgust, sick, ruin | 1.32% |

Table 1: Top 3 examples of the lexicon words from each category in the Moral Foundations dictionary present in our data, and their prevalence, measured as % of posts which contain words from that category

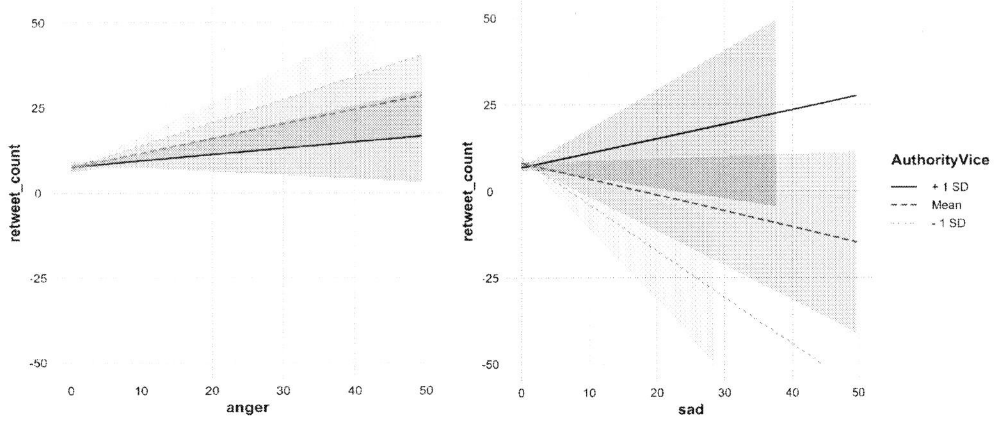


Figure 1: Interaction plots between retweet count and the usage of anger (left) and sadness (right) with authority-vice

## 3   Results and Discussion

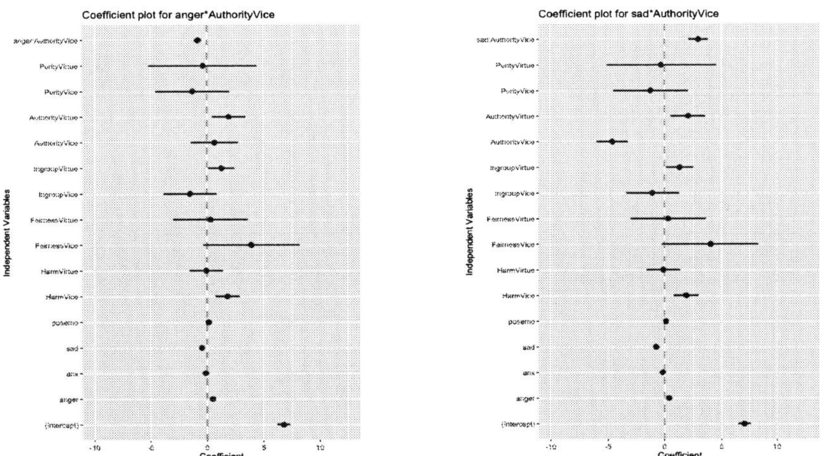


Figure 2: Coefficient charts with confidence intervals for regression analysis

We hypothesize that the presence of emotion and moral language in tweets would result in a significant effect on the retweet count (Brady et al., 2017). We report significant main effects and interactions of the independent variables and their effect on retweet count. Our multivariate regression analysis resulted in significant regression equation ($F(15, 526082) = 2.507, p < 0.001$) with an residual standard error of 278.9, indicating that each expression of anger contributes to a 0.50133 increase in retweet count as a main effect, but each expression of anger with authority-vice leads to a 0.81356 decrease in retweet count. The addition of the interaction term to the regression was found to be significant ($F = 6.682, p < 0.001$). Another significant regression equation was found ($F(15, 526082) = 2.838, p < 0.000$) with an residual standard error of 278.9, indicating that each expression of sadness contributes to a 0.73045 decrease in retweet count as a main effect, but each expression of sadness with authority-vice leads to a 2.92685 decrease in retweet count. The addition of the interaction term to the regression was found to be significant ($F = 11.643, p < 0$). These interactions are visualized in Figure 1. Other independent variables including anxiety and positive emotion for emotion and harm, fairness, purity for moral expression used together had no significant interaction effects on retweet count. All coefficients are presented in Figure 2.

## Conclusion and Future Work

The theoretical implications of these results showcase how the usage of emotion and moral language used together could affect engagement on social media, thereby affecting information contagion and diffusion through message sharing as retweeting. Our findings point towards how the expression of authority-vice (consisting of words such as `dissent`, `rebel`, `betray` etc.) in an emotionally charged environment could both negatively and positively affect message sharing, depending on the emotional context. In both significant interactions, the expression of authority-vice as moral language seems to change the predicting properties of the emotions as main effects. Additional implications of our findings are evident in the study of how content gets shared on social media. Our findings are consistent with the results of Brady et al. (2017), and showcase how moral and emotional expression used together leads to more information diffusion, especially during polarizing events. As part of future work, we will investigate more nuanced means, beyond moderated regressions, to characterize the role of emotional and moral language use on information contagion in more varied contexts.

## Acknowledgements

This research is part of a multi-phase study, which is funded by the Department of Defense's Army Research Office through federal grant #72487-RT-REP.

## References

Shelley Boulianne. 2019. Revolution in the making? social media effects across the globe. *Information, communication & society*, 22(1):39–54.

William J. Brady, Julian A. Wills, John T. Jost, Joshua A. Tucker, and Jay J. Van Bavel. 2017. Emotion shapes the diffusion of moralized content in social networks. *Proceedings of the National Academy of Sciences*, 114(28):7313–7318.

Jeremy A Frimer, Mark J Brandt, Zachary Melton, and Matt Motyl. 2019. Extremists on the left and right use angry, negative language. *Personality and Social Psychology Bulletin*, 45(8):1216–1231.

Jesse Graham, Jonathan Haidt, Sena Koleva, Matt Motyl, Ravi Iyer, Sean P Wojcik, and Peter H Ditto. 2013. Moral foundations theory: The pragmatic validity of moral pluralism. In *Advances in experimental social psychology*, volume 47, pages 55–130. Elsevier.

Marlon Mooijman, Joe Hoover, Ying Lin, Heng Ji, and Morteza Dehghani. 2018. Moralization in social networks and the emergence of violence during protests. *Nature human behaviour*, 2(6):389–396.

Stefan Stieglitz and Linh Dang-Xuan. 2012. Political communication and influence through microblogging–an empirical analysis of sentiment in twitter messages and retweet behavior. In *2012 45th Hawaii International Conference on System Sciences*, pages 3500–3509. IEEE.

Ben M Tappin and Ryan T McKay. 2019. Moral polarization and out-party hostility in the us political context. *Journal of Social and Political Psychology*, 7(1):213–245.

Yla R Tausczik and James W Pennebaker. 2010. The psychological meaning of words: Liwc and computerized text analysis methods. *Journal of language and social psychology*, 29(1):24–54.

# Mapping of Narrative Text Fields To ICD-10 Codes Using Natural Language Processing and Machine Learning


**Risuna Nkolele**
Wits University
School of CSAM
risunawisdom@gmail.com

**Turgay Celik**
Wits University
School of EIE
Turgay.Celik@wits.ac.za

**Simphiwe Zitha**
IBM Research Africa
Wits Lab
nhlanhla34@gmail.com



## Abstract

The assignment of ICD-10 codes is done manually, which is laborious and prone to errors. The use of natural language processing and machine learning approaches have been receiving increasing attention on automating the task of assigning ICD-10 codes. In this study we investigate the effect of different approaches on automating the task of assigning ICD-10 codes. To do this we use South African clinical dataset containing three narrative text fields (Clinical Summary, Presenting Complaints and Examination Findings). The following traditional machine learning algorithms, namely: Logistic Regression, Multinomial Naive Bayes, Support Vector Machine, Decision Tree, Random Forest and Extreme Gradient Boost were used as our classifiers. Our study results show the strong potential of automated ICD-10 coding from the narrative text fields. Extreme Gradient Boost outperformed other classifiers in automating the task of assigning ICD-10 codes based on the three narrative text fields with an accuracy of 79%, precision of 75% , and recall of 78%. While our worst classifier (Decision Tree) achieved the accuracy of 54%, precision of 60% and recall of 56%.


## 1 Introduction

The International Statistical Classification of Diseases and Related Health Problems 10th revision (ICD-10) code is a diagnostic classification system for diseases and health related problems recognized by the World Health Organization (WHO) [1]. ICD-10 codes are manually assigned by clinical coders [2]. Clinical coders spend time manually assigning ICD-10 codes and and due to the large data produced, this process becomes laborious and prone to errors [3]. The coding errors are associated with risks such as: billing mistakes, denied medical claims, misdiagnosis and withheld payments [4]. Thus, automating the task of assigning ICD-10 codes will make a significant contribution in the WHO healthcare system as this will help with improving the medical care system.

## 2 Dataset and Preprocessing

The dataset used in this study contains de-identified clinical records of 21460 discharges, with 2559 unique ICD-10 codes. Due to the data sparsity, we chose the ICD-10 codes that have the frequency of at least 100 discharges to carry out our study, 5148 clinical records remained with 21 unique ICD-10 codes. We perform various preprocessing phases (punctuation marks removal, special characters removal, stopwords removal and abbreviation expansion) to generate a normalized dataset. Finally, to measure the performance of our models, we use 10-folds cross-validation to train, validate, and test our models. Out of 5148 clinical records, 4634 were used for training, and validation, and 514 were used for testing.






*Proceedings of the 55th Annual Meeting of the Association for Computational Linguistics*, pages 131–135
Florence, Italy, July 28th, 2019. ©2019 Association for Computational Linguistics

## 3   Experiment Setup

The first phase in feature extraction is vocabulary building. To generate the vocabulary, we tokenize the narrative text fields in the normalize training dataset and we kept the word-document matrix with the counts of each term in one note. This is done by calculating the TF-IDF scores. After constructing the vocabulary, we construct a bag of words feature vector for each patient note. The vector dimension of each narrative text field is different.

### 3.1   Learning Algorithms and Metrics

We explore the use of a few learning algorithms for text classification, specifically, we train Logistic Regression, Multinomial Naive Bayes, Support Vector Machine with and without grid-search, Decision Tree, Random Forest as well as Extreme Gradient Boost. The feature vector constructed using bag of words are used as inputs for each algorithm. To measure our model performances, we performed several types of evaluation metrics used in multi-class classification: Precision, Recall, Accuracy and Confusion Matrix.

## 4   Results and Discussion

The following section presents the results and discussion. We present the results of our best and worst classifiers.

**Table 1:** Text classification performance representation for our best model(Extreme Gradient Boost) and worst model (Decision Tree). The description of the terminology used in this section: (Combination 1: Clinical Summary and Presenting Complaints, Combination 2: Clinical Summary and Examination Findings, Combination 3: Presenting Complaints and Examination Findings and Combination 4: Clinical Summary, Presenting Complaints and Examination Findings)

| Narrative Text Fields | Accuracy | Precision | Recall |
| --- | --- | --- | --- |
| Clinical Summary | 0.54 | 0.60 | 0.56 |
| Presenting Complaints | 0.54 | 0.60 | 0.56 |
| Examination Findings | 0.54 | 0.60 | 0.56 |
| Combination 1 | 0.60 | 0.56 | 0.54 |
| Combination 2 | 0.54 | 0.60 | 0.56 |
| Combination 3 | 0.54 | 0.60 | 0.56 |
| Combination 4 | 0.54 | 0.60 | 0.56 |

(a) Decision Tree performance

| Narrative Text Fields | Accuracy | Precision | Recall |
| --- | --- | --- | --- |
| Clinical Summary | 0.81 | 0.78 | 0.81 |
| Presenting Complaints | 0.81 | 0.78 | 0.81 |
| Examination Findings | 0.81 | 0.78 | 0.81 |
| Combination 1 | 0.81 | 0.78 | 0.81 |
| Combination 2 | 0.81 | 0.78 | 0.81 |
| Combination 3 | 0.73 | 0.68 | 0.71 |
| Combination 4 | 0.73 | 0.68 | 0.71 |

(b) Extreme Gradient Boost performance

The models performance were evaluated using 10-fold cross-validation technique. The total accuracy, precision, recall of all the models across all narrative text fields are compared in Table 1. Extreme Gradient Boost performs better amongst all the classifiers, which means it has the highest classification accuracy using the testing dataset. It correctly classifies 79% of the instances from all the predictions made, which means that 406 clinical records were correctly labeled out of the 514 clinical records across all classes. The model has the highest overall precision (75%); this implies that the Extreme Gradient Boost prediction is often correct and has a low misclassification rate. The Extreme Gradient Boost has a recall of (78%); this means that it has the highest proportion of correctly classifying ICD-10 codes. The Table 2, Figure 1 are obtained using our best machine learning model (Extreme Gradient Boost). The Extreme Gradient Boost outperformed the other models because its algorithm creates an ensemble of decision trees and average them together to obtain a more stable and accurate prediction. Extreme Gradient Boost avoids overfitting of the trees in the model as each data sample is split into different trees. Our worst model (Decision Tree) give the same results for all the narrative text fields, this implies that our model cannot distinguish difference between the vectors used for each field and it ends up predicting the same results for each narrative text.

**Table 2:** Extreme Gradient Boost-shows the calculated precision and recall of each class based on Clinical Summary.

| Narrative text | Precision | Recall | F1-score | Support |
|---|---|---|---|---|
| C15.X | 0.89 | 0.89 | 0.89 | 18 |
| C20.X | 0.75 | 0.75 | 0.75 | 12 |
| C25.X | 0.88 | 0.88 | 0.88 | 8 |
| C50.X | 0.82 | 1.00 | 0.90 | 47 |
| C73.X | 0.81 | 0.93 | 0.87 | 14 |
| E11.X | 0.00 | 0.00 | 0.00 | 9 |
| I10.X | 0.36 | 0.17 | 0.24 | 46 |
| I70.X | 0.64 | 0.93 | 0.76 | 58 |
| I71.X | 0.67 | 1.00 | 0.80 | 10 |
| I73.X | 0.33 | 0.05 | 0.08 | 21 |
| K35.X | 0.94 | 0.98 | 0.96 | 48 |
| K40.X | 0.87 | 0.93 | 0.90 | 14 |
| K43.X | 1.00 | 0.75 | 0.86 | 16 |
| K56.X | 0.80 | 0.92 | 0.86 | 13 |
| K80.X | 0.92 | 0.82 | 0.87 | 28 |
| N18.X | 0.83 | 0.96 | 0.89 | 26 |
| Q66.X | 1.00 | 0.95 | 0.98 | 21 |
| S42.X | 0.91 | 1.00 | 0.95 | 20 |
| S52.X | 1.00 | 0.82 | 0.90 | 22 |
| S72.X | 0.86 | 0.91 | 0.89 | 34 |
| S82.X | 0.94 | 1.00 | 0.97 | 29 |

Precision is referred as a percentage of the results which are relevant, meaning that if the model predicts an actual class, how often is the class correct. Table 2 demonstrates the performance of our best model based on Clinical Summary. The higher the precision value, the better the model is at predicting relevant class. We will look at the performance of our two most and less frequent ICD-10 codes. I70.X (58) and K35.X (48) have the highest frequency, Class C25.X (8) and E11.X (9) are marked as the least classes. Our most frequent classes have the precision of (0.67) and (0.94), respectively. While our least frequent ICD-10 codes have the precision of (0.88) and (0.00), respectively. Class K35.X and C25.X have the high precision meaning this classes are highly to be predicted correctly, lower misdiagnosis rate. Class I70.X has the least precision, meaning this class is often misclassified. Our model always misclassify class E11.X.

Recall is a measure of the proportion of the actual positives that are correctly classified.

This will help us outline which class has the highest and lowest proportion of being correctly classified. Both our most frequent classes (I70.X- 0.93 and K35.X- 0.98) have the highest recall values, while our two least frequent classes have least recall values (C25.X- 0.88 and E11.X - 0.00). This infers that both most frequent classes have the highest proportion of being correctly classified. Class C25.X have the lower proportion of being correctly classified and Class E11.X has 0% of being classified.

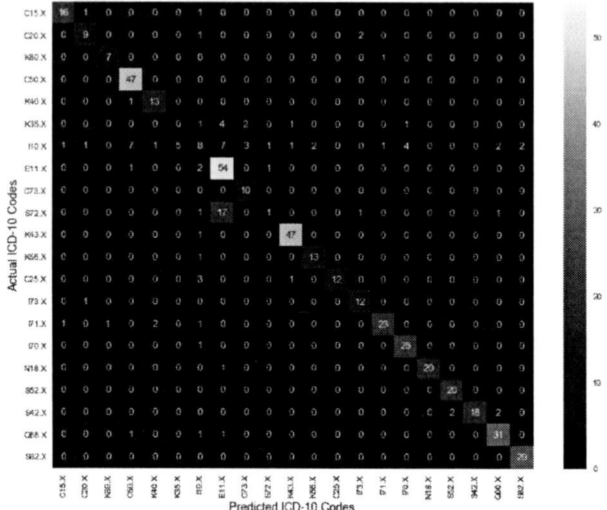

**Figure 1:** A confusion matrix describing the performance of Extreme Gradient Boost based on Clinical Summary

**Figure 1**, presents the confusion matrix of our best model based on the Clinical Summary. A confusion matrix is a table used to summarize pre-known predicted labels. It is used to evaluate a text classification models on the test data. We have 514 clinical records, but our model correctly classified 81% of clinical records (415), 19% (99) were misclassified. Our model was able to detect 83% (25/30) of the actual records in class I70.X and 0% for class K35.X. From our least frequent classes our model was able to detect 100% (12/12) actual labels for class C25.X and 64% (54/84) for class E11.X.

## 5   Conclusion and limitations

This study is motivated by the literature which has shown manual allocation of ICD-10 codes from narrative text fields is prone to errors, which sometimes results into misdiagnosis. In this study, we automated the process of allocating the ICD-10 codes from the narrative text fields extracted from Charlotte Maxeke Johannesburg Academic Hospital electronic discharge database system. We compared different traditional machine learning algorithms to check the most efficient algorithm for automating the task of assigning ICD-10 codes. We also highlight some limitations of this study. We considered only the 100 most frequent discharge summaries out of 21460 discharges present in the Electronic Discharge summary database system. Another important limitation is that the clinician allocated ICD-10 code is considered as the Gold Standard, this may lead to inaccuracies as the clinician may not have allocated the most appropriate ICD-10 code for a particular patient. However, this does not depict the accuracy of clinician coding and the real environment.

## Acknowledgements

The authors thank Dr. M Klipin and Mr. T Mbambala for their valuable help. This work is supported by DST-CSIR National e-Science Postgraduate Teaching and Training Platform.

## References

[1]  W. H. Organization et al., *The ICD-10 classification of mental and behavioural disorders: clinical descriptions and diagnostic guidelines*, Geneva: World Health Organization, **1992**.

[2]  R. Kavuluru, A. Rios, Y. Lu, *Artificial intelligence in medicine* **2015**, *65*, 155–166.

[3]  L. Virginio, J. C. dos Reis in International Conference on Data Integration in the Life Sciences, Springer, **2018**, pp. 122–134.

[4]  D. L. Adams, H. Norman, V. J. Burroughs, *Journal of the National Medical Association* **2002**, *94*, 430.

# Multitask Models for Controlling
# the Complexity of Neural Machine Translation


**Sweta Agrawal**
Department of Computer Science
University of Maryland
sweagraw@cs.umd.edu

**Marine Carpuat**
Department of Computer Science
University of Maryland
marine@cs.umd.edu


## Abstract


We introduce a machine translation task where the output is aimed at audiences of different levels of target language proficiency. We collect a novel dataset of news articles available in English and Spanish and written for diverse reading grade levels. We leverage this dataset to train multitask sequence to sequence models that translate Spanish into English targeted at an easier reading grade level than the original Spanish. We show that multitask models outperform pipeline approaches that translate and simplify text independently. [1]


## 1 Introduction

Generating text at the right level of complexity is important to make machine translation (MT) more accessible to non-native speakers, language learners (Petersen and Ostendorf, 2007; Allen, 2009) or people who suffer from language impairments (Carroll et al., 1999; Canning et al., 2000; Inui et al., 2003). Simplification has been used to improve MT by restructuring complex sentences into shorter and simpler segments that are easier to translate (Gerber and Hovy, 1998; Štajner and Popovic, 2016; Hasler et al., 2017). Closest to our goal, Marchisio et al. (2019) address the task of producing either simple or complex translations of the same input, using automatic readability scoring of parallel corpora. Our work shares their goal of controlling translation complexity, but considers a broader range of reading grade levels and simplification operations grounded in professionally edited text simplification corpora.

We collect examples of Spanish sentences paired with several English translations that span a range of complexity levels from the Newsela website, which provides professionally edited simplifications and translations. While Newsela dataset has been used to build English text simplification systems (Xu et al., 2016; Zhang and Lapata, 2017; Scarton and Specia, 2018; Nishihara et al., 2019; Zhong et al., 2020) and Spanish simplification systems (Štajner et al., 2018), we exploit the document level alignment between English and Spanish articles to construct evaluation and training samples for complexity controlled MT. By contrast with MT parallel corpora, the English and Spanish translations at different grade levels are only comparable. We adopt a multitask approach that trains a single encoder-decoder model to perform the two distinct tasks of machine translation and text simplification and evaluate it on Spanish-English complexity controlled MT. Our empirical study shows that multitask models produce better and simpler translations than pipelines of independent translation and simplification models. Scripts to replicate our model configurations and our cross-lingual segment aligner are available at https://github.com/sweta20/ComplexityControlledMT.

## 2 A Multitask Approach to Complexity Controlled MT

We define **complexity controlled MT** as a task that takes two inputs: an input language segment $s_i$ and a target complexity $c$ representing the desired reading grade level of the output. The goal is to generate a translation $s_o$ in the output language with complexity $c$.

---

[1] This paper is an abridged version of our work (Agrawal and Carpuat, 2019).






*Proceedings of the 55th Annual Meeting of the Association for Computational Linguistics*, pages 136–139
Florence, Italy, July 28th, 2019. ©2019 Association for Computational Linguistics

We model $P(s_o|s_i, c; \theta)$ as a neural encoder-decoder with attention (Bahdanau et al., 2015). Target complexity $c$ is incorporated as a special token appended to the beginning of the input sequence, which acts as a side constraint. Our multitask training configuration lets us exploit different types of training examples to train shared encoder-decoder parameters $\theta$. We use the following samples/tasks:

- Complexity controlled MT samples $(s_i, c_o, s_o)$: These are the closest samples to the task at hand, but are hard to obtain. They are used to defined the complexity-controlled MT loss, $\mathcal{L}_{CMT} = \sum_{(s_i, c_o, s_o)} \log P(s_o|s_i, c_o; \theta)$.

- MT samples $(s_i, s_o)$: These are sentence pairs drawn from parallel corpora. They are available in large quantities for many language pairs (Tiedemann, 2012) and are used to define the MT loss, $\mathcal{L}_{MT} = \sum_{(s_i, s_o)} \log P(s_o|s_i; \theta)$.

- Text simplification samples in the MT target language $(s_o, c_{s'_o}, s'_o)$ where $s'_o$ is a simplified version of complexity $c_{s'_o}$ for input $s_o$, which are likely to be available in much smaller quantities than MT samples and are used to define the simplification loss, $\mathcal{L}_{Simplify} = \sum_{(s_o, c_{s'_o}, s'_o)} \log P(s'_o|s_o, c_{s'_o}; \theta)$.

The multitask loss is simply obtained by summing the losses from individual tasks: $\mathcal{L}_{CMT} + \mathcal{L}_{MT} + \mathcal{L}_{Simplify}$.

## 3   Evaluation and Discussion

We extract segment pairs from the Newsela corpus which consists of English articles in their original form, 4 or 5 different versions re-written by professionals to suit different grade levels as well as optional translations of original and/or simplified English articles into Spanish. English and Spanish segments are aligned across complexity levels to create a bilingual dataset for training and evaluating complexity controlled MT systems. We report results using both translation and simplification metrics: BLEU (Papineni et al., 2002), SARI (Xu et al., 2016) and the Pearson Correlation between the complexity of NMT output and of reference translations (Heilman et al., 2008), where the reading grade level complexity of MT outputs and reference translations is estimated using the Automatic Readability Index (ARI).[2].

We contrast the multitask system with pipeline based approaches, where translation and simplification are treated as independent consecutive steps. In the first pipeline setup, the output from the translation model is fed as input to an English simplification model while in the second, the output from the Spanish simplification model is fed as input to an translation model.

Table 1 shows that compared to pipeline models, multitask models generate translations that better match human references according to BLEU. SARI suggests that multitask translations are simpler than baseline translations, and their resulting complexity correlates better with reference grade levels according to PCC. The "All tasks" model highlights the strengths of the multitask approach: combining training samples from many tasks yields improvements over the "Translate and Simplify" multitask model which is trained on the exact same data as the pipelines. However, even without additional training data, the multitask "Translate and Simpify" model improves over baselines mainly by simplifying the output more, which suggests that the

| Complexity cont. MT | BLEU | SARI | PCC |
|---|---|---|---|
| *Pipeline Baselines* | | | |
| Translate then Simplify | 21.98 | 30.4 | 0.436 |
| Simplify then Translate | 17.09 | 37.4 | 0.275 |
| *Multitask Models* | | | |
| Translate and Simplify | 22.51 | 44.8 | 0.572 |
| All Tasks | **22.75** | **45.0** | **0.608** |

Table 1: Compared to pipeline models, multitask models produce complexity controlled translations that better match human references (BLEU), that are simpler (SARI), and whose resulting complexity correlates better with the target grade level (PCC).

simplification component of the multitask model benefits from the additional MT training data. Table 2 illustrates simplification operations observed for a fixed grade 12 Spanish input into English with target grade levels ranging from 9 to 3. For lower grade levels such as 7 and 5, paraphrasing (e.g. "inaugurar"

---

[2]`https://github.com/mmautner/readability`

is translated as "set to open") and sentence splitting is observed. For the simplest grade level, the model deletes additional content such as "authoritations" and "historical".

| 12 | Ahora el museo Mauritshuis está por inaugurar una exposición dedicada a los autorretratos del siglo XVII, que destaca las similitudes y diferencias entre las fotos modernas y las obras de arte históricas. |
|---|---|
| 9 | Now the museum Mauritois is launching an exhibition dedicated to the 18th century author-itations, highlighting the similarities and differences between modern photos and historical artworks. |
| 7 | The museum is **now set to open** an exhibition dedicated to the 18th century authoritations, highlighting the similarities and differences between modern photos and historical artworks. |
| 5 | The museum is now set to open an exhibit dedicated to the 18th century ~~authoritations~~. **It highlights** the similarities and differences between modern photos and historical artworks. |
| 3 | The museum is now set to open an exhibit dedicated to the 18th century. It **shows** the similarities and differences between modern photos and ~~historical~~ art works. |

Table 2: Example of multi-task model outputs when translating grade 12 Spanish into increasingly simpler English: the multi-task model performs a wide range of simplification operations including <u>sentence splitting</u>, **paraphrasing** and deletion.

However, even when simplifying translations, multitask models are not yet able to exactly match the desired complexity level, and the gap between the complexity achieved and the target complexity increases with the amount of simplification required. Our datasets and models thus provide a foundation to investigate strategies for a tighter control on output complexity in future work using training objectives that explicitly addresses this gap or via modelling the type of lexical and syntactic operations performed when simplifying to a grade level.

## References


Sweta Agrawal and Marine Carpuat. 2019. Controlling text complexity in neural machine translation. In *Proceedings of the 2019 Conference on Empirical Methods in Natural Language Processing and the 9th International Joint Conference on Natural Language Processing (EMNLP-IJCNLP)*, pages 1549–1564.

David Allen. 2009. A study of the role of relative clauses in the simplification of news texts for learners of english. *System*, 37(4):585–599.

Dzmitry Bahdanau, Kyunghyun Cho, and Yoshua Bengio. 2015. Neural Machine Translation by Jointly Learning to Align and Translate. In *International Conference on Learning Representations (ICLR)*.

Yvonne Canning, John Tait, Jackie Archibald, and Ros Crawley. 2000. Cohesive generation of syntactically simplified newspaper text. In *International Workshop on Text, Speech and Dialogue*, pages 145–150. Springer.

John Carroll, Guido Minnen, Darren Pearce, Yvonne Canning, Siobhan Devlin, and John Tait. 1999. Simplifying text for language-impaired readers. In *Ninth Conference of the European Chapter of the Association for Computational Linguistics*.

Laurie Gerber and Eduard Hovy. 1998. Improving Translation Quality by Manipulating Sentence Length. In *Conference of the Association for Machine Translation in the Americas (AMTA)*.

Eva Hasler, Adrià de Gispert, Felix Stahlberg, Aurelien Waite, and Bill Byrne. 2017. Source sentence simplification for statistical machine translation. *Computer Speech & Language*, 45(Supplement C):221–235, September.

Michael Heilman, Kevyn Collins-Thompson, and Maxine Eskenazi. 2008. An analysis of statistical models and features for reading difficulty prediction. In *Proceedings of the third workshop on innovative use of NLP for building educational applications*, pages 71–79. Association for Computational Linguistics.

Kentaro Inui, Atsushi Fujita, Tetsuro Takahashi, Ryu Iida, and Tomoya Iwakura. 2003. Text simplification for reading assistance: A project note. In *Proceedings of the Second International Workshop on Paraphrasing*, pages 9–16, Sapporo, Japan, July. Association for Computational Linguistics.

Kelly Marchisio, Jialiang Guo, Cheng-I Lai, and Philipp Koehn. 2019. Controlling the reading level of machine translation output. In *Proceedings of Machine Translation Summit XVII Volume 1: Research Track*, pages 193–203.

Daiki Nishihara, Tomoyuki Kajiwara, and Yuki Arase. 2019. Controllable text simplification with lexical constraint loss. In *Proceedings of the 57th Annual Meeting of the Association for Computational Linguistics: Student Research Workshop*, pages 260–266.

Kishore Papineni, Salim Roukos, Todd Ward, and Wei-Jing Zhu. 2002. BLEU: A method for automatic evaluation of machine translation. In *Proceedings of the 40th Annual Meeting of the Association for Computational Linguistics*, Philadelphia, PA, July.

Sarah E Petersen and Mari Ostendorf. 2007. Text simplification for language learners: a corpus analysis. In *Workshop on Speech and Language Technology in Education*.

Carolina Scarton and Lucia Specia. 2018. Learning Simplifications for Specific Target Audiences. In *Proceedings of the 56th Annual Meeting of the Association for Computational Linguistics (Volume 2: Short Papers)*, volume 2, pages 712–718.

Sanja Štajner and Maja Popovic. 2016. Can text simplification help machine translation? In *Proceedings of the 19th Annual Conference of the European Association for Machine Translation*, pages 230–242.

Sanja Štajner, Marc Franco-Salvador, Paolo Rosso, and Simone Paolo Ponzetto. 2018. Cats: A tool for customized alignment of text simplification corpora. In *Proceedings of the Eleventh International Conference on Language Resources and Evaluation (LREC-2018)*.

Jörg Tiedemann. 2012. Parallel data, tools and interfaces in opus. In Nicoletta Calzolari (Conference Chair), Khalid Choukri, Thierry Declerck, Mehmet Ugur Dogan, Bente Maegaard, Joseph Mariani, Jan Odijk, and Stelios Piperidis, editors, *Proceedings of the Eight International Conference on Language Resources and Evaluation (LREC'12)*, Istanbul, Turkey, may. European Language Resources Association (ELRA).

Wei Xu, Courtney Napoles, Ellie Pavlick, Quanze Chen, and Chris Callison-Burch. 2016. Optimizing statistical machine translation for text simplification. *Transactions of the Association for Computational Linguistics*, 4:401–415.

Xingxing Zhang and Mirella Lapata. 2017. Sentence simplification with deep reinforcement learning. In *Proceedings of the 2017 Conference on Empirical Methods in Natural Language Processing*, pages 584–594, Copenhagen, Denmark, September. Association for Computational Linguistics.

Yang Zhong, Chao Jiang, Wei Xu, and Junyi Jessy Li. 2020. Discourse level factors for sentence deletion in text simplification. *ArXiv*, abs/1911.10384.

# Using Social Media For Bitcoin Day Trading Behavior Prediction

**Anna Paula Pawlickamaule and Kristen Johnson**
Department of Computer Science and Engineering
Michigan State University, East Lansing, MI 48824
`{pawlick5, kristenj}@msu.edu`

## Abstract

This abstract presents preliminary work in the application of natural language processing techniques and social network modeling for the prediction of cryptocurrency trading and investment behavior. Specifically, we are building models to use language and social network behaviors to predict if the tweets of a 24-hour period can be used to buy or sell cryptocurrency to make a profit. In this paper we present our novel task and initial language modeling studies.

## 1 Introduction

Since 2009, with the introduction of Bitcoin (BTC), cryptocurrency has increasingly gained in popularity. Many investors follow well-known cryptocurrency experts on Twitter and use their advice to guide personal investment strategies[1]. Because people are investing their money and Bitcoin prices can fluctuate quickly, resulting in real life financial gains or losses, models that can rapidly analyze trending discourse on Twitter would benefit investors.

To this end, we are in the process of developing models that use language and behavior extracted from tweets for predicting whether an investor should buy or sell their cryptocurrency. Our overall contributions upon completion of this initial work include a cryptocurrency dataset and models that incorporate both language and social network features for investment action prediction. The ultimate models are intended to comprise a weakly-supervised pipeline for day trading: given tweets from a 24-hour period, predict whether to buy or sell cryptocurrency based off of discussions from that day. This abstract presents our dataset and the initial language-based models of our eventual pipeline.

## 2 Related Works

The use of social media, specifically Twitter and its social network interactions, to show connections between online discourse and its effects on public opinion has been widely studied in NLP (Sridhar et al., 2015; Hasan and Ng, 2014; Abu-Jbara et al., 2013; Walker et al., 2012; West et al., 2014; Ritter et al., 2010) and a variety of social sciences (Bollen et al., 2011; Burch et al., 2015; Harlow and Johnson, 2011; Meraz and Papacharissi, 2013; Jang and Hart, 2015). There are many works on Twitter sentiment analysis, but closest to our work are those concerning Twitter sentiment and stock market predictions (Kouloumpis et al., 2011; Rao and Srivastava, 2012; Si et al., 2013).

There are relatively few works concerning cryptocurrency analysis and prediction. Of these, a majority use social media sentiment (Jain et al., 2018; Li et al., 2019), volume of tweets (Vidal, 2020), or both (Abraham et al., 2018) as the main feature for prediction. Furthermore, the prediction tasks are typically to predict cryptocurrency prices or whether the prices will rise or fall.

Sentiment is known to be difficult to predict on Twitter. Further, the volume of tweets can be falsely inflated by the actions of bots reporting currency prices, but not contributing to the discourse. Therefore, instead of sentiment or tweet volume, we aim to use the language directly extracted from tweets, their context, and features representing the social network behavior for a buy or sell (investment) prediction.



[1] `https://media.consensys.net/i-read-crypto-twitter-for-hours-everyday-here-are-40\`
`\-accounts-that-really-matter-cfecc681379d`



*Proceedings of the 55th Annual Meeting of the Association for Computational Linguistics*, pages 140–143
Florence, Italy, July 28th, 2019. ©2019 Association for Computational Linguistics

# 3 Datasets

## 3.1 Twitter Data Collection and Preprocessing

For this work we collected tweets related to cryptocurrency and BTC prices for trading. Rather than collect based on hashtag or keywords alone, we narrowed our research to specific time frames and user accounts. Tweets were scraped from January 2017, when Bitcoin surpassed $1,000 per coin, to its last all time high price in November 2013, until March 2020.

Within these time frames, three types of user accounts were identified for tweet collection to maximize presence of discourse for analysis and minimize tweet noise. These include influential cryptocurrency Twitter accounts, "influencers", which are well known as sources for investment information and thus should provide features for message propagation. Similarly, media accounts from traditional or online news sources are used. Lastly, we include users who frequently tweet about cryptocurrency and have at least ten thousand followers.

Before processing a total of 64,685 tweets were collected. Preprocessing consisted of two main steps. First, we standardized all tweets. This was done by controlling for capitalization, stemming, and removing URLs, character and white space noise, and stop words. Second, we removed irrelevant tweets, i.e., those tweets that do not discuss cryptocurrency trading. This was done by filtering for cryptocurrency-based keywords or hashtags (e.g., Bitcoin, BTC, Ethereum, crypto, cryptocurrency, blockchain, XRP, and altcoin), as well as identifying tweets that correspond to days with an increase or decrease of BTC price. After processing a total of 12,600 filtered tweets were used for experiments.

## 3.2 Testing Model Dataset

In this preliminary work, we aim to predict whether a user should buy or sell their cryptocurrency shares based on the current day's tweets. In order to create a labeled dataset for training and testing our models, we downloaded the price of Bitcoin from CoinMarketCap [2]. Using this information, we defined a momentum metric as:

$$momentum = \frac{Price_{close} - Price_{open}}{Price_{open}} \tag{1}$$

If the momentum on a given day increases or decreases by five percent on the following day, a script is used to automatically label the tweets as *buy* or *sell*, respectively. Using these labels, we train the models to predict a buy or sell trading behavior. To verify the accuracy of this approach to labeling, a human annotator was asked to label a subset of the tweets. We then compared the annotator labels to our automatically generated labels. The agreement with our automatically generated labels was 84.6%. We used this annotation approach in an attempt to have a fully automatic pipeline, i.e., a user could download tweets from the day, run the model, and get a prediction.

| Model | BOW | TF-IDF | DistilBERT |
|---|---|---|---|
| **Naive Bayes** | 66.54% | 61.89% | 52.89% |
| **Random Forest** | 78.24% | 77.18% | 77.12% |
| **Neural Network** | 50.11% | 49.8% | 70.17% |

Table 1: The columns represent the accuracy of each model when using either a bag-of-words (BOW), TF-IDF vector, or DistilBERT (Sanh et al., 2019) representation of the tweets as features.


# 4 Experimental Results

This section describes our initial models and features that will serve as baselines for improvement in future models. Table 1 shows the results of using Naive Bayes, Random Forest, and a simple neural network with two dense layers, with either BOW, TF-IDF, or DistilBERT representations of the tweets as features. For the experiment, the data was randomly shuffled and split into 80% training and 20% testing

---

[2]`https://coinmarketcap.com/`

sets in all the experiments. Interestingly, the Random Forest is more accurate than the hyperparameter-tuned Neural Network models. Further the accuracy of Naive Bayes decreased using DistilBert, but improved significantly the Neural Network. Based on this we are currently exploring a probabilistic graphical model and graphical neural network, in addition to non-language features that incorporate aspects of social network interaction that influences crypto market movements.

## 5   Future Work and Conclusion

This abstract presents our current work in progress. Predicting day trading behavior, i.e., whether to buy or sell stock, is a complicated task, especially in a volatile asset such as cryptocurrency. Our promising results show that language can be used to successfully model cryptocurrency trading behavior, however there is still room for improvement. We are in the process of adding more informative features extracted from Twitter, including temporal and social information, as well as contextual representations. Furthermore, we are exploring the use of economic framing as a predictive feature. We hope to show that how influential people speak on Twitter affects cryptocurrency trading and that this online discourse can be used for guiding personal investments.

## References


Jethin Abraham, Daniel Higdon, John Nelson, and Juan Ibarra. 2018. Cryptocurrency price prediction using tweet volumes and sentiment analysis. In *SMU Data Science Review: Vol. 1: No. 3, Article 1*.

Amjad Abu-Jbara, Ben King, Mona Diab, and Dragomir Radev. 2013. Identifying opinion subgroups in arabic online discussions. In *Proc. of ACL*.

Johan Bollen, Huina Mao, and Alberto Pepe. 2011. Modeling public mood and emotion: Twitter sentiment and socio-economic phenomena. In *Proc. of AAAI Conference on Weblogs and Social Media*.

Lauren M. Burch, Evan L. Frederick, and Ann Pegoraro. 2015. Kissing in the carnage: An examination of framing on twitter during the vancouver riots. *Journal of Broadcasting & Electronic Media*, 59(3):399–415.

Summer Harlow and Thomas Johnson. 2011. The arab spring— overthrowing the protest paradigm? how the new york times, global voices and twitter covered the egyptian revolution. *International Journal of Communication*, 5(0).

Kazi Saidul Hasan and Vincent Ng. 2014. Why are you taking this stance? identifying and classifying reasons in ideological debates. In *Proc. of EMNLP*.

Arti Jain, Shashank Tripathi, Harsh Dhardwivedi, and Pranav Saxena. 2018. Forecasting price of cryptocurrencies using tweets sentiment analysis.

S. Mo Jang and P. Sol Hart. 2015. Polarized frames on "climate change" and "global warming" across countries and states: Evidence from twitter big data. *Global Environmental Change*, 32:11–17, 5.

Efthymios Kouloumpis, Theresa Wilson, and Johanna Moore. 2011. Twitter sentiment analysis: The good the bad and the omg! In *Proc. of AAAI Conference on Weblogs and Social Media*.

Tianyu Ray Li, Anup S. Chamrajnagar, Xander R. Fong, Nicholas R. Rizik, and Feng Fu. 2019. Sentiment-based prediction of alternative cryptocurrency price fluctuations using gradient boosting tree model. *Frontiers in Physics*, 7:98.

Sharon Meraz and Zizi Papacharissi. 2013. Networked gatekeeping and networked framing on #egypt. *The International Journal of Press/Politics*, 18(2):138–166.

Tushar Rao and Saket Srivastava. 2012. Analyzing stock market movements using twitter sentiment analysis. In *Proc. of International Conference on Advances in Social Networks Analysis and Mining*.

Alan Ritter, Colin Cherry, and Bill Dolan. 2010. Unsupervised modeling of twitter conversations. In *Proc. of NAACL*.

Victor Sanh, Lysandre Debut, Julien Chaumond, and Thomas Wolf. 2019. Distilbert, a distilled version of bert: smaller, faster, cheaper and lighter.

Jianfeng Si, Arjun Mukherjee, Bing Liu, Qing Li, Huayi Li, and Xiaotie Deng. 2013. Exploiting topic based twitter sentiment for stock prediction. In *Proc. of 51st Annual Meeting of the Association for Computational Linguistics*.

Dhanya Sridhar, James Foulds, Bert Huang, Lise Getoor, and Marilyn Walker. 2015. Joint models of disagreement and stance in online debate. In *Proc. of ACL*.

Tiago Vidal. 2020. How traders can use twitter to anticipate bitcoin price moves, volume. 02.

Marilyn A. Walker, Pranav Anand, Robert Abbott, and Ricky Grant. 2012. Stance classification using dialogic properties of persuasion. In *Proc. of NAACL*.

Robert West, Hristo S Paskov, Jure Leskovec, and Christopher Potts. 2014. Exploiting social network structure for person-to-person sentiment analysis. *TACL*.

# HausaMT v1.0: Towards English–Hausa Neural Machine Translation


**Adewale Akinfaderin**
Data Duality
waleakinfaderin@gmail.com



## Abstract

Neural Machine Translation (NMT) for low-resource languages suffers from low performance because of the lack of large amounts of parallel data and language diversity. To contribute to ameliorating this problem, we built a baseline model for English–Hausa machine translation, which is considered a task for low–resource language. The Hausa language is the second largest Afro–Asiatic language in the world after Arabic and it is the third largest language for trading across a larger swath of West Africa countries, after English and French. In this paper, we curated different datasets containing Hausa–English parallel corpus for our translation. We trained baseline models and evaluated the performance of our models using the Recurrent and Transformer encoder–decoder architecture with two tokenization approaches: standard word–level tokenization and Byte Pair Encoding (BPE) subword tokenization.


## 1   Introduction

Hausa is a language spoken in the western part of Africa. It belongs to the Afro–Asiatic phylum and it is the second most spoken native language on the continent, after Swahili. The language is spoken by more than 40 million people as a first language and about 15 million people use it as a second and third language. Most of the speakers are concentrated in Nigeria, Niger and Chad – all resulting to both anglophone and francophone influences (Sabiu et al., 2018; Eberhard et al., 2019). Our work on curating datasets and creating evaluation benchmark for English–Hausa Neural Machine Translation (NMT) is inspired by the socio–linguistic facts of the Hausa language. Hausa has been referred to as the largest internal political unit in Africa. There has been extensive linguistic academic research on Hausa and the language benefits from the existence of trans–border communication in the West African Sahel belt and the availability of international radio stations like the BBC Hausa and Voice of America Hausa (Odoje, 2013).

The exponential growth of social media platforms have eased communication among users. However, the advances in technological adoption have also informed the need to translate human languages. In low–resource countries, the language inequality can be ameliorated by using machine translation to bridge gaps in technological, political and socio–economic advancements (Odoje, 2016). The recent successes in NMT over Phrased–Based Statistical Machine Translation (PBSMT) for high–resource data conditions can be leveraged to explore best practices, data curation and evaluation benchmark for low–resource NMT tasks (Bentivogli et al., 2016; Isabelle et al., 2017). Using the JW300, Tanzil, Tatoeba and Wikimedia public datasets, we trained and evaluated baseline NMT models for Hausa language.

## 2   Related Works

***Hausa Words Embedding***:   Researchers have recently curated datasets and trained word embedding models for the Hausa language. The results from this trained models have been


4th Widening NLP Workshop, Annual Meeting of the Association for Computational Linguistics, ACL 2020





*Proceedings of the 55th Annual Meeting of the Association for Computational Linguistics*, pages 144–147
Florence, Italy, July 28th, 2019. ©2019 Association for Computational Linguistics

promising, with approximately 300% increase in prediction accuracy over other baseline models (Abdulmumin & Galadanci, 2019).

***Masakhane***:  Due to the linguistic complexity and morphological properties of languages native to continent of Africa, using abstractions from successful resource–rich cross–lingual machine translation tasks often fail for low–resource NMT task. The Masakhane project was created to bridge this gap by focusing on facilitating open–source NMT research efforts for African languages (∀, Orife et al., 2020).

## 3  Dataset Description

For the HausaMT task, we used the JW300, Tanzil, Tatoeba and Wikimedia public datasets. The JW300 dataset is a crawl of the parallel data available on Jehovah Witness' website. Most of the data are from the magazines, *Awake!* and *Watchtower*, and they cover a diverse range of societal topics in a religious context (Agić & Vulić, 2019). The Tatoeba database is a collection of parallel sentences in 330 languages (Raine, 2018). The dataset is crowdsourced and published under a Creative Commons Attribution 2.0 license. The Tanzil dataset is a multilingual text aimed at producing a highly verified multi-text of the Quran text (Zarrabi-Zadeh et al., 2007). The Wikimedia dataset are parallel sentence pairs extracted and filtered from noisy parallel and comparable wikipedia copora (Wolk & Marasek, 2014). For this work, we trained on two datasets which are: 1) the JW300 as our baseline, and 2) All the datasets combined. The number of tokens, number of sentences and statistical properties of the datasets are in Table 1.

| Dataset | Sentence Length (Mean ± Std) | | Tokens | | Sentences |
|---|---|---|---|---|---|
| | English | Hausa | English | Hausa | |
| JW300 | 18.11 ± 10.53 | 20.14 ± 11.57 | 4,051,322 | 4,506,787 | 223,723 |
| All* | 19.71 ± 24.31 | 21.28 ± 24.60 | 6,919,805 | 7,471,256 | 351,024 |

Table 1: Dataset summary.*Combination of JW300, Tanzil, Tatoeba and Wikimedia datasets.

## 4  Experiments and Results

For our baseline model, we trained a recurrent-based model with the Long Short-Term Memory (LSTM) network as our encoder and decoder type with the Luong attention mechanism (Luong et al., 2015). To achieve an improved benchmark, we also trained a Transformer encoder–decoder model. The Transformer is based on attention mechanism and the training time is significantly faster than architectures based on convolutional or recurrent networks (Vaswani et al., 2017). For the hyperparameters used to train both the recurrent and transformer based architecture, we used an embedding size of 256, hidden units of 256, batch size of 4096 and an encoder and decoder depth of 6 respectively.

| Dataset | Model | BPE | | Word | |
|---|---|---|---|---|---|
| | | *dev* | *test* | *dev* | *test* |
| JW300 | Recurrent | 20.06 | 19.39 | 25.36 | 24.75 |
| | Transformer | **21.33** | **20.38** | **28.71** | **28.06** |
| All | Recurrent | 31.89 | 33.48 | 40.78 | 42.29 |
| | Transformer | **31.91** | 32.42 | **44.42** | **45.98** |

Table 2: BLEU scores for BPE and word-level tokenization. Best scores of the Transformer model against the Recurrent are highlighted in bold

To preprocess the parallel corpus, we used the standard word–level tokenization and Byte Pair Encoding (BPE) (Gage, 1994). The BPE is a subword tokenization which has become a successful choice in translation tasks. The model was trained based on the 4000 BPE tokens used on a recent machine translation study for South African languages (Martinus & Abbott, 2019). To train our model, the Joey NMT minimalist toolkit, which is open source and based on PyTorch was used (Kreutzer et al., 2019). The models were trained using a Tesla P100 GPU. The model training for the baseline and repeated tasks (datasets & tokenization type) took between 5-9 hours for each run.

## 5 Conclusion and Future Work

Evaluating the model on the test set, we observed that the word–level tokenization outperform the BPE by a BLEU score factor of ~1.27–1.42 times (Table 2). The qualities of the English to Hausa translations using both word–level and BPE subword tokenizations were rated positively by first language speakers. Table 3 shows some of the translations example.

| | |
|---|---|
| **Source:** | This is normal, because they themselves have not been anointed. |
| **Reference:** | Hakan ba abin mamaki ba ne don ba a shafa su da ruhu mai tsarki ba. |
| **Hypothesis:** | Wannan ba daidai ba ne, domin ba a shafe su ba. |
| **Source:** | A white - haired man in a frock coat appears on screen. |
| **Reference:** | Wani mutum mai furfura ya bayyana da dogon kwat a majigin. |
| **Hypothesis:** | Wani mutum mai suna da wani mutum mai suna da ke cikin mota yana da nisa a cikin kabari |
| **Source:** | Why is that of vital importance? |
| **Reference:** | Me ya sa hakan yake da muhimmanci? |
| **Hypothesis:** | Me ya sa wannan yake da muhimmanci? |

Table 3: Example Translations.

A significant portion of both the training and test datasets are from the the JW300 parallel data, which are religious texts. We acknowledge that for us to reach a viable state of real-world translation quality, we need to evaluate our model on "general" Hausa data. However, parallel data for other out-of-domain areas does not exist. High-yielding avenue for future work include evaluating on English texts and crowd-sourcing L1 speakers to manually evaluate the quality of the translations by editing. The post edited translation can then be used as the reference to calculate the evaluation metric. Other future work include carrying out an empirical study to explore the effect of word–level and subword tokenizations. Other methods such as the linguistically motivated vocabulary reduction (LMVR) have shown to perform better for languages in the Afro–Asiatic family (Ataman & Federico, 2018). The datasets, pre–trained models, and configurations are available on Github.[1]

## Acknowledgements

The author would like to thank Gabriel Idakwo for the qualitative analysis of the translations.

## References

David M. Eberhard, Gary F. Simons, and Charles D. Fennig (eds.). 2019. *Ethnologue: Languages of the world. twenty-second edition.* URL: http://www.ethnologue.com.

Ibrahim T. Sabiu, Fakhrul A. Zainol, and Mohammed S. Abdullahi. 2018. *Hausa People of Northern Nigeria and their Development.* Asian People Journal (APJ), eISSN : 2600-8971, Volume 1, Issue 1, PP 179-189.

Clement Odoje. 2013. *Language Inequality: Machine Translation as the Bridging Bridge for African languages.* 4, 01.

---

[1]https://github.com/WalePhenomenon/Hausa-NMT

Clement Odoje. 2016. *The Peculiar Challenges of SMT to African Languages* . s. ICT, Globalisation and the Study of Languages and Linguistics in Africa, PP 223.

Luisa Bentivogli, Arianna Bisazza, Mauro Cettolo, and Marcello Federico. 2016. *Neural versus Phrase-Based Machine Translation Quality: a Case Study.* Proceedings of the 2016 Conference on Empirical Methods in Natural Language Processing, PP 257-267, Austin, Texas.

Pierre Isabelle, Colin Cherry,and George Foster. 2017. *A Challenge Set Approach to Evaluating Machine Translation.* Proceedings of the 2017 Conference on Empirical Methods in Natural Language Processing, PP 2486âĂŞ2496, Copenhagen, Denmark.

Idris Abdulmumin and Bashir S. Galadanci. 2019. *hauWE: Hausa Words Embedding for Natural Language Processing.* 2019 2nd International Conference of the IEEE Nigeria Computer Chapter, PP. 1-6, Zaria, Nigeria.

∀, Iroro F. O. Orife, Julia Kreutzer, Blessing Sibanda, Kathleen Siminyu, Laura Martinus, Jamiil Toure Ali, Jade Abbott, Vukosi Marivate, Salomon Kabongo, Musie Meressa, Espoir Murhabazi, Orevaoghene Ahia, Elan van Biljon, Arshath Ramkilowan, Adewale Akinfaderin, Alp ÃŰktem, Wole Akin, Ghollah Kioko, Kevin Degila, Herman Kamper, Bonaventure Dossou, Chris Emezue, Kelechi Ogueji, and Abdallah Bashir. 2020. *Masakhane – Machine Translation For Africa.* To appear in the Proceedings of the AfricaNLP Workshop, International Conference on Learning Representations (ICLR 2020).

Željko Agić and Ivan Vulić. 2019. *JW300: A Wide-Coverage Parallel Corpus for Low-Resource Languages.* Proceedings of the 57th Annual Meeting of the Association for Computational Linguistics, PP 3204âĂŞ3210, Florence, Italy.

Paul Raine. 2018. *Building Sentences with Web 2.0 and the Tatoeba Database.* Accents Asia, 10(2), PP 2-7.

Hamid Zarrabi-Zadeh, Abbas Ahmadi, Morteza Bagheri, Yousef Daneshvar, Mohammad Derakhshani, Mohammad Fakharzadeh, Ehsan Fathi, Yusof Ganji, Mojtaba Haghighi, Nasser Lashgarian, Zahra Mousavian, Mohsen Saboorian, Yaser Shanjani, Mohammad-Reza Nikseresht, and Mahdi Mousavian. 2007. *Tanzil Project.* URL: `http://tanzil.net/docs/home`.

Krzysztof Wolk and Krzysztof Marasek. 2014. *Building Subject-aligned Comparable Corpora and Mining it for Truly Parallel Sentence Pairs.* Procedia Technology, Volume 18, PP 126-132.

Ashish Vaswani, Noam Shazeer, Niki Parmar, Jakob Uszkoreit, Llion Jones, Aidan N. Gomez, ÅĄukasz Kaiser, and Illia Polosukhin. 2017. *Attention is All you Need.* In 31st Conference on Neural Information Processing Systems (NIPS 2017), Long Beach, CA, USA.

Philip Gage. 1994. *A New Algorithm for Data Compression.* C Users J., 12(2), PP. 23âĂŞ38.

Laura Martinus and Jade Abbott. 2019. *A Focus on Neural Machine Translation for African Languages.* CoRR, abs/1906.05685. URL: `http://arxiv.org/abs/1906.05685`.

Julia Kreutzer, Joost Bastings, and Stefan Riezler. 2019. *Joey NMT: A Minimalist NMT Toolkit for Novices.* Proceedings of the 2019 EMNLP and the 9th IJCNLP (System Demonstrations), pages 109âĂŞ114, Hong Kong, China.

Duygu Ataman and Marcello Federico. 2018. *An Evaluation of Two Vocabulary Reduction Methods for Neural Machine Translation.* Proceedings of AMTA 2018, vol. 1: MT Research Track, Pp 97-110, Boston, MA.

Thang Luong, Hieu Pham, and Christopher D. Manning. 2015. *Effective Approaches to Attention-based Neural Machine Translation.* Proceedings of the 2015 Conference on Empirical Methods in Natural Language Processing, Pp 1412 - 1421, Lisbon, Portugal.

# Outcomes of coming out: Analyzing stories of LGBTQ+


**Tanvi Anand***
Manipal Institute of Technology
MAHE, Manipal, India
tanviaanand@gmail.com

**Krithika Ramesh***
Manipal Institute of Technology
MAHE, Manipal, India
kramesh.tlw@gmail.com



## Abstract

The Internet is frequently used as a platform through which opinions and views on various topics can be expressed. One such topic that draws controversial attention is LGBTQ+ rights. This paper attempts to analyze the reaction that members of the LGBTQ+ community face when they reveal their gender or sexuality, or in other words, when they 'come out of the closet'. We aim to classify the experiences shared by them as positive or negative. We collected data from various sources, primarily Twitter. We have applied deep learning techniques and compared the results to other classifiers, and the results obtained from applying classical sentiment analysis techniques to it.


## 1 Introduction

People who belong to the LGBTQ community often have inhibitions about sharing their sexual or gender identity with others, as it isn't always received favorably. Through our research, we attempt to gauge the reaction that a person of the LGBTQ+ community receives on 'coming out of the closet', that is to say, when they reveal their sexual/gender orientation to someone. The dataset consists of 696 preprocessed statements by people who came out of the closet and shared their experiences online. We've tested a variety of unsupervised and supervised learning techniques on this data to assess the sentiment of the reaction. The primary motivation for this research work is to provide a more effective method for social media surveys that assess the receptiveness to the LGBTQ+ community.

## 2 Dataset

The dataset is compiled from two sources, with Twitter being the primary source. A part of the dataset is composed of tweets extracted using the Twitter API. The tweets contained the hashtags #comingout, #outofthecloset and their tense variations, as used by (Anand et al., 2019). The remainder of the dataset was gathered from a forum [1] that catered specifically to allowing people to share their experience of coming out of the closet. In total, there are 696 items present in this dataset. The dataset was manually annotated according to whether or not the immediate reaction (of the person being spoken about in the text) was negative or positive. For example, an item like "My mom kicked me out of the house and called me a sinner when I told her I was gay" would be a negative reaction by the "mom". The annotation was done by two people, a student of gender studies and the other a student of clinical psychology. An item was marked as pos, for positive, if it conveyed acceptance or support of their sexuality or gender identity, and neg, for negative, if any form of dissent was expressed toward this reveal. 37.35% of the items were tagged pos. The preprocessing pipeline for cleaning the tweets is as follows

- **Tokenization and Removal of Hyperlinks** The data was initialized split into tokens, using a specific set of punctuation as delimiters. Any hyperlinks attached to the tweet, punctuation marks, digits and special characters were removed.

---


* denotes equal contribution.
[1] https://whenicameout.com/





*Proceedings of the 55th Annual Meeting of the Association for Computational Linguistics*, pages 148–150
Florence, Italy, July 28th, 2019. ©2019 Association for Computational Linguistics

| Classifier | MNB | RF | Log Reg | LSVM | MLP | Bi-LSTM | LSTM | GRU |
| --- | --- | --- | --- | --- | --- | --- | --- | --- |
| Accuracy | 78.15% | 75.28% | 79.88% | 77.58% | 79.31% | 85.71% | 78.57% | 80% |

Table 1: Classification Results

- **Segmentation of Hashtags** We use the ekphrasis [2] library to segment and isolate the words contained in a hashtag. For example, the phrase '#outandproud' is separated into three words, and, 'out', 'and', 'proud' are treated as individual tokens and added to the preprocessed data (Baziotis et al., 2017). Often, a lot of useful information is lost when these words from the hashtags are not taken into consideration.

- **Removal of stopwords** We use the corpus of stopwords imported from the NLTK [3] library to filter them out.

- **Lemmatization** We use the wordnet lemmatizer from the NLTK library to get word lemmas.

## 3 Methodology

The objective is to classify the sentiment into two categories - pos or neg. We trained different models for this task and attempted to draw a comparison between traditional machine learning techniques (Kibriya et al., 2004), (Joachims, 1998), (Indra et al., 2016), (Breiman, 2001) and deep learning models (Zhang et al., 2018). These algorithms rely on feature extraction using methods such as the bag-of-words, or the TF-IDF approach to build a vocabulary using which the classifier attempts to categorize the data. However, they are susceptible to failure as the approaches for feature extraction do not take into account the order of the words, merely the frequency with which they occur. These approaches also have other drawbacks, such as not being able to detect the similarity between words, or the semantic relation between them.

In light of this, deep learning models could potentially prove to be better alternatives, and we test this theory with the use of a range of architectures, such as the Multilayer Perceptron (MLP), LSTMs (both unidirectional and bidirectional) and Gated Recurrent Units (GRUs). The architecture for the LSTMs and GRUs utilizes an embedding of the same size as that of the vocabulary, with 400 dimensions to it. There are 100 hidden units in the sequence model, the output of which is flattened and subsequently passed through 3 hidden layers, of 128, 64 and 32 units, with a dropout value of 0.5. We have utilized the sigmoid activation function in the output layer and the adam optimizer. The dataset is split in a 9:1 ratio training:test set ratio, with 10% of the data being reserved for evaluating the effectiveness of the model on unseen data.

The hyperparameters for the probabilistic machine learning models were chosen using grid search, whereas the hyperparameters for the deep learning models were chosen using manual hyperparameter tuning.

| Text | Label | MNB | RF | SVM | Log Reg | MLP | Bi-LSTM | GRU | LSTM |
| --- | --- | --- | --- | --- | --- | --- | --- | --- | --- |
| Came out to Mum and Dad and Sister today. 100% support from my wonderful sister. Mum and Dad are processing but say the love me. Such a relief #comingout #TransAwarenessWeek | pos | pos | pos | pos | pos | pos | pos | pos | pos |
| When I came out, I realized what disappointment looked like on a person's face. My mom's. Today… we're still working through it. | neg | neg | pos | pos | neg | neg | neg | pos | neg |
| When I came out to my best friend, he said, "Well, about god damn time." He knew long before me. | pos | pos | pos | pos | pos | pos | pos | pos | pos |
| I didn't come out. I was outed by my high school vice-principal, first to my mom, then to the entire student body. | neg | neg | pos | neg | neg | neg | neg | neg | neg |

Table 2: Sample predictions for classifiers

## 4 Results and Conclusion

The classification accuracy for various methods are shown in Table 2. The deep learning models are shown to outperform these classical machine learning algorithms by a significant margin, owing to the

---

[2] https://pypi.org/project/ekphrasis/

[3] https://www.nltk.org/

fact that the deep learning models consider the structure of the sentence and semantic relations.

In this work, we explored various methods to test their effectiveness in surveying and evaluating data to measure the degree of acceptance that the LGBTQ+ community receives from family, friends, and society in general on revealing their identity to them. We look to delve further into this work by testing other deep learning architectures to obtain better results, and to find a way to be able to generalize these models so that they may be used in surveying data related to similar social topics as well.

## References


Tanvi Anand, Krithika Ramesh, and Sanjay Singh. 2019. Out of the closet: Lexicon based sentiment analysis on tweets about. In *TENCON 2019-2019 IEEE Region 10 Conference*, pages 731–736.

Christos Baziotis, Nikos Pelekis, and Christos Doulkeridis. 2017. Datastories at semeval-2017 task 4: Deep lstm with attention for message-level and topic-based sentiment analysis. In *Proceedings of the 11th international workshop on semantic evaluation (SemEval-2017)*, pages 747–754.

Leo Breiman. 2001. Random forests. *Mach. Learn.*, 45(1):5–32, October.

ST Indra, Liza Wikarsa, and Rinaldo Turang. 2016. Using logistic regression method to classify tweets into the selected topics. In *2016 International Conference on Advanced Computer Science and Information Systems (ICACSIS)*, pages 385–390. IEEE.

Thorsten Joachims. 1998. Text categorization with support vector machines: Learning with many relevant features. In *European conference on machine learning*, pages 137–142. Springer.

Ashraf M Kibriya, Eibe Frank, Bernhard Pfahringer, and Geoffrey Holmes. 2004. Multinomial naive bayes for text categorization revisited. In *Australasian Joint Conference on Artificial Intelligence*, pages 488–499. Springer.

Lei Zhang, Shuai Wang, and Bing Liu. 2018. Deep learning for sentiment analysis: A survey. *Wiley Interdisciplinary Reviews: Data Mining and Knowledge Discovery*, 8(4):e1253.

# An Evaluation of Subword Segmentation Strategies for Neural Machine Translation of Morphologically Rich Languages


**Aquia Richburg**
University of Maryland
arichbu1@umd.edu

**Ramy Eskander**
Columbia University
rnd2110@columbia.edu

**Smaranda Muresan**
Columbia University
smara@columbia.edu

**Marine Carpuat**
University of Maryland
marine@cs.umd.edu


## Abstract


Byte-Pair Encoding (BPE) (Sennrich et al., 2016) has become a standard pre-processing step when building neural machine translation systems. However, it is not clear whether this is an optimal strategy in all settings. We conduct a controlled comparison of subword segmentation strategies for translating two low-resource morphologically rich languages (Swahili and Turkish) into English. We show that segmentations based on a unigram language model (Kudo, 2018) yield comparable BLEU and better recall for translating rare source words than BPE.


## 1 Problem Overview

While applying BPE segmentation is the default strategy in neural Machine Translation (MT) (Sennrich et al., 2016; Sennrich and Zhang, 2019), prior work suggests that tokenization and segmentation choices matter when processing morphologically-rich languages. Güler and Cüneyd Tantuğ (2020) show that segmentation strategies that more explicitly represent the compositionality of words result in word embeddings that improve text classifiers and language models for Turkish. When translating Arabic into English, Oudah et al. (2019) show that the Penn Arabic Treebank segmentation yields the best translation quality with statistical MT models, while word-based translation outperforms other techniques (including BPE) for neural MT models. Others have attempted to model morphological inflections as part of novel neural MT architectures, especially when translating into morphologically rich languages such as Arabic, Czech and Turkish (Ataman et al., 2020). Banerjee and Bhattacharyya (2018) construct a hybrid subword segmentation strategy by combining BPE with the morphological analyzer Morfessor for translations into Hindi and Bengali. Tamchyna et al. (2017) and Huck et al. (2017) also directly model morphological inflections in the target language for Czech and German.

In this work, we measure the impact of input representations when translating from two low-resource morphologically rich languages, Turkish and Swahili, into English.

- We compare BPE with unigram language model (LM) tokenization (Kudo, 2018). These methods differ in how they generate the closed set of subwords that will define the neural MT model vocabulary, and in how a given sequence is segmented into subwords. **BPE** is the most naïve approach inspired by compression strategies, and defines a subword vocabulary by greedily merging most frequent character sequences. BPE tokenization is a simple deterministic process which consists in applying the learned merge operations greedily. **Unigram LM segmentation** prunes an initial subword space of all substrings observed during training based on their contribution to a unigram LM loss. New inputs are tokenized by finding the sequence of subwords that maximize the unigram LM probability of the input sequence.

- We also evaluate how initial segmentations of the data impact the subword model: we compare a standard rule-based tokenization with morpheme segmentations obtained using the MorphAGram **unsupervised morphological segmentation system** (Eskander et al., 2020).

151


*Proceedings of the 55th Annual Meeting of the Association for Computational Linguistics*, pages 151–155
Florence, Italy, July 28th, 2019. ©2019 Association for Computational Linguistics

| | SW-EN | | | | TR-EN | | | |
| | BPE | | Unigram LM | | BPE | | Unigram LM | |
| | ANALYSIS1 | ANALYSIS2 | ANALYSIS1 | ANALYSIS2 | Newstest16 | Newstest17 | Newstest16 | Newstest17 |
|---|---|---|---|---|---|---|---|---|
| *Baseline Segmentation* | | | | | | | | |
| Tokenization | **28.26 ± 0.15** | **29.17 ± 0.17** | **28.22 ± 0.19** | **28.98 ± 0.12** | **16.95 ± 0.07** | **16.75 ± 0.15** | **16.97 ± 0.13** | **16.75 ± 0.06** |
| *Morpheme Segmentation* | | | | | | | | |
| Multi-way Cascaded | 25.35 ± 0.39 | 26.26 ± 0.31 | 24.35 ± 0.11 | 25.33 ± 0.07 | 16.68 ± 0.11 | 16.35 ± 0.09 | 16.75 ± 0.07 | 16.35 ± 0.09 |
| Three-way Cascaded | 26.07 ± 0.31 | 26.68 ± 0.26 | 24.60 ± 0.95 | 25.45 ± 0.78 | 16.79 ± 0.17 | 16.54 ± 0.11 | 16.71 ± 0.04 | 16.42 ± 0.11 |
| Multi-way Standard | 25.24 ± 0.14 | 26.37 ± 0.10 | 23.88 ± 0.23 | 25.04 ± 0.17 | 16.68 ± 0.13 | 16.59 ± 0.09 | 16.69 ± 0.06 | 16.33 ± 0.10 |
| Three-way Standard | 25.73 ± 0.31 | 26.71 ± 0.16 | 25.44 ± 0.13 | 26.36 ± 0.07 | 16.83 ± 0.11 | 16.66 ± 0.12 | 16.70 ± 0.11 | 16.44 ± 0.07 |
| Multi-way Scholar-Seeded | 25.35 ± 0.36 | 26.30 ± 0.48 | 24.34 ± 0.12 | 25.21 ± 0.11 | 15.64 ± 0.12 | 15.54 ± 0.09 | 15.74 ± 0.16 | 15.39 ± 0.08 |
| Three-way Scholar-Seeded | 25.90 ± 0.19 | 26.83 ± 0.26 | 25.08 ± 0.26 | 26.04 ± 0.24 | 16.08 ± 0.08 | 15.89 ± 0.11 | 16.19 ± 0.05 | 15.65 ± 0.03 |

Table 1: BLEU scores of SW-EN and TR-EN systems using (a) BPE or unigram LM subword segmentations (columns), on top of data that is (b) either tokenized or segmented into morphemes (rows). Averages taken over 5 random initializations.

## 2 Empirical Study

**Tasks and Data**   Our translation tasks are {Swahili, Turkish} (SW,TR) into English. The SW-EN data comes from the IARPA MATERIAL program[1] with 24400 sentence pairs for training, and test sets are extracted from the MATERIAL ANALYSIS sets. The validation set is held-out data from MATERIAL BUILD. The Turkish-English data comes from the WMT news translation task (Bojar et al., 2017) with 207373 sentence pairs for training, and using newstest2016 and newstest2017 as test sets. We use newsdev2016 as a validation set. We apply tokenization and true-casing using the Moses toolkit.

**Neural MT Models**   are attentional encoder-decoders (Bahdanau et al., 2014), with 2 LSTM layers and 512-dimensional hidden layers and embeddings. We utilize source-target-softmax weight tying and layer normalization. Training uses Adam with an initial learning rate of 0.001.

**Subword Models**   Based on prior work and preliminary experiments, we apply joint source-target subword segmentation model to the tokenized true-cased text.[2] Unigram language model segmentations are obtained using SentencePiece (Kudo and Richardson, 2018), with a vocabulary size of 8000 and 16000 for SW-EN and TR-EN. BPE models are built using subword-nmt (Sennrich et al., 2016), with 10000 and 30000 merge operations for SW-EN and TR-EN, respectively.

**Morphological Analysis**   We use MorphAGram (Eskander et al., 2020; Eskander et al., 2016), an unsupervised framework based on Adaptor Grammars (Johnson et al., 2007) where word structure is modeled as a probabilistic context free grammar (PCFG), with the following configuration:

- **Grammar**: In the *PrStSu+SM* grammar used here, a word is modeled as a sequence of prefixes, a stem and suffixes, where *Pr*, *St* and *Su* stand for *Prefix*, *Stem* and *Suffix*, in order, where a sub-morph level is added, denoted by *SM*.
- **Number of segments per word**: Complex affixes can be further split into simple affixes (multi-way segmentation) or kept as whole segments (three-way segmentation: prefix+stem+suffix)
- **Learning setup** The *Standard* setup is language-independent, while the *Scholar-Seeded* setup uses initial affixes compiled from grammar resources. The *Cascaded* setup simulates the *Scholar-Seeded* setup in a language-independent manner by learning the seeded affixes.

As an example, a Swahili sentence is segmented as follows by the Three-way Scholar-Seeded model:
*Taarifa kamili itatolewa na Waziri Mkuu baada ya kuwa wamepangiwa vituo vya kazi.*
*Taarif+a ka+mili ita+tolew+a na Waziri Mkuu baada ya kuw+a wame+pangiw+a vi+tu+o vya kazi.*

**Results**   For both language pairs, we obtain comparable BLEU scores (Papineni et al., 2002) between BPE and unigram LM subword segmentations, and the baseline tokenization outperform the MorphAGram segmented variants (Table 1). The baseline tokenization improves BLEU by +2.48–2.72 for SW-

---

[1] https://www.iarpa.gov/index.php/ research-programs/material

[2] Preliminary results indicate that morpheme-based models yield higher BLEU score than word-based but both are worse than BPE and unigram language models; thus, we only present results with the combination of subwords and morphemes.

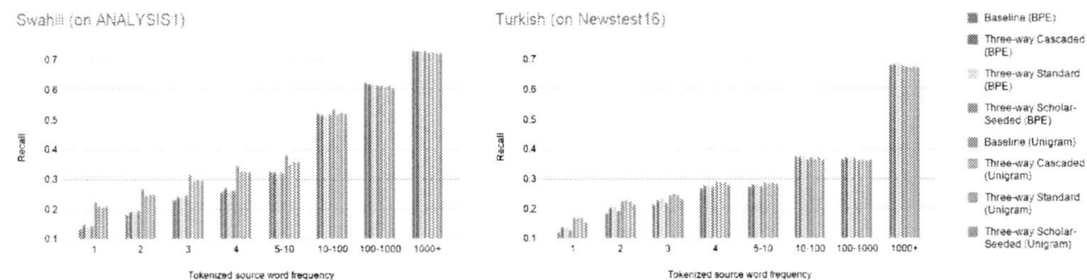


Figure 1: Unigram LM models yield higher recall for low frequency source words than BPE models. At higher frequencies BPE is comparable or greater than unigram LM.

EN and +0.19–1.28 for TR-EN compared to the morpheme-based segmentation. Among morpheme-based segmentations, three-way outperform multi-way splits, and the best BLEU scores are obtained with language-independent learning set-ups (Standard or Cascaded), although BLEU deltas are small.

To quantify the impact of segmentation beyond BLEU, we word align the tokenized test sets using the Berkeley Aligner (Liang et al., 2006) and use the compare-mt tool (Neubig et al., 2019) to calculate unigram recall binned by source word frequency. Figure 1[3] shows that unigram LM subwords improve recall over BPE subwords for all tokenizations for words seen fewer than 10 times by +3.8-6.9% for SW-EN and +0.08-3.6% for TR-EN. As source frequency increases, the recall delta decreases until BPE models reach comparable recall as unigram models (1% higher recall) for very frequent words (1000+). With BPE subwords, starting from MorphAGram segmentations reach slightly greater recall than using standard tokenization, whereas with unigram LM, the baseline tokenization outperforms MorphAGram.

These findings are consistent with the distribution of subwords generated by BPE vs. the unigram LM. We bin standard tokenized source words in the training set according to frequency and compute the type-to-token ratio (TTR) of subwords generated by the respective segmentation strategy within bins. The lower TTR obtained with unigram LM subwords for all frequency bins suggests that it captures the training set distribution better than BPE subwords (Figure 2).

**Conclusion** Our controlled comparison suggests that the unigram LM subwords are more effective than BPE when translating low-resource morphologically-rich languages. While they yield comparable BLEU scores, unigram LM subwords improves unigram recall when translating rare source words. Segmenting words into morphemes helps translate rare words better when using BPE models, but these benefits disappear with unigram LM subwords, where the baseline tokenization performs best.

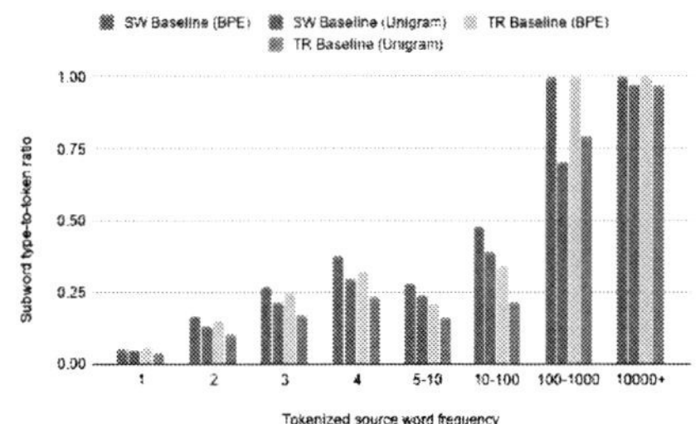


Figure 2: Unigram LM subwords yield lower Type-to-Token Ratios than BPE subwords.

## Acknowledgments

This research is supported in part by the Office of the Director of National Intelligence (ODNI), Intelligence Advanced Research Projects Activity (IARPA), via contract #FA8650-17-C-9117. The views and conclusions contained herein are those of the authors and should not be interpreted as necessarily representing the official policies, either expressed or implied, of ODNI, IARPA, or the U.S. Government. The U.S. Government is authorized to reproduce and distribute reprints for governmental purposes notwithstanding any copyright annotation therein.

---

[3]The values for recall between three-way and multi-way splits are comparable, so we only report three-way splits for clarity.

## References

Christophe Andrieu, Nando De Freitas, Arnaud Doucet, and Michael I Jordan. 2003. An Introduction to MCMC for Machine Learning. *Machine learning*, 50(1-2):5–43.

Duygu Ataman, Wilker Aziz, and Alexandra Birch. 2020. A latent morphology model for open-vocabulary neural machine translation. In *International Conference on Learning Representations*.

Dzmitry Bahdanau, KyungHyun Cho, and Yoshua Bengio. 2014. Neural machine translation by jointly learning to align and translate. *arXiv preprint arXiv:1409.0473*.

Tamali Banerjee and Pushpak Bhattacharyya. 2018. Meaningless yet meaningful: Morphology grounded subword-level NMT. In *Proceedings of the Second Workshop on Subword/Character LEvel Models*, pages 55–60, New Orleans, June. Association for Computational Linguistics.

Ondřej Bojar, Rajen Chatterjee, Christian Federmann, Yvette Graham, Barry Haddow, Shujian Huang, Matthias Huck, Philipp Koehn, Qun Liu, Varvara Logacheva, Christof Monz, Matteo Negri, Matt Post, Raphael Rubino, Lucia Specia, and Marco Turchi. 2017. Findings of the 2017 conference on machine translation (wmt17). In *Proceedings of the Second Conference on Machine Translation, Volume 2: Shared Task Papers*, pages 169–214, Copenhagen, Denmark, September. Association for Computational Linguistics.

Kaj Bostrom and Greg Durrett. 2020. Byte Pair Encoding is Suboptimal for Language Model Pretraining. *arXiv e-prints*, page arXiv:2004.03720, April.

Ramy Eskander, Owen Rambow, and Tianchun Yang. 2016. Extending the Use of Adaptor Grammars for Unsupervised Morphological Segmentation of Unseen Languages. In *Proceedings of he Twenty-Sixth International Conference on Computational Linguistics (COLING)*, Osaka, Japan.

Ramy Eskander, Francesca Callejas, Elizabeth Nichol, Judith Klavans, and Smaranda Muresan. 2020. Morphagram: Evaluation and framework for unsupervised morphological segmentation. In *Proceedings of the Eleventh International Conference on Language Resources and Evaluation (LREC 2020)*.

Chengyue Gong, Di He, Xu Tan, Tao Qin, Liwei Wang, and Tie-Yan Liu. 2018. Frage: Frequency-agnostic word representation. In *Advances in neural information processing systems*, pages 1334–1345.

Gökhan Güler and A Cüneyd Tantuğ. 2020. Comparison of turkish word representations trained on different morphological forms. *arXiv*, pages arXiv–2002.

Matthias Huck, Simon Riess, and Alexander M. Fraser. 2017. Target-side word segmentation strategies for neural machine translation. In *WMT*.

Sébastien Jean, Kyunghyun Cho, Roland Memisevic, and Yoshua Bengio. 2015. On using very large target vocabulary for neural machine translation. In *Proceedings of the 53rd Annual Meeting of the Association for Computational Linguistics and the 7th International Joint Conference on Natural Language Processing (Volume 1: Long Papers)*, pages 1–10.

Mark Johnson, Thomas L. Griffiths, and Sharon Goldwater. 2007. Adaptor Grammars: a Framework for Specifying Compositional Nonparametric Bayesian Models. In B. Sch"olkopf, J. Platt, and T. Hoffman, editors, *Advances in Neural Information Processing Systems 19*, pages 641–648, Cambridge, MA. MIT Press.

Diederik P Kingma and Jimmy Ba. 2014. Adam: A method for stochastic optimization. *arXiv preprint arXiv:1412.6980*.

Taku Kudo and John Richardson. 2018. Sentencepiece: A simple and language independent subword tokenizer and detokenizer for neural text processing. In *EMNLP*.

Taku Kudo. 2018. Subword regularization: Improving neural network translation models with multiple subword candidates. In *Proceedings of the 56th Annual Meeting of the Association for Computational Linguistics (Volume 1: Long Papers)*, pages 66–75.

Percy Liang, Ben Taskar, and Dan Klein. 2006. Alignment by agreement. In *Proceedings of the Main Conference on Human Language Technology Conference of the North American Chapter of the Association of Computational Linguistics*, HLT-NAACL '06, page 104–111, USA. Association for Computational Linguistics.

Minh-Thang Luong, Ilya Sutskever, Quoc Le, Oriol Vinyals, and Wojciech Zaremba. 2015. Addressing the rare word problem in neural machine translation. In *Proceedings of the 53rd Annual Meeting of the Association for Computational Linguistics and the 7th International Joint Conference on Natural Language Processing (Volume 1: Long Papers)*, pages 11–19.

Graham Neubig, Zi-Yi Dou, Junjie Hu, Paul Michel, Danish Pruthi, Xinyi Wang, and John Wieting. 2019. compare-mt: A tool for holistic comparison of language generation systems. *CoRR*, abs/1903.07926.

Mai Oudah, Amjad Almahairi, and Nizar Habash. 2019. The impact of preprocessing on Arabic-English statistical and neural machine translation. In *Proceedings of Machine Translation Summit XVII Volume 1: Research Track*, pages 214–221, Dublin, Ireland, August. European Association for Machine Translation.

Kishore Papineni, Salim Roukos, Todd Ward, and Wei-Jing Zhu. 2002. Bleu: a method for automatic evaluation of machine translation. In *Proceedings of the 40th annual meeting on association for computational linguistics*, pages 311–318. Association for Computational Linguistics.

Maja Popović. 2015. chrF: character n-gram f-score for automatic MT evaluation. In *Proceedings of the Tenth Workshop on Statistical Machine Translation*, pages 392–395, Lisbon, Portugal, September. Association for Computational Linguistics.

Ivan Provilkov, Dmitrii Emelianenko, and Elena Voita. 2019. Bpe-dropout: Simple and effective subword regularization. *arXiv preprint arXiv:1910.13267*.

Rico Sennrich and Biao Zhang. 2019. Revisiting low-resource neural machine translation: A case study. In *Proceedings of the 57th Annual Meeting of the Association for Computational Linguistics*, pages 211–221.

Rico Sennrich, Barry Haddow, and Alexandra Birch. 2016. Neural machine translation of rare words with subword units. In *Proceedings of the 54th Annual Meeting of the Association for Computational Linguistics (Volume 1: Long Papers)*, pages 1715–1725, Berlin, Germany, August. Association for Computational Linguistics.

Aleš Tamchyna, Marion Weller-Di Marco, and Alexander Fraser. 2017. Modeling target-side inflection in neural machine translation. In *Proceedings of the Second Conference on Machine Translation*, pages 32–42, Copenhagen, Denmark, September. Association for Computational Linguistics.

Sami Virpioja, Ville T Turunen, Sebastian Spiegler, Oskar Kohonen, and Mikko Kurimo. 2011. Empirical comparison of evaluation methods for unsupervised learning of morphology. *TAL: traitement automatique des langues*, 52(2):45–90.

# Enhanced Urdu Word Segmentation using Conditional Random Fields and Morphological Context Features


**Aamir Farhan, Mashrukh Islam and Dipti Misra Sharma**
Language Technologies Research Centre
International Institute of Information Technology
Hyderabad, India
{aamir.farhan, mashrukh.islam}@research.iiit.ac.in, dipti@iiit.ac.in



## Abstract

Word segmentation is a fundamental task for most of the NLP applications. Urdu adopts Nastalique writing style which does not have a concept of space. Furthermore, the inherent non-joining attributes of certain characters in Urdu create spaces within a word while writing in digital format. Thus, Urdu not only has space omission but also space insertion issues which make the word segmentation task challenging. In this paper, we improve upon the results of Zia, Raza and Athar (2018) by using a manually annotated corpus of 19,651 sentences along with morphological context features. Using the Conditional Random Field sequence modeler, our model achieves $F_1$ score of 0.98 for word boundary identification and 0.92 for sub-word boundary identification tasks. The results demonstrated in this paper outperform the state-of-the-art methods.


## 1   Introduction

Word segmentation is the first and foremost task for NLP applications, such as sentence parsing, part-of-speech tagging and machine translation. Word segmentation can be explicitly challenging for languages which do not have a delimiter to mark word boundary in their writing system. Urdu is one such language which is written in Arabic script using Nastalique writing system. Conventionally, Nastalique writing system adopts writing in a continuous fashion without any space characters. However, when Urdu is written in digital format, white space is used to mark word boundary as well as sub-word boundary in order to get correct shaping of a non-joining character, as discussed in the next section. Due to this absence of an objective delimiter, Urdu faces complex issues in word segmentation. This paper explains the problem of word segmentation in Urdu and presents an enhanced model for solving the tokenization problem using Conditional Random Fields (CRFs) along with morphological context features.

## 2   Literature Survey

Several rule-based methods have been used for tokenization issues in Urdu. Durrani and Hussain (2010) broadly descirbed the Word Segmentation issues and proposed various hybrid methods to solve the problem. One of them being a rule-based dictionary lookup with maximum matching. Another hybrid method involved statistical modeling using n-grams along with hueristics to identify the top 10 segmentations of an input string of Urdu characters. Their hybrid method achieved error detection rate of 85.8% for space omission and space insertion errors. Zia et al. (2018) proposed a CRF based model for Urdu Word Segmentation along with a publicly available corpus.




*Proceedings of the 55th Annual Meeting of the Association for Computational Linguistics*, pages 156–159
Florence, Italy, July 28th, 2019. ©2019 Association for Computational Linguistics

## 3   Urdu Writing System

Urdu is written in cursive Arabic script, also known as Nastalique. Urdu characters aquire different shapes according to the their respective positions in a word. The characters can be divided into two categories, *joiners* and *non-joiners*. Depending upon their position in a sequence, a joiner can have four shape variants: 1) initial 2) medial 3) final and 4) isolated form. Non- joiners only have two forms, final and isolated.

Conventionally, Urdu does not have a concept of white space as a word delimiter. A white space is instead used while typing to prevent a character from joining to its subsequent character. This ensures that correct shape of a character is maintained. For example, Urdu typists learn to insert a white space within the word خوش قسمت (Fortunate) to get the correct shape of ش. Without space, it appears like خشکسمت which is visually incorrect.

Thus Urdu writing system has space insertion issues when a white space is inserted within a word to get correct shape of a character and space omission issues when the joiners connect to each other in the Nastalique writing style.

## 4   Word Segmentation Model

To solve the aforementioned issues in the Urdu writing system, we present the word segmentation problem as a sequence labelling task where each character in the input sequence is assigned one of the following labels: 1) B : Beginning of a word  2) S : Beginning of a sub-word 3) O : Others

### 4.1   Corpus

The system presented by Zia et al. (2018) was trained using a manually crafted corpus of 4,325 sentences which is relatively small when compared to benchmark corpora of languages like Arabic and Chinese. We manually annotated a much bigger corpus of 19,651 sentences from Urdu news journals. We used white space to mark word boundary and Zero Width Non-Joiner (ZWNJ) to mark sub-word boundary, consistent with the rules proposed by Rehman et al. (2011).  The corpus covered most Urdu morphological constructions. For training and testing purposes, we have split the data in the following terms : 17,400 sentences for training and 2250 for testing.

### 4.2   Features

We crafted context features in terms of N-grams to capture the morphological context of a character in a sequence. The features involve unicode class of the character along with N-grams up to four preceding and four succeeding characters. We also incorporated a boolean feature in terms of whether a character belongs to Urdu script or not. For example, for the character م in the phrase الزام لگاکر will have the following set upto 4-grams as part of its features

$$\text{['c+م الگاک ', 'c+م لگا , 'c+م لگ', 'c+م ', 'c+مل', 'c+لـ', 'c+الزام', 'c-الزام', 'c-لزام', 'c-زام', 'c-ام', 'c-ام', 'c-ا', 'c=م']}$$

### 4.3   Model

Since the word segmentation problem is now transformed to a sequence labeling problem, we adopted a Conditional Random Field (CRF) model proposed by Lafferty et al. (2001). CRF is a framework for building probabilistic models to label sequence data. The model is defined as $P(\mathbf{y_1...y_n}|\mathbf{X})$ where $\mathbf{X}$ is a sequence of input and $\{y_1...y_n\}$ is a sequence of predicted labels. The labels, as described above, belong to the set, $L = \{B, S, O\}$.

# 5 Results

For evaluation metrics, we used precision, recall and $F_1$ measures. On a testing data set of 2250 sentences, our model achieved $F_1$ score of 0.98 for label B (word boundary), 0.92 for label S ( sub-word boundary) and 0.99 for label O (others). The results show significant improvement in the $F_1$ scores as compared to the previous methods primarily because of two factors:

- Significantly larger data size and richness of the new training corpus.
- The new engineered features which consider N-grams up to four preceding and four succeeding characters.

| Label | Precision | Recall | $F_1$ Score |
|---|---|---|---|
| O | 0.99 | 0.99 | 0.99 |
| B | 0.98 | 0.98 | 0.98 |
| S | 0.90 | 0.93 | 0.92 |

Table1: Test results corresponding to each label

| | O | B | S |
|---|---|---|---|
| O | 137294 | 1126 | 3 |
| B | 1080 | 47586 | 29 |
| S | 5 | 16 | 300 |

Table2:  Confusion  matrix for sequence labeling

# 6 Limitations and Future Scope

The model proposed in this project is trained using a manually crafted corpus which is relatively small compared to segmentation benchcmark corpora of resource rich languages like Arabic and Chinese. The model also heavily depends on manually engineered features for determinig word and sub-word boundaries. We have explored the usage of neural models like Bi-LSTM for this task. Since the neural models are data hungry, we plan to expand our annotated corpus and explore suitable character embeddings which can be fed to a Bi-LSTM RNN. We also plan to tag special grammatical constructions in Urdu like the *Izafa* constructions and add this label to our annotation schema as well.

**References**

Durrani, N., & Hussain, S. (2010, June). Urdu word segmentation. In Human Language Technologies: The 2010 Annual Conference of the North American Chapter of the Association for Computational Linguistics (pp. 528-536). Association for Computational Linguistics.

Zia, Raza and Athar (2018). Urdu Word Segmentation using Conditional Random Fields(CRFs). Proceedings of the 27th International Conference on Computational Linguistics. Association for Computational Linguistics.

Afzal, M., & Hussain, S. (2001). Urdu computing standards: development of Urdu Zabta Takhti (UZT) 1.01. InMulti Topic Conference, 2001. IEEE INMIC 2001. Technology for the 21st Century. Proceedings. IEEE International(pp. 216-222). IEEE.

Cai, D., & Zhao, H. (2016). Neural word segmentation learning for Chinese. arXiv preprint arXiv:1606.04300.

Lafferty, J., McCallum, A., & Pereira, F. C. (2001). Conditional random fields: Probabilistic models for segmenting and labeling sequence data.

Monroe, W., Green, S., & Manning, C. D. (2014). Word segmentation of informal Arabic with domain adaptation. In Proceedings of the 52nd Annual Meeting of the Association for Computational Linguistics (Volume 2: Short Papers) (Vol. 2, pp. 206-211).

Rehman, Z., Anwar, W., & Bajwa, U. I. (2011). Challenges in Urdu text tokenization and sentence boundary dis-ambiguation. In Proceedings of the 2nd Workshop on South Southeast Asian Natural LanguageProcessing (WSSANLP) (pp. 40-45).

Ping, G., & Yu-Hang, M. (1994). The adjacent matching algorithm of Chinese automatic word segmentation and its implementation in the QHFY Chinese-English system. In Proceedings of the 1994 International Conference on Chinese Computing, Singapore (Vol. 301, p. 94).

Wong, P. K., & Chan, C. (1996, August). Chinese word segmentation based on maximum matching andword binding force. In Proceedings of the 16th conference on Computational linguistics-Volume 1 (pp. 200-203). Association for Computational Linguistics.

Green, S., & DeNero, J. (2012, July). A class-based agreement model for generating accurately inflected transla-tions. In Proceedings of the 50th Annual Meeting of the Association for Computational Linguistics: Long Pa-pers-Volume 1 (pp. 146-155). Association for Computational Linguistics.

Sornlertlamvanich, V. 1995. Word Segmentation for Thai in a Machine Translation System (in Thai), Papers on Natural Language Processing, NECTEC, Thailand

# Flexible Non-Autoregressive Neural Machine Translation
## via Repositioning Edit Operations


**First Author**
Affiliation / Address line 1
Affiliation / Address line 2
Affiliation / Address line 3
`email@domain`

**Second Author**
Affiliation / Address line 1
Affiliation / Address line 2
Affiliation / Address line 3
`email@domain`


## Abstract


We introduce an iterative text refinement model to reduce the decoding space of non-autoregressive models by disentangling the token prediction and relative position prediction. We show that our model achieves promising performance on the English-German translation task.


## 1 Introduction

Most sequence generation models generate sequences from left to right in an autoregressive way, where the model prediction at each time step is conditioned on its previous predictions (Sutskever et al., 2014; Bahdanau et al., 2015). A wide range of non-autoregressive (NAR) sequence generation models have been proposed to accelerate the sequence generation process by generating all tokens in parallel (Gu et al., 2017; Lee et al., 2018; Gu et al., 2019). While allowing for highly parallel sequence generation, such models ignore the dependencies among target tokens which causes lower accuracy than their autoregressive counterparts.

Lee et al. (2018) propose to generate the sequence by iteratively refining the previously generated target sequence to capture the dependencies among target tokens. However, at each decoding step, the model still needs to predict both the identities of the tokens to be generated and the relative position of the generated tokens in parallel, which makes the action space at each step too large to be effectively modeled. Thus the resulting model suffers from inefficient training, token repetition, and inadequacy issues (Wang et al., 2019).

In this work, we propose to reduce the action space at each decoding step by disentangling the predictions of token identities and their relative positions. We introduce an iterative refinement model which generates target sequences by alternately applying three types of operations – reposition, deletion, and insertion: at each iteration, the model first inserts several tokens into the input sequence in parallel to form an intermediate sequence, adjusts the relative positions of the inserted tokens, and deletes token when necessary. We train the model using imitation learning. To train each policy predictor, we use the model outputs from each other as the input sequence and train the predictors to imitate an oracle policy. Experiments on the English-German translation task show that our model outperforms a strong NAR baseline introduced by Gu et al. (2019).

## 2 Approach

### 2.1 Problem Formulation

We formulate the iterative generation problem as a Markov Decision Process defined by $(\mathcal{Y}, \mathcal{A}, \mathcal{E}, \mathcal{R}, \boldsymbol{y}^0)$, where a state $\boldsymbol{y}$ in the state space $\mathcal{Y}$ corresponds to a sequence of tokens $\boldsymbol{y} = (y_1, y_2, ..., y_L)$ from the vocabulary $\mathcal{V}$ up to length $L$, and $\boldsymbol{y}^0 \in \mathcal{Y}$ is the initial sequence. For standard sequence generation tasks $\boldsymbol{y}^0$ is an empty sequence $(\langle s \rangle, \langle /s \rangle)$, while for lexically constrained generation tasks $\boldsymbol{y}^0$ is the constraint sequence $(\langle s \rangle, c_1, ..., c_k, \langle /s \rangle)$ where $k$ is the number of lexical constraints.

At the $i$-th decoding iteration, the model takes the initial sequence or output from the previous iteration as the input sequence $\boldsymbol{y}^{i-1}$, chooses an action $\boldsymbol{a}^i \in \mathcal{A}$ to refine the sequence $\boldsymbol{y}^i = \mathcal{E}(\boldsymbol{y}^{i-1}, \boldsymbol{a}^i)$, and receives a reward $r^i = \mathcal{R}(\boldsymbol{y}^i)$. The model learns a policy $\pi$ that maps the input sequence $\boldsymbol{y}^{i-1}$ to a




*Proceedings of the 55th Annual Meeting of the Association for Computational Linguistics*, pages 160–163
Florence, Italy, July 28th, 2019. ©2019 Association for Computational Linguistics

probability distribution $P(\mathcal{A})$ over the action space $\mathcal{A}$. We define a refinement action $a \in \mathcal{A}$ based on three basic operations – reposition, deletion, and insertion:

**Reposition & Deletion**  We combine the reposition and deletion operations. For each position in the input sequence $\boldsymbol{y}_{1\ldots n}$, the reposition and deletion policy $\pi_{rpsdel}(r\,|\,i, \boldsymbol{y})$ predicts an index $r \in [0, n]$: if $r > 0$, we place the $r$-th input token $y_r$ at the $i$-th output position, otherwise we delete the token at that position. We constrain $\pi_{rpsdel}(1\,|\,1, \boldsymbol{y}) = \pi_{rpsdel}(n\,|\,n, \boldsymbol{y}) = 1$ to maintain sequence boundaries.

**Insertion**  Similar to Gu et al. (2019), the insertion operation consists of two phases: (1) *placeholder prediction:* given an input sequence $\boldsymbol{y}_{1\ldots n}$, the placeholder predictor $\pi_{plh}(p\,|\,i, \boldsymbol{y})$ predicts the number of placeholders to be inserted between two neighboring tokens $(y_i, y_{i+1})$; (2) *token prediction:* given the output of the placeholder predictor, the token predictor $\pi_{tok}(t\,|\,i, \boldsymbol{y})$ replaces each placeholder with an actual token.

   **Combined Action:**  Given an input sequence $\boldsymbol{y}_{1\ldots n}$, an single-step action can be decomposed into three phases: reposition and delete tokens, insert placeholders, and replace placeholders with tokens. More formally, we define an action as a sequence of reposition, deletion, and insertion steps $a = (\boldsymbol{r}, \boldsymbol{p}, \boldsymbol{t})$, where each step contains a set of basic operations applied in parallel:

$$\boldsymbol{r} = \{r_1, ..., r_n\}$$
$$\boldsymbol{p} = \{p_1, ..., p_{n-1}\}$$
$$\boldsymbol{t} = \{t_1, ..., t_m\}$$

where $m = \sum_i^{n-1} p_i$. We define the policy as

$$\pi(\boldsymbol{a}|\boldsymbol{y}) = \prod_{r_i \in \boldsymbol{r}} \pi_{rpsdel}(r_i\,|\,i, \boldsymbol{y}) \cdot \prod_{p_i \in \boldsymbol{p}} \pi_{plh}(p_i\,|\,i, \boldsymbol{y}') \cdot$$
$$\prod_{t_i \in \boldsymbol{t}} \pi_{tok}(t_i\,|\,i, \boldsymbol{y}'')$$

where the intermediate outputs $\boldsymbol{y}' = \mathcal{E}(\boldsymbol{y}, \boldsymbol{r})$ and $\boldsymbol{y}'' = \mathcal{E}(\boldsymbol{y}', \boldsymbol{p})$.

## 2.2  Model

We base our model on the standard Transformer encoder-decoder model (Vaswani et al., 2017) and extract the decoder representations $(\boldsymbol{h}_1, ..., \boldsymbol{h}_n)$ to make the following policy predictions:

**Reposition & Deletion Classifier**  gives a categorical distribution over the index of the input token to be placed at each output position:

$$\pi_{rpsdel}(r\,|\,i, \boldsymbol{y}) = \mathrm{softmax}(\boldsymbol{h}_i \cdot [\boldsymbol{b}, \boldsymbol{e}_1, ..., \boldsymbol{e}_n]) \tag{1}$$

where $\boldsymbol{e}_i$ is the embedding of the $i$-th token in the input sequence, and $\boldsymbol{b} \in \mathbb{R}^{d_{model}}$ is used to predict whether to delete the token.

**Placeholder Classifier**  gives a categorical distribution over the number of placeholders to be inserted between every two consecutive positions:

$$\pi_{plh}(p\,|\,i, \boldsymbol{y}) = \mathrm{softmax}([\boldsymbol{h}_i\,;\,\boldsymbol{h}_{i+1}] \cdot \boldsymbol{W}^{plh}) \tag{2}$$

where $\boldsymbol{W}^{plh} \in \mathbb{R}^{(2d_{model}) \times (K+1)}$.

**Token Classifier**  predicts the actual tokens to fill in the place of each placeholder:

$$\pi_{tok}(t\,|\,i, \boldsymbol{y}) = \mathrm{softmax}(\boldsymbol{h}_i \cdot \boldsymbol{W}^{tok}) \tag{3}$$

where $\boldsymbol{W}^{tok} \in \mathbb{R}^{d_{model} \times |\mathcal{V}|}$.

## 3   Evaluation and Future Work

We evaluate our model on WMT'14 English-German translation task (Bojar et al., 2014). We apply standard preprocessing steps including normalization, tokenization, true-casing, and BPE (Sennrich et al., 2016) with 32,000 joint operations. During training, we apply sequence-level knowledge distillation from autoregressive (AR) teacher models as widely used in non-autoregressive generation (Gu et al., 2017; Lee et al., 2018; Gu et al., 2019). Specifically, when training the non-autoregressive models, we replace the reference sequences in the training data with translation outputs from an AR teacher model trained on the same parallel data.

|      | BLEU  | latency (ms) |
|------|-------|--------------|
| AR   | 27.30 | 308.64       |
| LevT | 26.86 | 113.12       |
| Ours | 26.70 | 109.05       |

Table 1: BLEU scores and the latency per sentence of the autoregressive (AR) baseline, LevT, and our model on English-German translation task.

We compare our model with the LevT model proposed in Gu et al. (2019), which only includes insertion and deletion operations while our model includes an additional reposition operation. For both our model and LevT, we use the base Transformer model (Vaswani et al., 2017) with $d_{model} = 512$, $d_{hidden} = 2048$, $n_{heads} = 8$, $n_{layers} = 6$, and dropout $= 0.3$. We tie the source and target embeddings with the output layer weights (Press and Wolf, 2017; Nguyen and Chiang, 2018). Both models are trained using the Adam optimizer (Kingma and Ba, 2015) with initial learning rate of 0.0005 for maximum 300,000 steps with a batch size of 64,800 tokens.

As shown in Table 1, we evaluate the models using BLEU and decoding latency per sentence. Both LevT and our model achieves close performance to the AR baseline with 3x speedup. Our model achieves comparable BLEU to LevT (the difference is not significant[1]) while being 4% times faster.

Further improvements could be achieved by combining the cross-entropy objective with a bag-of-word objective introduced in Xu et al. (2019) when training the insertion model to reduce the penalty on the insertion model for generating tokens in the wrong relative order. Another interesting future avenue is to train the insertion network with additional bilingual dictionary data or unsupervised lexicon induction to improve low-resource machine translation.

## References


Dzmitry Bahdanau, Kyunghyun Cho, and Yoshua Bengio. 2015. Neural machine translation by jointly learning to align and translate. In *Proceedings of the 3th International Conference on Learning Representations*.

Ondřej Bojar, Christian Buck, Christian Federmann, Barry Haddow, Philipp Koehn, Johannes Leveling, Christof Monz, Pavel Pecina, Matt Post, Herve Saint-Amand, Radu Soricut, Lucia Specia, and Aleš Tamchyna. 2014. Findings of the 2014 workshop on statistical machine translation. In *Proceedings of the Ninth Workshop on Statistical Machine Translation*, pages 12–58, Baltimore, Maryland, USA, June. Association for Computational Linguistics.

Jonathan H. Clark, Chris Dyer, Alon Lavie, and Noah A. Smith. 2011. Better hypothesis testing for statistical machine translation: Controlling for optimizer instability. In *Proceedings of the 49th Annual Meeting of the Association for Computational Linguistics: Human Language Technologies*, pages 176–181, Portland, Oregon, USA, June. Association for Computational Linguistics.

Jiatao Gu, James Bradbury, Caiming Xiong, Victor O. K. Li, and Richard Socher. 2017. Non-autoregressive neural machine translation. *CoRR*, abs/1711.02281.

Jiatao Gu, Changhan Wang, and Junbo Zhao. 2019. Levenshtein transformer. In *Advances in Neural Information Processing Systems 32*, pages 11181–11191. Curran Associates, Inc.

Diederik P. Kingma and Jimmy Ba. 2015. Adam: A method for stochastic optimization. In *Proceedings of the 3th International Conference on Learning Representations*.


---

[1] We conduct pair-wise statistical significance test using paired bootstrap (Clark et al., 2011) with $p < 0.05$.

Jason Lee, Elman Mansimov, and Kyunghyun Cho. 2018. Deterministic non-autoregressive neural sequence modeling by iterative refinement. In *Proceedings of the 2018 Conference on Empirical Methods in Natural Language Processing*, pages 1173–1182, Brussels, Belgium, October-November. Association for Computational Linguistics.

Toan Q. Nguyen and David Chiang. 2018. Improving lexical choice in neural machine translation. In *Proceedings of the 2018 Conference of the North American Chapter of the Association for Computational Linguistics: Human Language Technologies*, pages 334–343. Association for Computational Linguistics.

Ofir Press and Lior Wolf. 2017. Using the output embedding to improve language models. In *Proceedings of the 15th Conference of the European Chapter of the Association for Computational Computational*, pages 157–163. Association for Computational Linguistics.

Rico Sennrich, Barry Haddow, and Alexandra Birch. 2016. Neural machine translation of rare words with subword units. In *Proceedings of the 54th Annual Meeting of the Association for Computational Linguistics*, pages 1715–1725. Association for Computational Linguistics.

Ilya Sutskever, Oriol Vinyals, and Quoc V Le. 2014. Sequence to sequence learning with neural networks. In *Advances in neural information processing systems*, pages 3104–3112.

Ashish Vaswani, Noam Shazeer, Niki Parmar, Jakob Uszkoreit, Llion Jones, Aidan N. Gomez, Lukasz Kaiser, and Illia Polosukhin. 2017. Attention is all you need. *CoRR*, abs/1706.03762.

Yiren Wang, Fei Tian, Di He, Tao Qin, ChengXiang Zhai, and Tie-Yan Liu. 2019. Non-autoregressive machine translation with auxiliary regularization. In *Proceedings of the AAAI Conference on Artificial Intelligence*, volume 33, pages 5377–5384.

Weijia Xu, Xing Niu, and Marine Carpuat. 2019. Differentiable sampling with flexible reference word order for neural machine translation. In *Proceedings of the 2019 Conference of the North American Chapter of the Association for Computational Linguistics: Human Language Technologies, Volume 1 (Long and Short Papers)*, pages 2047–2053, Minneapolis, Minnesota, June. Association for Computational Linguistics.